FISHES OF INDIANA

D1522236

INDIANA NATURAL SCIENCE
Gillian Harris, editor

INDIANA UNIVERSITY PRESS
Bloomington and Indianapolis

FISHES
of INDIANA

–*A Field Guide*–

THOMAS P. SIMON

ILLUSTRATIONS BY
JOSEPH R. TOMELLERI

This book is a publication of

Indiana University Press
601 North Morton Street
Bloomington, Indiana 47404-3797 USA

iupress.indiana.edu

Telephone orders   800-842-6796
Fax orders   812-855-7931
Orders by e-mail   iuporder@indiana.edu

© 2011 by Thomas P. Simon and Joseph R. Tomelleri
All rights reserved

No part of this book may be reproduced or utilized in
any form or by any means, electronic or mechanical,
including photocopying and recording, or by any
information storage and retrieval system, without
permission in writing from the publisher. The Association
of American University Presses' Resolution on Permissions
constitutes the only exception to this prohibition.

This book is printed on acid-free paper.

Manufactured in China

Library of Congress Cataloging-in-Publication Data

Simon, Thomas P.
  Fishes of Indiana : a field guide / Thomas P.
Simon ; illustrations by Joseph R. Tomelleri.
     p. cm. — (Indiana natural science)
  Includes bibliographical references and index.
  ISBN 978-0-253-22308-1 (pbk. : alk. paper)
 1. Fishes—Indiana—Identification. I. Title.
  QL628.I6S56 2011
  597.09772—dc22
                                    2010046736

1   2   3   4   5   16   15   14   13   12   11

*ALL MY LOVE TO MY WIFE, BETH, AND MY
CHILDREN, TOM, CAMERON, LIA, AND ZACHARY,
FOR ALL OF THEIR ENCOURAGEMENT AND SUPPORT.
REMEMBERING DAYS IN THE FIELD WITH FISH!*

GOING FISHING
Zachary J. Simon

Took a short cut down
To Jackson Creek
Brother, sister and me
Leaves crunching
Birds making hoopla
Climbing over fallen trees
Beware of red sinking sand
Throwing rocks
Shoveling for fish
At snake cove
We caught a fish
The only one we've caught today
Let it go, on its way
Sister finds bluebells
Brother sucks the honey out
Water is as muddy as a pig
Up to my knees
Deep as can be
Oh what creek fun!

Contents

~~~~~~

Preface

For the past 25 years, preparation of the *Fishes of Indiana* has been on the forefront of my research program; however, while the forthcoming natural history text is being completed, the need to have a guide to assist students, anglers, and others in the identification of the various species occurring in Indiana is an obvious need. The premise of this field guide is to provide taxonomic traits necessary to identify the various species in Indiana and to provide information on the natural history and distribution of each species. This book is written for the professional and the public, especially when simplified terms could be used; however, a glossary of terms is included.

My goal was to make the field guide as useful as possible for students and anglers seeking to identify an individual fish either in the laboratory or at the lake. This book is designed to be a lightweight, condensed version of the forthcoming professional work. This field guide includes an illustrated key to all of the families, genera, and species of fishes that have ever occurred within the political boundaries of Indiana. Several species included in the key and species accounts are considered extirpated, extinct, or hypothetical.

Despite the numerous field trips in which I have participated, one thing is certain: there are still many surprises to be found. Perhaps species we thought were extirpated were just so rare that they went undetected. Better equipment, searching in previously unsurveyed areas, and more focused searches in the appropriate habitats may uncover further gems. Even in the last 5 years, species that were thought to be extirpated from the state have been found. Populations of Alligator gar (*Atractosteus spatula*), Popeye shiner (*Notropis anogenus*), Banded pygmy sunfish (*Elassoma zonatum*), and Variegate darter (*Etheostoma variatum*), among others, have recently been found after a century of suspected extirpation. I encourage other naturalists, anglers, hobbyists, students, and scientists to pursue what else might be discovered. One thing is certain: species distributions will change, and unless continued monitoring is done, these changes will cause the loss of precious aquatic treasures that exist beneath our waters. My hope is that this guide will be useful to future generations of fish biologists, ichthyologists, naturalists, and anglers who want to know more about the fishes inhabiting the waters of our Indiana, and that it will stimulate others to investigate these fascinating organisms.

Acknowledgments

The completion of a project of this magnitude would not be possible without the assistance of numerous people. For field assistance, I have enjoyed the companionship of numerous students, colleagues, and professionals. Naming the many people involved in my research in this small space certainly would unintentionally miss someone highly valued. Many thanks to Larry Page, Brooks Burr, and the late Karl Lagler, who provided mentorship, training, and schooling on the fine points of collecting and documenting important results. Larry Page, Brooks Burr, Robert Wallus, and Robert Jenkins verified many species identifications and assisted in curating specimens. Numerous curators allowed access to museum collections that contained important historic information: Susan Jewett and Jeffrey Clayton, United States National Museum (USNM), William Pearson, University of Louisville (UL); Douglas Nelson and Gerry Smith, University of Michigan (UMMZ); Mark Kibby, Ohio State University Museum of Biodiversity (OSUM); Mike Retzer and Lawrence Page, Illinois Natural History Survey (INHS); William Eschmeyer and Dave Catania, California Academy of Sciences (CAS)—includes collections from Stanford University (SU) and Indiana University (IU); John Whitaker, Indiana State University (ISU); Ron Richards, Indiana State Museum (INSM); John Iverson, Earlham College (EC); Jeffrey Davis, Cincinnati Museum of Natural History (CMNH); Ronald Hellenthal, University of Notre Dame Department of Biology Museum of Natural History (NDNH); Brooks Burr, Southern Illinois University at Carbondale (SIUC); Barry Chernoff, Field Museum of Natural History (FMNH); David Etnier, University of Tennessee (UT); Jay Hatch, Bell Museum of Natural History, University of Minnesota (BMNH); Hank Bart and Nelson Rios, Tulane University (TU); Neil Douglas, University of Louisiana–Monroe (ULM); the late George Becker, University of Wisconsin–Stevens Point (UWSP); Bernie Kuhajda, University of Alabama (UAIC); Lee Hartle, Georgia Museum of Natural History (UGAMNH); John Friel, Cornell University (CU); Karsten Hartel, Museum of Comparative Zoology, Harvard University (MCZ); C. Lavett Smith and Robert Daniels, New York State Museum–Albany (NYSM); Scott Schaefer, American Museum of Natural History (AMNH); Claude Baker, Indiana University Southeast; Andy Bentley, Natural History Museum and Biodiversity Research Center, University of Kansas (KU); John Lundberg and Mark Sabaj Perez, the Academy of Natural Sciences, Philadelphia (ANSP); Carter Gilbert, Florida Museum of Natural History (FMNH); Patrice Provost, Museum of Natural History Paris (MNHP); Nick Mandrak, Royal Ontario Museum (ROM); and Patrick Campbell, Natural History Museum, London (BMNH). Ronda Dufour, Stephanie Worden, Charles Morris, and Thomas Cervone assisted in compiling information. Illustrations were completed by Joseph Tomelleri, obtained from government publications, and used with permission from others.

Abbreviations

ABD	air bladder depth
ADFL	adipose fin length
BDA	body depth at anus
BDE	body depth at eyes
BDP1	body depth at pectoral fin
CFL	caudal fin length
ChiBL	chin barbel length
cm	centimeter(s)
CPD	caudal peduncle depth
DELT	deformities, eroded fins, lesions, or tumors
DFL	dorsal fin length
ED	eye diameter
FL	fork length
ft	feet
g	gram(s)
GD	greatest depth
ha	hectare
HD	head depth
HL	head length
HW	head width
kg	kilogram(s)
km	kilometer(s)
lbs	pound
m	meter(s)
MandL	mandible length
MaxBL	maxillary barbel length

MBL   mandibular barbel length

mm   millimeter(s)

SL   standard length

TL   total length

FISHES OF INDIANA

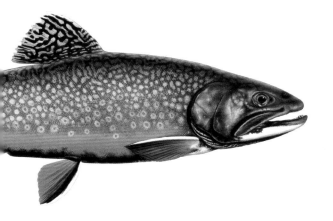

Table 1. Species List of Indiana Fishes.

Noting distribution and habitats of fishes in the major drainages of Indiana.

| Ep = extirpated | N = native species | NI = possibly introduced, but considered native |
| E = extinct | I = introduced | X = known to frequent this habitat type |

Species	COMMON NAME	Lowland	Upland	Big River	Stream	Creek	Lacustrine	Subterranean	Lake Michigan	Kankakee River	Maumee River	Wabash River	White River	Ohio River	Page(s)
Petromyzontidae															
Ichthyomyzon bdellium	Ohio lamprey	X	X	X	X									N	93
Ichthyomyzon castaneus	Chestnut lamprey	X	X	X	X							N		N	96
Ichthyomyzon fossor	Northern brook lamprey		X		X	X			N	N	N	N	N		96
Ichthyomyzon unicuspis	Silver lamprey	X	X	X	X				N	N	N	N	N	N	96
Lampetra aepyptera	Least brook lamprey				X	X						N		N	98
Lampetra appendix	American brook lamprey		X		X	X			N	N	N	N	N	N	98
Petromyzon marinus	Sea lamprey	X		X	X	X	X		I						98
Polyodontidae															
Polyodon spathula	Paddlefish	X		X			X		Ep		Ep	N	N	N	100
Acipenseridae															
Acipenser fulvescens	Lake sturgeon	X		X			X		N		Ep	N	N	Ep	104
Scaphirhynchus platorynchus	Shovelnose sturgeon	X		X								N	N	N	104

continued

1

Table 1 *continued*

Species	COMMON NAME	Habitats							Drainage						Page(s)
		Lowland	Upland	Big River	Stream	Creek	Lacustrine	Subterranean	Lake Michigan	Kankakee River	Maumee River	Wabash River	White River	Ohio River	
Lepisosteidae															102
Atractosteus spatula	Alligator gar	X		X			X								104
Lepisosteus oculatus	Spotted gar	X		X			X		N	N	N	Ep	N	N	106
Lepisosteus osseus	Longnose gar	X	X	X	X				N	N	N	N	N	N	106
Lepisosteus platostomus	Shortnose gar	X		X					N			N	N	N	108
Amiidae															
Amia calva	Bowfin	X		X	X		X		N	N	N	N	N	N	110
Hiodontidae															109
Hiodon alosoides	Goldeye	X		X								N	N	N	110
Hiodon tergisus	Mooneye	X		X					N		N	N		N	110
Anguillidae															109
Anguilla rostrata	American eel	X		X	X				N	N	N	N	N	N	110
Clupeidae															112
Alosa alabamae	Alabama shad	X		X										N	112
Alosa chrysochloris	Skipjack herring	X		X					I	N		N	N	N	114
Alosa pseudoharengus	Alewife	X		X			X		I					1	114
Dorosoma cepedianum	Gizzard shad	X	X	X	X		X		N	N	N	N	N	N	114
Dorosoma petenense	Threadfin shad	X		X			X					1	1	N	114
Catostomidae															116
Carpiodes carpio	River Carpsucker	X	X	X	X							N	N	N	122
Carpiodes cyprinus	Quillback	X	X	X	X		X		N	N	N	N	N	N	122
Carpiodes velifer	Highfin carpsucker	X	X	X	X						N	N	N	N	122

Scientific name	Common name												Page
Catostomus catostomus	Longnose sucker	X			X		N					N	124
Catostomus commersonii	White sucker	X	X		X	X	N	N	N	N	N	N	124
Cycleptus elongatus	Blue sucker	X		X					N	N		N	124
Erimyzon oblongus	Creek chubsucker	X			X		N	N	N		N	N	126
Erimyzon sucetta	Lake chubsucker	X			X	X	N	N	N	N	N	N	126
Hypentelium nigricans	Northern hogsucker	X	X		X		N		N		N	N	126
Ictiobus bubalus	Smallmouth buffalo	X			X		N		N	N	N	N	128
Ictiobus cyprinellus	Bigmouth buffalo	X			X		N	N	N	N	N	N	128
Ictiobus niger	Black buffalo	X			X		N		N	N	N	N	128
Minytrema melanops	Spotted sucker	X		X		X	N		N	N	N	N	128
Moxostoma anisurum	Silver redhorse	X			X		N		N	N	N	N	130
Moxostoma breviceps	Smallmouth redhorse	X			X		N		N	N	N	N	130
Moxostoma carinatum	River redhorse	X	X		X		N		N	N	N	N	130
Moxostoma duquesnei	Black redhorse	X			X		N		N	N	N	N	132
Moxostoma erythrurum	Golden redhorse	X			X	X	N		N	N	N	N	132
Moxostoma lacerum	Harelip sucker	X								E			132
Moxostoma macrolepidotum	Shorthead redhorse	X			X		N		N	N	N	N	134
Moxostoma valenciennesi	Greater redhorse	X			X		N		Ep	N	N	Ep	134
Cyprinidae													136
Campostoma anomalum	Common stoneroller	X			X		N		N				150
Campostoma pullum	Central stoneroller	X	X		X		N		N	N	N	N	150
Campostoma oligolepis	Largescale stoneroller	X			X		N		N				150
Carassius auratus	Goldfish	X			X		1	1	1	1	1	1	152
Chrosomus eos	Northern redbelly dace				X					1		1	152
Chrosomus erythrogaster	Southern redbelly dace	X				X	N	N	N		N		152
Clinostomus elongatus	Redside dace	X		X			N	N	N		N		154

continued

Table 1 continued

Species	COMMON NAME	Lowland	Upland	Big River	Stream	Creek	Lacustrine	Subterranean	Lake Michigan	Kankakee River	Maumee River	Wabash River	White River	Ohio River	Page(s)
					Habitats						Drainage				
Couesius plumbeus	Lake chub	X					X		N						154
Ctenopharyngodon idella	Grass carp	X		X			X		I	I		I	I	I	154
Cyprinella lutrensis	Red shiner	X			X	X				I		NI	N	NI	156
Cyprinella spiloptera	Spotfin shiner		X	X	X	X		X	N	N		N	N	N	156
Cyprinella nov. cf. spiloptera	Tippecanoe shiner		X		X						N		N		158
Cyprinella whipplei	Steelcolor shiner		X		X	X				N		N	N		158
Cyprinus carpio	Carp	X	X	X	X	X	X		I	I	I	I	I	I	158
Ericymba buccata	Silverjaw minnow		X		X	X			N	N	N	N	N	N	158
Erimystax dissimilis	Streamline chub		X		X							N			160
Erimystax x-punctata	Eastern gravel chub		X		X						Ep	N			160
Hybognathus hayi	Cypress minnow	X			X										160
Hybognathus nuchalis	Mississippi silvery minnow	X		X	X							N	N	N	162
Hybopsis amblops	Bigeye chub		X		X	X				Ep		N	N		162
Hybopsis amnis	Pallid shiner		X		X	X			N	N			N		162
Hypophthalmichthys molitrix	Silver carp	X		X								I	I	I	164
Hypophthalmichthys nobilis	Bighead carp	X		X								I	I	I	164
Luxilus chrysocephalus	Striped shiner		X		X	X			N	N	N	N	N	N	164
Luxilus cornutus fontinalis	Common shiner		X		X	X			N	N	N				166
Lythrurus fasciolaris	Scarletfin shiner		X	X	X	X								N	166
Lythrurus fumeus	Ribbon shiner	X			X	X			N			N	N	N	166
Lythrurus umbratilis	Redfin shiner	X	X		X	X			N	N	N	N	N	N	168
Lythrurus nov. cf. umbratilis	Silver creek shiner	X	X		X	X			N	N	N	N	N	N	168

Scientific name	Common name														Page
Macrhybopsis hyostoma	Shoal chub	X	X			X	X						N		N	168
Macrhybopsis storeriana	Silver chub	X	X			X	X						N	N	N	170
Nocomis biguttatus	Hornyhead chub			X	X	X	X		N				N	N	N	170
Nocomis micropogon	River chub	X	X			X	X	X	N				N	N		170
Notemigonus crysoleucas	Golden shiner	X		X	X	X	X		N	Ep	Ep		N	N		172
Notropis anogenus	Pugnose shiner	X						X	N			Ep	N			172
Notropis ariommus	Popeye shiner			X	X	X	X						N			172
Notropis atherinoides	Emerald shiner	X	X	X	X	X	X		N	N		N	N	N	N	174
Notropis blennius	River shiner	X	X		X	X	X		N			N	N	N	N	174
Notropis boops	Bigeye shiner					X	X					N	N		N	174
Notropis buchanani	Ghost shiner	X	X			X	X					N	N	N	N	174
Notropis chalybaeus	Ironcolor shiner	X			X		X	X	N	1	1					176
Notropis dorsalis	Bigmouth shiner			X		X	X		N	N			N			176
Notropis heterodon	Blackchin shiner	X				X	X	X	N	N	N	N				178
Notropis heterolepis	Blacknose shiner	X				X	X	X	N	N	N	N				178
Notropis hudsonius	Spottail shiner	X		X	X	X	X	X	N	N	N	N				178
Notropis percobromus	Carmine shiner			X	X	X	X					N	N			180
Notropis photogenis	Silver shiner			X	X	X	X					N	N	N	N	180
Notropis rubellus	Rosyface shiner			X	X	X	X					N	N	N	N	180
Notropis shumardi	Silverband shiner	X	X			X	X		N	N		N	N		N	182
Notropis stramineus	Sand shiner	X		X	X	X	X		N			N	N	N	N	182
Notropis texanus	Weed shiner	X				X	X	X	N	N			N	N	N	182
Notropis volucellus	Mimic shiner	X	X		X	X	X		N	N		N	N	N	N	184
Notropis wickliffi	Channel shiner	X	X		X	X	X					N	N	N	N	184
Opsopoeodus emiliae	Pugnose minnow	X		X		X	X	X	N		N	N	N	N	N	184
Phenacobius mirabilis	Suckermouth minnow		X		X	X	X	X	N		N	N	N	N	N	186

continued

Table 1 *continued*

Species	COMMON NAME	Habitats							Drainage						Page(s)
		Lowland	Upland	Big River	Stream	Creek	Lacustrine	Subterranean	Lake Michigan	Kankakee River	Maumee River	Wabash River	White River	Ohio River	
Pimephales notatus	Bluntnose minnow	X	X	X	X	X			N	N	N	N	N	N	186
Pimephales promelas promelas	Fathead minnow	X	X		X	X		X	N	N	N	N	N	N	186
Pimephales vigilax	Bullhead minnow	X	X	X	X				N	N		N	N	N	188
Rhinichthys cataractae	Longnose dace								N		Ep				188
Rhinichthys obtusus	Western blacknose dace		X			X			N	N	N	N	N	N	188
Scardinius erythrophthalmus	Rudd	X			X		X		I						190
Semotilus atromaculatus	Creek chub	X	X		X	X			N	N	N	N	N	N	190
Cobitidae															190
Misgurnus anguillicaudatus	Oriental weatherfish	X			X		X		I						191
Ictaluridae															192
Ameiurus catus	White catfish	X		X			X		N			I	I	I	196
Ameiurus melas	Black bullhead	X	X		X	X	X		N	N		N	N	N	196
Ameiurus natalis	Yellow bullhead	X	X		X	X	X		N	N		N	N	N	198
Ameiurus nebulosus	Brown bullhead	X	X		X		X		N			N	N	N	198
Ictalurus furcatus	Blue catfish	X		X								N	N	N	198
Ictalurus punctatus	Channel catfish	X	X	X	X		X		N		N	N	N	N	200
Noturus eleutherus	Mountain madtom		X		X							N	N	N	200
Noturus flavus	Stonecat		X		X	X			N	N		N	N	N	200
Noturus gyrinus	Tadpole madtom	X	X		X	X	X		N	N	N	N	N	N	202
Noturus miurus	Brindled madtom	X	X		X	X					N	N	N	N	202
Noturus nocturnus	Freckled madtom	X	X		X	X						N	N	N	202
Noturus stigmosus	Northern madtom		X		X						N	N		N	204
Pylodictis olivaris	Flathead catfish	X	X	X	X		X		N		I	N	N	N	204

Scientific name	Common name						Page
Osmeridae							204
Osmerus mordax	Rainbow smelt		X			I	210
Salmonidae							206
Coregonus alpenae	Longjaw cisco		X			E	210
Coregonus artedii	Cisco or Lake herring		X			N	212
Coregonus clupeaformis	Lake whitefish		X			N	212
Coregonus hoyi	Bloater		X			N	212
Coregonus johannae	Deepwater cisco		X			E	214
Coregonus kiyi kiyi	Kiyi		X			N	214
Coregonus nigripinnis	Blackfin cisco		X			E	214
Coregonus reighardi	Shortnose cisco		X			Ep	214
Coregonus zenithicus	Shortjaw cisco		X			Ep	216
Prosopium cylindraceum	Round whitefish		X			N	216
Oncorhynchus gorbuscha	Pink salmon		X			I	216
Oncorhynchus kisutch	Coho salmon		X			I	218
Oncorhynchus mykiss	Rainbow trout or Steelhead		X		I	I	218
Oncorhynchus tshawytscha	Chinook salmon		X			I	218
Salmo salar	Atlantic salmon			X	I		220
Salmo trutta	Brown trout			X	I		220
Salvelinus fontinalis	Brook trout		X			N	220
Salvelinus namaycush namaycush	Lake trout		X			N	222
Esocidae							
Esox americanus vermiculatus	Grass pickerel	X	X			N	224
Esox lucius	Northern pike	X	X		N	N	224
Esox m. masquinongy	Great Lakes muskellunge	X	X			N	224
Esox masquinongy ohioensis	Ohio River muskellunge	X	X		I	N	224

continued

Table 1 continued

| | | Habitats | | | | | | | Drainage | | | | | | |
Species	COMMON NAME	Lowland	Upland	Big River	Stream	Creek	Lacustrine	Subterranean	Lake Michigan	Kankakee River	Maumee River	Wabash River	White River	Ohio River	Page(s)
Umbridae															223
Umbra limi	Central mudminnow	X			X	X	X		N	N	N	N	N	N	226
Percopsidae															226
Percopsis omiscomaycus	Trout-perch	X			X				N		Ep			N	228
Aphredoderidae															228
Aphredoderus sayanus	Pirate perch	X		X	X	X			N	N	N	N	N	N	228
Amblyopsidae															230
Amblyopsis spelaea	Northern cavefish		X					X					N	N	230
Typhlichthys subterraneus	Southern cavefish	X					X						N		229
Lotidae															230
Lota lota	Burbot	X		X	X		X		N		N	N		NI	232
Fundulidae															234
Fundulus catenatus	Northern studfish		X		X	X							N		234
Fundulus diaphanus menona	Banded killifish	X					X		N	N	N				234
Fundulus dispar	Northern starhead topminnow	X			X		X		N	N		N	N		236
Fundulus notatus	Blackstripe topminnow	X			X	X	X		N	N	N	N	N	N	236
Fundulus olivaceus	Blackspotted topminnow		X		X	X				N		N	N	N	233
Poeciliidae															236
Gambusia affinis	Western mosquitofish	X			X	X	X		1		1	1	1	1	238
Atherinopsidae															240
Labidesthes sicculus	Brook silverside	X	X		X		X		N	N	N	N	N	N	240
Menidia beryllina	Inland silverside	X		X										1	240

Family / Species	Common name										Status	Page
Muglidae												239
Mugil cephalus	Striped mullet	X			X						N	240
Moronidae												242
Morone americana	White perch	X	X		X	X						244
Morone chrysops	White bass	X	X	X	X	X				N	N	244
Morone mississippiensis	Yellow bass	X			X	X				N	N	244
Morone saxatilis	Striped bass	X	X		X				1	1	1	246
Percidae												248
Ammocrypta clara	Western sand darter	X	X		X			N		Ep	N	256
Ammocrypta pellucida	Eastern sand darter		X		X		N			N	N	256
Crystallaria asprella	Crystal darter		X		X					Ep	Ep	256
Etheostoma asprigene	Mud darter	X		X	X			N		N	N	258
Etheostoma nov. cf. asprigene	Tangle darter	X	X	X						N	N	258
Etheostoma blennioides	Eastern greenside darter		X	X	X		N			N	N	258
Etheostoma caeruleum	Rainbow darter		X	X	X	X	N	N		N	N	260
Etheostoma camurum	Bluebreast darter		X	X				N		N	N	260
Etheostoma chlorosoma	Bluntnose darter	X	X	X	X		?			N	N	260
Etheostoma exile	Iowa darter	X	X	X	X		N	N		N	N	262
Etheostoma flabellare flabellare	Barred fantail darter	X		X			N	N		N	N	262
Etheostoma flabellare lineolatum	Striped fantail darter	X	X	X	X		N	N		N	N	262
Etheostoma gracile	Slough darter	X		X	X	X				N	N	264
Etheostoma histrio	Harlequin darter		X	X	X						N	264
Etheostoma maculatum	Spotted darter		X	X				N		N	N	264
Etheostoma microperca	Least darter	X	X		X		N			N	N	266
Etheostoma nigrum nigrum	Johnny darter	X	X	X	X	X	N	N		N	N	266
Etheostoma nov. cf. nigrum	Scaly darter	X			X	X	N	N		N	N	266

continued

Table 1 *continued*

Species	COMMON NAME	Habitats							Drainage						Page(s)
		Lowland	Upland	Big River	Stream	Creek	Lacustrine	Subterranean	Lake Michigan	Kankakee River	Maumee River	Wabash River	White River	Ohio River	
Etheostoma pholidotum	Prairie darter		X		X	X						N	N		268
Etheostoma proeliare	Cypress darter	X			X	X								N	268
Etheostoma spectabile	Orangethroat darter		X		X	X				N	N	N	N	N	268
Etheostoma squamiceps	Spottail darter		X			X						N		N	270
Etheostoma tippecanoe	Tippecanoe darter		X		X							N	N		270
Etheostoma variatum	Variegate darter		X	X	X									N	270
Etheostoma nov. cf. zonale	Jade darter		X		X					N					272
Etheostoma zonale	Banded darter		X		X									N	272
Perca flavescens	Yellow perch	X	X	X	X		X		N	N	N	N	I	I	272
Percina caprodes	Logperch	X	X	X	X	X	X		N	N	N	N	N	N	274
Percina copelandi	Channel darter		X		X						N	N	Ep	N	274
Percina evides	Gilt darter		X		X						Ep	N	Ep	Ep	274
Percina maculata	Blackside darter		X	X		X	X		N	N	N	N	N	N	276
Percina phoxocephala	Slenderhead darter		X		X				N	N		N	N	N	276
Percina sciera sciera	Dusky darter	X	X		X	X						N	N	N	276
Percina shumardi	River darter	X		X	X				N		N	N	N	N	278
Percina uranidea	Stargazing darter	X		X		X						Ep			278
Percina vigil	Saddleback darter		X			X						Ep	Ep		278
Percina zebra	Manitou darter	X	X		X		X		N			N			280
Sander canadense	Sauger	X		X	X				N		N	N	N	N	280
S. vitreus	Walleye	X		X	X				N		N	N	N	N	280

Family / Species	Common name															Page
Elassomatidae																282
Elassoma zonatum	Banded pygmy sunfish	X											N			288
Centrarchidae																283
Ambloplites rupestris	Rock bass	X	X			X		N			N	N	N	N	N	288
Centrarchus macropterus	Flier	X		X		X						N	N	N	N	288
Lepomis cyanellus	Green sunfish	X	X	X		X	X	N	N		N	N		N	N	290
Lepomis gibbosus	Pumpkinseed							N	N	N	N			N		290
Lepomis gulosus	Warmouth	X	X		X	X		N	N	N	N		N	N	N	290
Lepomis humilis	Orangespotted sunfish	X	X			X			N	N			N	N	N	292
Lepomis macrochirus	Bluegill	X	X	X		X		N	N	N	N	N	N	N	N	292
Lepomis megalotis	Longear sunfish	X	X	X		X	X		N		N		N	N	N	292
Lepomis microlophus	Redear sunfish	X		X		X						N	N	N	N	292
Lepomis miniatus	Redspotted sunfish	X				X		1			1		NI?	1	N	294
Lepomis pellastes	Northern longear sunfish	X	X			X		1			1		N	N	N	294
Lepomis symmetricus	Bantam sunfish	X		X		X		N		N	N		EP	N		294
Micropterus dolomieu	Smallmouth bass	X		X		X		N		N	N		N	N	N	296
Micropterus punctulatus	Spotted bass	X		X	X								N	N	N	296
Micropterus salmoides	Largemouth bass	X	X		X			N		N	N		N	N	N	296
Pomoxis annularis	White crappie	X	X	X	X	X		N		N	N		N	N	N	298
Pomoxis nigromaculatus	Black crappie	X	X	X	X	X		N		N	N		N	N	N	298
Cottidae																298
Cottus bairdii	Mottled sculpin		X	X		X	X	N		N	N		N	N		300
Cottus nov. cf. bairdii	Bluethroat sculpin		X	X			X							N	N	302
Cottus carolinae	Banded sculpin		X	X		X	X							N	N	302
Cottus cognatus	Slimy sculpin	X				X		N			N					304
Myoxocephalus thompsoni	Deepwater sculpin	X				X		N			N					304

continued

Table 1 *continued*

Species	COMMON NAME	Lowland	Upland	Big River	Stream	Creek	Lacustrine	Subterranean	Lake Michigan	Kankakee River	Maumee River	Wabash River	White River	Ohio River	Page(s)
Gobiidae															306
Apollonia melanostomus	Round goby						X		I						307
Gasterosteidae															306
Culaea inconstans	Brook stickleback	X	X			X	X		N		N	N	N		309
Gasterosteus aculeatus	Threespine stickleback						X		I						308
Pungitius pungitius	Ninespine stickleback						X		N						308
Sciaenidae															310
Aplodinotus grunniens	Freshwater drum	X		X	X		X		N	1	N	N	N	N	310

Introduction:
Purpose and Plan of the Book

The variety of landscapes and drainages occurring within Indiana has provided a rich assortment of habitats and a diverse fish fauna. Fish have been well studied over the last 200 years by many well-known scientists. At the turn of the twentieth century and until the middle of this present period, Indiana University was among the primary training centers for fisheries science. Yet, despite the large amount of training and research that occurred at Indiana University, a fish guide to the species occurring in the state had never been prepared. Past studies of the fish fauna have included annotated checklists, distribution studies, or special treatments contained within governmental reports and scientific monographs.

Indiana is a very diverse state and there is no comparison to other northern states. This diversity is a result of the Great Lakes to the north, the Ohio River to the south, and the Wabash River flowing from central to western margins of the state. Indiana possesses the highest fish diversity north of the Ohio River (Table 2). There have been 227 species of fishes documented within our political boundaries. This diverse fish assemblage makes Indiana's one of the most species-rich and diverse faunas in North America. The three most diverse states are Alabama (Boschung and Mayden 2004), Tennessee (Etnier and Starnes 1993), and Kentucky (Burr and Warren 1986). There are over 950 species of freshwater fish occurring in North America, including southern Mexico (Page and Burr 1991). Several species new to science are recognized within this work or were raised from synonymy; thus, they were not included in those previous estimates in Simon et al. (2002).

The richness and the variety of the fish fauna is a result of the gradient of cold to warm waters. Swift, turbulent waters occur in the northeast, while basic-gradient lowland streams occur in the southwest. The standing waters include small wetland, pannes, and ponds in the dunes of Lake Michigan and inland lakes and reservoirs in the central and southern regions. The unique features of the karst streams of south-central Indiana include a variety of caves and spectacular waterfalls. Some fish species are relics of the Pleistocene glaciation that created the deep, clear waters of the Great Lakes, while other portions of Indiana were not recently affected by the last glaciation event. These species occur in the karst streams and cave habitats. During the Wisconsin glaciation, the land was covered by a mile-thick ice sheet that followed previously flattened terrain further pushing surface soils, creating moraines. Many of these northern moraines became the impoundment for natural lakes and wetlands. Large freshwater fish species characteristic of large rivers, such as the Ohio and Wabash rivers, include the Paddlefish, Lake sturgeon, Bowfin, and Mooneye. In the Great Lakes are included other coldwater species such as the whitefish, Lake and Brook trout, Trout-perch, and Longnose sucker.

TABLE 2. FISH DIVERSITY AMONG STATES IN
THE NORTHEASTERN UNITED STATES.

| State | SPECIES RICHNESS | | | |
	Native	Endemic	Exotic	Total
Connecticut	26	0	50	63
Delaware	41	0	10	51
Illinois	191	0	17	208
Indiana	203	1	24	227
Maine	52	0	21	73
Maryland	93	1	13	107
Massachusetts	66	0	18	84
Michigan	184	0	23	207
Minnesota	139	0	33	159
New Hampshire	48	0	6	54
New Jersey	61	0	24	85
New York	130	0	7	137
Ohio	138	0	24	162
Pennsylvania	190	0	16	206
Rhode Island	21	0	11	32
Vermont	77	0	15	92
Virginia	196	6	18	220
West Virginia	170	1	8	179
Wisconsin	146	0	13	159

The state of Indiana has been extensively modified over most of its area and virtually none of the waters exist in presettlement condition. The landscape has been extensively modified, including the draining of wetlands, the channelization of headwater streams, and elimination of riverine wetlands including the great marshes of northern and southwestern Indiana. The former wetlands of the St. Joseph River, Great Marsh of the Calumet area wetlands, and the Grand Marsh of the Kankakee River are mostly memories recorded in history. The Black Swamp of the Maumee River and the extensive wetland complex along the Wabash River have been drained, ditched, and channelized. Many of the wetland species that occupied these areas have experienced either reduction in population abundance or were extirpated.

The invasion, release and importation, and stocking of non-indigenous and alien species into the Great Lakes caused widespread decline in biological quality of native fish faunas. The construction of the Welland Canal bypassed the former natural barrier caused by Niagara Falls. This breach enabled the spread of Sea lamprey, Alewife, and Threespine stickleback. The collapse of the Lake trout fisheries of Lake Michigan and the reduction in the whitefish fisheries was a result of overfishing and the parasitic Sea lamprey. The intentional stocking of Rainbow smelt and Pacific salmons was to provide additional fishing opportunities, while the accidental importation of Round goby and Oriental weatherfish in ship ballast has deteriorated the quality of world-class fisheries. The discharge of effluents from mining, manufacturing, and wastewater has polluted surface waters. Toxic effects from herbicides, pesticides, metals, and nutrients have impacted surface waters and created the anoxic zone in the Gulf of Mexico.

Perhaps the greatest future threat to biological diversity in Indiana is the invasion of exotic and alien fish species. Impacts are yet undetermined from the Asian carps that have invaded most of the large and great rivers in the eastern and central United States. Many of these species were intentionally raised in the aquaculture industry and escaped confinement. If changes in the fish assemblages of the Ohio and Mississippi river drainages will resemble that of the Great Lakes, we can anticipate severe destruction. The Great Lakes fauna is represented by species richness and composition that reflects watersheds from all over the world, including Southeast Asia, the Pacific Northwest, the Atlantic Slope, the Caspian and Black seas, and the Adriatic.

The ecology and conservation of native fish species is a priority of this work. Of all the fish species known to have occurred within Indiana, the majority of the species are currently stable (83.4%); however, several species are extinct (6 species), localized (12 species), or either very rare or imperiled (20 species). A single species is endemic and found only in specialized habitats within the state.

Despite the extensive work that has occurred in our state, many species are poorly known. Additional life history studies of ecological patterns are needed to understand basic biological needs. The species in most need of study include the minnows and darters. These species are perhaps the most interesting of our fauna but are also among the smallest, as they rarely exceed 3–4 inches (75–100 mm) in total length. With the publication of this work, our understanding of distribution patterns will be better understood and this will enable professional biologists, hobbyists, and anglers to enjoy the natural habitats and features of Indiana. My hope is that this work will stimulate you to inquire about what lives in your local streams and lakes. Who knows—perhaps our work will benefit better management and restoration of ecological processes that will enhance and protect rare species.

How to Use This Guide

The book is divided into a series of sections, with the introductory material providing needed technique information, keys to families, and background information on our fish fauna. Although my series *Reproductive Biology and Early Life History of Fishes in the Ohio River Drainage* provides detailed early life history identification accounts for many Indiana species, included here is a pictorial guide to early life history stages for all families. The proper way to use this guide is to look at the family key first, then to migrate to the species key. For families with monotypic genera, no attempt has been made to incorporate this species-level information into the family key. The **species account** section provides diagnostic family information, including a key to species within that family, then habitat and species diversity information within each family.

The **species account** section provides written distribution description for the species entire range, but the map shows only its range in Indiana watersheds. Common state and provincial abbreviations are used for geographic places. The maps are based on U.S. Geological Survey delineated watersheds adopted for management of the various hydrologic units. These maps are created to facilitate quick determination of species occurrence based on over 18,000 collections from all ninety-two counties in the state. The gray-scale watersheds do not necessarily represent the species occurrence as "everywhere" within the watershed, rather which watershed has that species found at least "somewhere" within the drainage area. These records might have been based on recent collections (post-1985) or museum information, literature citations, or studies that were viewed from others (pre-1985). For this project, no attempt was made to differentiate distribution based on temporal information.

The taxonomic diagnostic information presented for each species is meant to provide additional supplemental traits to ensure accurate identification. Each species has morphometric, meristic, and pigmentation information to assist in identification. Perhaps the greatest aid to accurate identification is the illustrations prepared by Joseph R. Tomelleri. These beautiful drawings are intentionally presented opposite each species account and distribution map so that quick identification can be readily available. These illustrations are taxonomically accurate and precise.

Lastly, supplemental species account information is provided that includes species conservation status, habitat preferences, diet, reproductive biology, and maximum size of adults. The **conservation status** is based on published papers by Simon et al. (2002), which represent each species status within Indiana. This conservation status is based on my personal opinions and does not reflect those of the state of Indiana nor the federal government. The **habitat preference** information is a summary of the major habitat types, including waterbody type, substrate, and stream cover preferences. **Diet** is based on definitions by Goldstein and Simon (1999) and classifies species based on dominant food, feeding behavior, and morphological features. **Reproductive guild** definitions are based on the concept and definition of Balon (1975) and further classified by Simon (1999). Lastly, the **maximum adult size** for each species is from Lee et al. (1980), which may not represent the maximum size of individuals from Indiana.

INDIANA
FISHES AND WATERS

Figure 1. Watersheds of the state of Indiana showing hydrologic units for each of the drainage subdivisions.

Waters of Indiana and Fish Associations

The political boundaries of Indiana comprise three basins, the Great Lakes basin, the Illinois or Mississippi river basin, and Ohio River basin (Figure 1). The Great Lakes basin includes the northern third of the state and includes all streams draining toward Lakes Michigan and Erie. The principal drainages of Lake Michigan include the Calumet and St. Joseph rivers, while the principal Lake Erie drainage is the Maumee River. The Mississippi River basin comprises the northwestern portion of the state, including the Illinois River basin, which is drained by the Kankakee and Iroquois river watersheds. The Illinois River eventually drains into the Mississippi River basin. The third basin is the Ohio River, which drains more than two-thirds of Indiana. The principal tributaries include the Wabash, Whitewater, and minor tributaries that drain directly into the Ohio River. Wabash River principal tributaries include the Salamonie, Mississinewa, Eel, Tippecanoe, Sugar, White, and Patoka rivers. The Whitewater River drains into the Great Miami River and enters the Ohio River in the southeastern-most portion of the state. The minor tributaries that drain directly into the Ohio River include the Little Blue, Blue, Anderson, and Pigeon rivers.

These three basins are contained within six ecoregions (Woods et al. 1998). Ecoregions are ecological mosaics of land use, land cover, geological history, and soil types. The Central Corn Belt Plain includes the Lake Michigan and Calumet River drainages of northwestern Indiana and the Kankakee and Iroquois rivers. The Northern Indiana Till Plain comprises the St. Joseph River including the Pigeon and Elkhart rivers as the primary drainages. The Huron-Erie Lake Plain contains the Maumee River drainage including the St. Joseph, St. Marys, and Auglaize rivers. The largest ecoregion is the Eastern Corn Belt Plain, which encompasses central and portions of southeastern Indiana including the upper Wabash, West Fork White, East Fork White, Muscatatuck, Lost, and Whitewater rivers. The Interior River Lowland includes the middle and lower Wabash River and tributaries such as the Vermillion, Sugar, Eel (lower), and Patoka rivers. These streams are basic gradient and have been extensively channelized. The last ecoregion is the Interior Plateau, which includes the minor tributaries of the Ohio River. These streams are principally karst streams that have bedrock substrates.

GEOLOGICAL DRAINAGE DEVELOPMENT

The present northern drainages are recent pathways that were established less than 10,000 years ago when the last glacier traversed the state (Page and Burr 1986). The landform of southern Indiana has been determined by the southern-most glaciation event, called the Illinoian, which covered the Blue River and most of the East Fork White River. The drainage history during the Illinoian has been obscured by the more recent Wisconsin glaciation. The Wisconsin glacier extensively altered the land mass by depositing large amounts of glacial till. The weight of the mile-high ice followed paths of least resistance, scouring the land, and created moraines and glacial pothole lakes.

During the early stages of the glacial ice retreat, two difference drainage ways were created in the eastern part of Indiana (Gerking 1945). The Whitewater River and the East Fork White River drained the south and western parts of the glacial melt water. Fall Creek drained the central melt waters west toward the Mississippi River. Walnut Creek, Sugar Creek, and the Wabash River drained the western area. As the ice melted, flowages were created. Large proglacial lakes drained south into the Mississippi River basin. For example, Lake Chicago in the Lake Michigan basin drained into the Illinois River and Lake Maumee in the Lake Erie Basin drained south into the Wabash River and Ohio River through the Little Wabash River.

Ice in the Lake Michigan lowland retreated about 13,000 years ago northward to Cheboygan County, Michigan, and may have cleared the Straits of Mackinaw (Farrand et al. 1969; Evenson et al. 1976). When ice advanced in the Lake Michigan basin into the waters of Lake Chicago, the principal drainage was southward through the Chicago outlet (Underhill 1986). Additional connections were created by the three lobes of the Wisconsin glacier. The Michigan lobe, the Saginaw lobe, and the Huron-Erie lobe penetrated Indiana from the northwest, north, and northeast. The Saginaw lobe was the first to retreat. The water associated with this lobe was drained by the upper Tippecanoe River. During this time, the Tippecanoe River valley was likely connected with the Iroquois and Kankakee drainages. When the Michigan lobe retreated, there was unobstructed flow westerly between the future Illinois and Wabash drainages. As the Saginaw lobe melted and retreated northward, the St. Joseph River valley was the primary drain and provided connections between the Kankakee and Illinois rivers. This is perhaps one of the most important drains that enabled fishes to enter the Great Lakes from the Mississippi River valley (Leverrett and Taylor 1915; Gerking 1945). No new drainages were created when the Michigan lobe retreated.

The Great Lakes began to form as the three lobes retreated. Leverrett and Taylor (1915) and Coleman (1922) described the various stages in the development of the Great Lakes. The development of present-day Lake Michigan went through several proglacial stages including Lake Chicago (draining through the Chicago Outlet), followed by Lake Algonquin (draining southwest through the Chicago Outlet) and the Nipissing Great Lakes (draining east through the Ottawa River prior to uplift and then easterly through Port Huron after the uplift).

The Huron-Erie lobe was the first to retreat, creating Lake Maumee (Underhill 1986). This lake was a proglacial lake that existed just southwest of the present Lake Erie and extended to as far west as Fort Wayne. Lake Maumee flowed south from the ice front with an outlet at Fort Wayne south to the Wabash River at Huntington. As the ice retreated, the level of Lake Maumee lowered while the area of the lake increased, producing a series of proglacial lakes. These stages of proglacial lakes included Lakes Arkona, Whittlesey, Wayne, Warren, and Lundy. During the development of Lake Erie, the proglacial Lake Maumee drained by way of the Maumee and Wabash rivers (Coleman 1922). As development progressed, this drain was abandoned and the drain went through the Maumee River and flowed northeasterly. As Lake Maumee was formed, the Michigan lobe of the glacier retreated into the northwest part of the state. Lake Chicago was formed by melting ice between the ice border and the last moraine. The outlet for this lake drained south into the Illinois River through the area of Chicago (Gerking 1945).

Present-day streams, such as the Ohio River, greatly enlarged as the former Teays River was blocked by the ice mass (Page and Burr 1986). Prior to the Wisconsin glaciation, the Wabash River was larger than the Ohio River, which was only a small tributary. The Ohio River increased in drainage area during this period, as the upper Teays River drainage pattern changed. A glacial refugia remained near Martinsville southward to the Ohio River. This area formed an important recolonization point post-glaciation. The characteristics of glacial meltwater were turbid, cold, and variable flows. These stream types would be preferred by coldwater species, such as trout, salmon, and pike. These waters would be well oxygenated but probably too cold for many species to use as a migration corridor.

A series of stream captures and stream piracies enabled exchange of adjacent watershed fish faunas (Gerking 1945). Stream capture usually occurs in headwaters of two closely spaced streams from adjacent watersheds. Local flooding caused streams to be inundated, thus enabling species to move or exchange between former land barriers. This is a particularly simple change for headwater fish species but would not be a common mechanism for large river species.

FISH FAUNAL RELATIONSHIPS

The fishes of the Great Lakes include a diverse fauna, which drains the tributaries of Lakes Erie and Michigan and the deep waters of Lake Michigan (Table 1). The Lake Michigan drainage includes 143 species, while the Maumee River drainage includes 110 species. The Coregonine fishes are endemic to the Great Lakes (Koelz 1929) and include *Coregonus alpenae, C. johannae, C. nigripinnis,* and *C. reighardi* that have been extirpated. The Coregonine fishes have been extensively studied (Lindsey and Woods 1970; Todd and Smith 1980; Todd 1981;

Todd et al. 1981), yet the postulated recent common ancestor and origin of the species complex has not been solved. With the extinction of several species, the evolutionary hypotheses will be difficult to reconstruct.

The Wabash River is the most diverse watershed with 151 native fish species (Table 1). This could well have the most native fish species of any drainage in the Ohio River basin. The two principal tributaries, the West Fork White River including the lower White River and the East Fork White River, include 126 species. Three fish species, including a single species that is now extinct, have been extirpated from the Wabash River drainage. The Harelip sucker (*Moxostoma lacerum*) was always considered rare. The species was known from the Tippecanoe River; however, it is not known what caused its demise. Some speculate that the extinction may have been due to either habitat changes or environmental degradation.

Several darters were last collected from the lower Wabash River near New Harmony in the late 1890s (Gerking 1945). The Crystal darter (*Crystallaria asprella*), Stargazing darter (*Percina uranidea*), and Saddleback darter (*Percina vigil*) are large river fish that are found on riffle habitats (Page 1983; Kuehne and Barbour 1983). Few riffle habitats remain in the lower Wabash River, perhaps as a result of river meandering.

The Illinois River basin within Indiana contains 102 species. The watershed was once a large wetland complex but has been drained and extensively altered. Despite the widespread changes, the species composition has not resulted in widespread extirpations. Only the Bigeye chub (*Hybopsis amblops*) has been extirpated from the drainage; however, the species has expanded its range elsewhere in the White River.

The Ohio River basin includes 149 species. The riverine wetland habitats, which existed in the tributary mouths of the minor tributaries, have been inundated with the construction of the navigation lock and dams. The loss of riverine wetlands and the barriers created by the lock and dams has impacted Alabama shad (*Alosa alabamae*) and American eel (*Anguilla rostrata*) and has restricted the movement of Lake sturgeon, Paddlefish, and Crystal darter. The increased depth of the main stem Ohio River has created a variety of habitat types that are difficult to study; however, with the use of a variety of gear types, populations of Northern madtom (*Noturus stigmosus*) and Channel darter (*Percina copelandi*) have been discovered in deep main channel waters. The Variegate darter (*Etheostoma variatum*) and Redside dace (*Clinostomus elongatus*) are limited to the Whitewater and Greater Miami rivers. The Redside dace is isolated in headwater streams above Brookville Reservoir northward into Ohio and a relict population of the species is found in Miami County. The Variegate darter occurs from Brookville southward to the Ohio River, but the species does not occur farther south into the Greater Miami River. A record for the species exists from near the Blue River mouth. This record has been confirmed by observing the actual preserved specimen; however, the habitat does not appear to be consistent with the swift current and large cobble and boulder substrates that the species prefers. It is unlikely that persisting populations continue to exist in the Blue River.

RANGE REDUCTION

The Alligator gar (*Atractosteus spatula*) was collected in the East Fork White River during 2007 from multiple locations but had not been previously collected from the Wabash River drainage since the turn of the nineteenth century. The species was associated with the extensive riverine wetlands surrounding the Wabash River, but with the draining of these wetlands the species had been locally extirpated. Recent population collections from the East Fork White River and from the Ohio River near Madison indicate that the species is still present.

The Popeye shiner (*Notropis ariommus*) and Channel darter originally were described from the White River near Indianapolis (Cope 1867; Jordan 1877). The Popeye shiner has not been collected from the White River since the end of the nineteenth century (Cope 1868). The Popeye shiner has recently been collected from the Vernon Fork Muscatatuck River, a tributary of the East Fork White River. The Channel darter is an inhabitant of large, deep rivers and has not been collected in the White River since Jordan's (1877) description. Since Jordan, only a single record of the Channel darter was published by Carney et al. (1993); however, upon inspection of the specimen at the

Illinois Natural History Survey, it was determined that the specimen was actually a Slenderhead darter (*Percina phoxocephala*) (T. P. Simon and B. E. Fisher, unpublished data). The species is present in the main stem Ohio and Maumee rivers.

The Banded pygmy sunfish was originally known from the lower Wabash River in the extensive backwater swamps. The species was reported by Forbes and Richardson (1905, 1920) but has only recently been found in tributaries of the lower Wabash River, Knox County. The species' current status is unknown due to the lack of adequate surveys in cypress swamps along the lower Ohio River. Surveys since the early 1990s have not found any recent specimens with the exception of the Dee Shee River. The draining of the extensive backwater wetlands along the lower Wabash River is the probable cause of this species range reduction.

Seven fish species have either been extirpated from the Wabash River or experienced range reductions, including the Northern brook lamprey (*Ichthyomyzon fossor*), Lake sturgeon (*Acipenser fulvescens*), Lake herring (*Coregonus artedii*), Greater redhorse (*Moxostoma valenciennesi*), Northern madtom, Spotted darter (*Etheostoma maculatum*), and Gilt darter (*Percina evides*). Three species have increased their range, including the Eastern sand darter (*Ammocrypta pellucida*), Harlequin darter (*Etheostoma histrio*), and Tippecanoe darter (*E. tippecanoe*). The reason for increasing ranges is primarily due to better targeted sampling in specific habitats.

The Northern brook lamprey is known in Indiana from the Galena River, Lake Michigan basin, and a few locations in the Tippecanoe River, Fulton County (T. P. Simon, unpublished data). Aggressive lampricide treatment of streams to control Sea lamprey populations in the Lake Michigan basin may have caused the local extirpation of native non-parasitic lampreys.

Lake sturgeon was once known from the Wabash River near Cayuga throughout the main channel of the Wabash River (Blatchley 1938). Due to the species' large size and difficulty of collecting individuals from main channel habitats, little is known of the species' status in the Wabash River. It is assumed that the species has been locally extirpated from the Wabash

River, but a small recovering population exists in the East Fork White River beneath Williams Dam (T. P. Simon, unpublished data; B. E. Fisher, pers. comm.). This may be the sole remaining population in the Ohio River basin. The species is not known from the Ohio River except from individuals marked and re-captured from the East Fork White River populations.

The Lake herring has seen extensive range reduction as a result of cultural eutrophication and the loss of the thermo-cline in many glacial lakes (Pearson 2001). The species has been locally extirpated from most of the known lakes within the Tippecanoe River system.

The Greater redhorse is rare in the Wabash River drainage and was previously known from only a few locations in Vigo County (Whitaker and Wallace 1973) and from the Eel River watershed upstream of Logansport (Braun 1984). Sampling at previously known collection localities in the Wabash River and tributaries (Vigo County) has shown that the species has been locally extirpated. Currently, the species is found only in the Eel River watershed near Logansport and has not been collected anywhere else in the Ohio River drainage. The species is present in the St. Joseph (Lake Michigan) and Maumee river drainages and Lake Michigan.

The Northern madtom has not been collected from the Tippecanoe River since the late 1800s (Gerking 1945). The species has been recently reported from the Tippecanoe River, but specimen identity is unconfirmed. As a result, the current status of the species is unknown. The Northern madtom has been collected from the main stem Ohio River near Evansville at water depths of 18.6 m (Simon 2007).

My record of Spotted darter was the last individuals col-lected from the Tippecanoe River. These specimens were col-lected in 1985 from a large riffle downstream of Winamac, Fulton County, and reported by Carney et al. (1993; T. P. Simon, unpublished data). The species has not been collected from the Tippecanoe River since, but the species has been found in the East Fork White River, downstream of Shoals (Simon 2007), and is still common in the Blue River in Perry County.

The Gilt darter was originally found throughout the West Fork White River from Marion to Morgan counties (Margulies et al. 1980). The species type locality is the West Fork White

River near Indianapolis. The Gilt darter has been extirpated from its type locality but is considered currently stable, being found in the middle Tippecanoe River from Rochester to Lake Shafer (Simon 2007).

The Eastern sand darter has remained stable or increased in distribution throughout the Wabash River but has not expanded in the White River watershed (B. E. Fisher, pers. comm.). The species is found in the Tippecanoe River and from the Wabash River main stem upstream to the Eel River, including many tributaries. The species has also been found in the St. Joseph River upstream of the Maumee River mouth. The species is found over clean sand with moderate current.

Harlequin darter populations were considered extirpated from Indiana for more than a century (Whitaker and Gammon 1988). However, in the early 1990s, Simon and Kiley (1993) found the species in the lower White River and upper East Fork White River watershed. Harlequin darter prefer habitats with woody debris in moderate to fast-flowing waters. The Harlequin darter has been collected continuously from the Patoka River mouth up the Wabash River to the mouth of the White River, continuing upstream in the East Branch White River to Columbus terminating in Sugar Creek. The species is currently expanding into the West Fork White River and occurs as far upstream as Richland Creek (Simon 2007).

Lastly, the Tippecanoe darter has probably not expanded its range greatly, but more efficient sampling techniques and targeted sampling in select habitats have enabled more species records (Simon 2005). Trautman (1981) found in Ohio that population abundance can change dramatically based on annual recruitment. The Tippecanoe darter is found in the Tippecanoe River from Delong (Marshland) to the Wabash River mouth (Jordan and Evermann 1890) and has been collected in the lower East Fork White River downstream of Williams Dam to Shoals (Simon 2007).

ALIEN INVASION

The first alien invasion occurred with the intentional stocking and transplant of food fishes. Many species have been transplanted outside of their natural range into waters that were not suitable for continued existence. For example, Brook trout were transplanted to almost every coolwater stream in northern Indiana; however, none of these populations have survived. The Carp (*Cyprinus carpio*) and Goldfish (*Carassius auratus*) were transplanted into almost every watershed in North America. These species became established and naturalized into the main stem rivers and streams. These species were introduced by the federal government, intending that they might become food or game fish. Both species reach very large sizes and contribute to commercial fisheries in their native ranges.

The Carp has been introduced widely in North America, and there is no drainage or state that does not provide habitat for this species. Carp are ubiquitously found throughout Indiana, virtually in every drainage system. Goldfish are much less successful in colonizing North American streams and rivers. They are nearly absent from Indiana, with the exception of the Lake Michigan basin. Typically Goldfish are found only in the most degraded habitats in the White River watershed, that is, White River canal in downtown Indianapolis, and are common in the Grand Calumet River.

The recently introduced Asiatic aliens may prove to be much more devastating to native fish species than Carp and Goldfish. Four large Asian species have been imported into the aquaculture industry and have escaped into the wild. The Grass carp, *Ctenopharyngodon idella,* also known as the White amur, was imported into Alabama and Arkansas from eastern Asia in 1963 to control aquatic vegetation (U.S. Fish and Wildlife Service, unpublished data). An adult Grass carp has been reported to eat 45 kg (99.2 lbs) of vegetation per day. The Grass carp is widespread in the Wabash and lower White rivers. Individuals have been caught by anglers as far north as Lafayette (Tippecanoe County) and to the East and West Forks White River junction.

The Bighead carp, *Hypophthalmichthys nobilis,* was brought to Arkansas in 1972 from eastern China by a private fish farmer to control plankton in culture ponds. The species escaped in the early 1980s. The Bighead carp feeds near the surface of rivers, on organisms such as zooplankton and aquatic insect larvae and adults, and has been observed schooling with other filter-feeding species such as Paddlefish. The Bighead carp also competes directly with other native species, such as Bigmouth buffalo (*Ictiobus cyprinellus*), Gizzard shad (*Dorosoma cepedianum*), all early life stages of native fish species, and native unionid mussels. Individual Bighead carp are known to grow to be about 39.5 kg (88 lbs) and 1.2 m (4 ft) long. Bighead carp have been collected from the middle Wabash River, the middle West Fork White River, and from the lower White River near Petersburg, Gibson County.

The Silver carp, *Hypophthalmichthys molitrix,* was brought by an Arkansas fish farmer to the United States from Asia in 1973 to control phytoplankton and possibly for use as a food fish. Silver carp have been introduced into sewage lagoons to control algae. The Silver carp escaped in the early 1980s into the Mississippi River basin. This fish is a very proficient feeder that has gill rakers that are fused into sponge-like porous plates. Silver carp can consume two to three times their weight in plankton each day. Because of its preferred food items, the Silver carp competes with all native fish larvae and juveniles, adult Paddlefish, Bigmouth buffalo, Gizzard shad, and native mussels. These fish can grow to be over 1 m (3.3 ft) in length and about 27.24 kg (60 lbs).

The most recent escaped Asian carp is the Black carp, *Mylopharyngodon piceus,* which was brought to the United States in the early 1970s from eastern Asia. The Black carp and Grass carp resemble each other. The Black carp can be identified by its fused pharyngeal teeth that are used in crushing shells of mollusks and crustaceans. In the 1980s, Black carp was imported for use as a food fish and to control the spread of trematodes (parasites) in snails at catfish farms. The only known record of escape occurred in 1994 in Missouri, when thirty or more Black carp escaped with several thousand Bighead carp into the Osage River in Missouri. Black carp have reached the size of 1.29 m (4.3 ft) and over 35.87 kg (79 lbs).

The effect of the new wave of Asian carp on the North American fish assemblages has still not been fully realized. It is unclear when population numbers from the second invasion will stabilize. Asian carps have the potential of affecting phytoplankton, zooplankton, and molluscan assemblages. In addition, these carps may also change the biomass and structure of native fish assemblages. The four recent Asian species' prolific spawning capacity and large size can reduce native species' biomass. The change in species composition, expansion and range reduction, and the intentional introductions and escape of non-indigenous species have affected the native fish fauna of Indiana. Introductions through ship ballast water have changed the Great Lakes fauna, while the escape of Asian carps through the aquaculture industry will profoundly change the Mississippi and Ohio river basins.

Field Study and Collection of Fishes

The study of fish, that is, ichthyology, is based on the study of variation within species. This requires the acquisition of fish specimens so that a variety of sizes can be studied. There are a variety of purposes for collecting fish. For the professional ichthyologist, the primary goal is to study the diversity and natural history of species. It is imperative that specimens be collected during different seasons, over different years, and from different places so that variation can be understood. Systematics (i.e., study of evolutionary relationships) and taxonomy (i.e., study of variation and recognition of different kinds) are among the primary questions investigated by ichthyologists. Spatial scale enables understanding of species range, status, and conservation needs. Thus, the need is for numerous specimens to fulfill the requirement for taxonomic comparison of varieties and descriptions.

Another objective of fish collections is to account for changes in the condition of streams and watersheds. Aquatic and fisheries biologists are interested in understanding change in population and communities. This can be for the purposes of best management practices or for formulating watershed plans for restoration and protection of ecological function. During the course of these watershed surveys, specimens are retained as vouchers from each site to enable accurate verification of species identified in the field. Vouchers are important records, since once deposited into a museum collection, each specimen serves as a long-term record of occurrence. Questions on taxonomic veracity can be checked since these specimens remain for perpetuity. Fish are indicators of environmental condition and reflect changes from human-induced changes.

A third purpose for collecting fish is for research on behavior, life history, and determining natural processes occurring during the annual species life cycle. These life history and distribution studies are conducted temporally over multiple years so that variation in response to flow, temperature, and other habitat variables can be studied. Specimens for these types of studies are often collected at the same site for a period of months. Often, a set number of specimens are required so that a certain number of individuals are removed from the population. The key to these studies is to not harvest so many individuals that the population is harmed but instead to ensure that sustainable observation is capable of being performed. For some rare species this requires photographic recording in the field and release of the individual. These photographic records become vouchers for the study. In other cases, only the species of interest is preserved for further study. These species-specific studies include investigations of habitat use, thermal preference, age, growth, survivorship, reproductive biology, diet, early life history, resource partitioning, and energetics.

Lastly, non-professionals have much to contribute to the study of fish. Amateurs and hobbyists that maintain fish in aquaria have made important observations on courtship and spawning behavior, selection of nest or spawning sites, early life history culture, growth, and survivorship of captive adults. The most important requirement is to be diligent in recording observations and be specific when describing actions. Particular note should be taken to describe as a good reporter—the who, what, when, where, why, and how of observations. There are outlets to share these observations in places like *American Currents,* the journal of the North American Native Fishes Association, or by contacting professionals and asking for assistance in collaboration and publication. A good photograph or "home movie" documenting the event is very important.

SAMPLING APPROACHES AND STUDY DESIGN

Despite the variety of collection methods and gear choices available to collectors, the common requirement is to collect a representative sample from the appropriate study reach. A representative sample requires that all available habitats are sampled in proportion to the amount occurring at the site. Fish of all species are captured and not differentially netted by the collection crew, so that minnows and darters are equally tried for as are large individual Largemouth bass. If the desire is to compare stream condition, the species relative abundance or spatial distribution must reflect that observed in the stream; thus standard collection methods need to be established and followed. These methods are usually based on specific distance or efforts that vary with watershed size (i.e., drainage area), stream width, or lake surface area. With increasing waterbody size is a concomitant increase in distance and time sampling.

The collector should assume that fish are found in every unique habitat. Fish vary with position in the water column (surface and bottom), habitat cycle (i.e., riffle, run, pool), cover type (i.e., submerged vegetation, woody debris, boulders, shallow shoal areas, undercut banks, exposed root masses and fibrous root mats, deep pools), and with position in the watershed (i.e., headwater streams, lakes, wetlands, and large rivers).

COLLECTING AND OBSERVING FISHES

The objectives for collecting fish are varied, but the clear point is that much still remains to be learned. Non-game species are particularly understudied, and these species are perhaps the most interesting and particularly amenable to captivity. Students and those interested in making contributions to specific species should start with surrogate or common forms, thus perfecting culture and captivity requirements prior to embarking on large-scale projects with threatened or endangered species.

One important point for professionals and amateurs is to be sure that the proper forms, applications, and requirements are met from your local state agency prior to going into the field and collecting specimens. For example, common sense minnow seines can be used to collect specimens with a valid fishing license. To use any other gear type, such as electrofishing equipment, hoop nets, or trap nets, would require a scientific purposes permit. Severe penalties can be imposed if these guidelines are not followed. Likewise, the disposition of the live fish is important. Individuals cannot be transported across state lines nor can game species be retained. Live fish cannot be sold under any circumstances unless a bait dealer's license or commercial license for the holding and sale is secured.

COLLECTING WITH NETS

The "common sense" minnow seine is the most well-known method for fish collection (Figure 2). The net includes a rectangular panel of various lengths and widths (usually made of nylon) that are connected to two poles or brails. The top of the rectangular net has a series of floats arranged equidistance along the top and a series of lead weights along the bottom line. The top line is called the float line and the bottom line the lead line. The size of the net varies with the purpose of the study and the size of the stream. Small seines are always used in small streams or in large streams with fast current.

The common sense minnow seine is perhaps the most variable piece of equipment for capturing fish since it depends on the ability and expertise of the collector. The approach is dependent on keeping the lead line on the bottom so that fish are not able to get beneath, while keeping the float line positioned so that individuals cannot jump over or swim over the top.

There are two basic techniques used to corral fish and herd them to shallows. The "set and kick" and "haul" procedures have several different modifications that will ensure success; however, both techniques are employed in a direction downstream to the current. The reason is because fish are usually oriented facing upstream, so when the seine engages the individual the tendency is to swim into the net rather than away from the net.

The set and kick procedure is used in shallow, flowing portions of the stream. These moving areas are called riffles or swift runs. The procedure requires a minimum of two people. One person sets the net and ensures that the lead line is touching the bottom at all places. The net is extended usually three-quarters the maximum extent of the length forming a U-shape in the lead line. The brails are held at 45- to 60-degree angles to the person's body. This person usually stands inside the net, facing upstream, so that the arms are outstretched as the brails are positioned into an inverted V-shape. The individual in very swift water may stand on the lead line to ensure that the bottom line remains without gaps. The second person moves upstream outside of the margins of the net and is known as the "kicker." The kicker moves upstream after the net is set about 6–10 ft (2–3 m) upstream or may move in very swift water only 3 ft (1 m). The kicker proceeds to bury his or her feet into the substrate and then kick down into it, dislodging stones, kicking woody debris and leaf packs, or using hands to move large boulders. The kicker moves as an ice-skater in a zig-zag pattern, alternating feet moving back and forth, so that the bottom in front of the entire width of the net is disturbed. The kicker moves quickly back and forth and toward the established net. Once they reach the net, the person in the net moves outside and the kicker and holder each take a brail. As they lift the net, they slide the lead line forward and then simultaneously lift the net, giving ground to the flow, and pick the net up out of the water. If additional people are available, two or more kickers may be used working side by side toward the net.

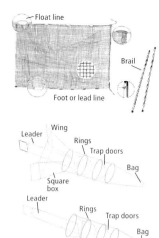

Figure 2. Example nets including common sense minnow seine (*top*), fyke net (*center*), and cast net (*bottom*).

The haul method is used in slow-moving or standing water. A variety of approaches can be used depending on the amount of bottom cover or "snags." Ideally, the net is positioned so that a slight bow or U-shape is created in the net. Two people are positioned so that one is on each brail. The net haul is initiated by dropping the net into place so that the lead line is maintained in contact with the bottom. The two seiners proceed so that they are both moving downstream at the same speed. If the net is pulled too fast, the lead line will lift from the bottom; too slow and the U-shape cannot be maintained. This type of seining requires much skill since the seiners must maintain proper speed and simultaneously keep a look out for snags and a place to withdraw the net.

The seine attempt is completed by either dragging the net to shore or by hoisting the net out of the water with a rapid downstream movement and lifting simultaneously. The former method requires that the collector on the deep end move to shore quickly in front of the shallow end of the seine, while the latter method requires cooperation and a simultaneous lifting of the lead line. Variations of this approach include placing a third person on the shoreline where the seiners are going to emerge and having the third person use his or her feet to kick fish into the seine as the fish try to escape. This person can assist in grabbing the lead line and making sure that it stays on the bottom as the brails beach the seine. The most important action is not speed but maintaining lead line contact with the bottom by manipulating the slope of the brails. Most fish attempt to escape as the seine is drawn into shore since the bottom is uneven and the opportunities for escape are increased. Another approach is to form a J-shape in the seine so that the highest portion of the J is extended into the deepest portion of the waters. This enables individual fish that attempt to run into deep waters to hit the edge of the net and does not allow escape.

Inevitably, the net will get snagged. Once the net is snagged do not tug at the net since this will cause tears and a greater chance of damage. Instead, once a snag is observed, find where the snag is stuck and back the seine off of the submerged object and lift the lead line off the object. Once the object is cleared, the net can be dropped back into place and seining can be continued. Most likely individuals that were in the net will escape, or a net lift can be done to check and determine what may have been captured. A third person can help by either flanking the seine to pull it off of submerged objects or "scouting ahead" of the advancing crew to notify them in advance of snags.

There are many different sizes and shapes of seines. For example, standard sizes may include 10, 15, 20, or 25 ft lengths that are usually 4–6 ft in height. The floats may be few or of high-density styrene or polypropylene. Lead lines may contain few numbers of lead weights or may possess a continuous chain along the bottom. Many lake studies use a "bag" seine, which has an extra panel in the center of the net that forms a bag that funnels all of the individuals from the panels into the middle and ultimately into the bag. The bag usually is a smaller mesh size than the panels, but all seines usually have mesh less than 0.5 inches (12.5 mm) to be legal. Most mesh seines have less than ⅛-inch mesh. The smaller the mesh the most likely smaller individuals will be retained; however, in swift water the smaller mesh creates more friction and greater resistance. Likewise, the amount of weight on the lead line depends on the substrate, size of the seine, and flow. On sand substrates, heavy weights will cut down into the soft substrates, causing the seine to be filled with sand. On large gravel substrates and swift flow, the heavier weight helps maintain contact with the substrate. Thus, a series of tradeoffs are observed and the best approach is to have a variable set of alternatives that either allows removal of weights or several seines permanently outfitted so choices in gear can be made.

Additional types of less commonly used nets include hoop nets, gill nets, trammel nets, fyke nets, dip nets, or cast nets (Figure 2). Hoop, gill, trammel, and fyke nets are passive gear types since they are placed into the stream in shallow areas along shore and left for a set period of time. Many sets are 24 hours in duration and then nets are retrieved and reset. The gill nets are large panels similar to a single seine but are anchored in place and marked with a float line and buoy. These nets are fished from shallow to deep, while "experimental" gill nets have a variety of mesh sizes along a single unit. The small mesh is positioned close to shore, while larger mesh sizes are in the deepest depths. These nets are usually 125 ft in length and contain five 25 ft sections. The mesh includes square mesh that ranges from ¾-, 1-, 1¼-, or 1½-, to 2-inch diagonal mesh. The method is successful when the fish swim into the net and gill themselves as they ram through the mesh sizes. Fish with spines or sharp fin rays are likewise captured by entanglement in the mesh. Trammel nets are effectively a double gill net that has two different size mesh. These nets are floated downstream or are stationary positioned. Fish are captured by passing through the larger mesh and then as they hit the smaller mesh, which entangles the individual, a pocket is formed around them.

Hoop nets and fyke nets are either round, square, or D-shaped (Figure 2). These nets have two wings and a center panel that proceed from the mouth of the net to funnel fish into the net's throat. Nets are usually fished parallel to shore so that the center panel connects two nets. The side wings proceed into deep and shallow water. The net has a series of hoops that reduce in size with distance from the mouth and are connected by a series of passages that allow one-way passage through the net to the tied or cod end of the net. Fish typically move through the series of passages to the cod end, which is staked and marked with a buoy. Depending on the size of the mesh many different kinds of fish can be collected, but these nets are best for catfish, sunfish, and large suckers. The advantage of the gear is that the fish collect themselves by swimming along the center or panel wings into the net. This increased activity usually occurs during nocturnal migration and movements from deep to shallows in moderate- to large-sized rivers and lakes.

Cast nets and dip nets are active gears since these nets require the collector to either throw or "cast" the net (Figure 2). The cast net is circular and has a long drawstring and a series of weights along the outer margin. The net is fished by casting it, similar to a discus, and allowing it to sink. The net is retrieved by pulling hard on the drawstring, which causes the weighted sink line to form a purse, capturing all of the individuals that were in the water column. This gear is not very effective but is successful in capturing surface species. Dip nets include a variety of shapes and sizes from a rectangular "sweep net" to a D-shaped net. The D-net is useful for scraping along bank habitats, especially in exposed tree roots, while the sweep net is useful for collecting in submerged aquatic plants. The net is either positioned in current so that the collector can kick downstream into the net or is repeatedly jabbed into the submerged plants, allowing the plants to be filtered through the mesh. Nets are effective methods that have decreased efficiency over other methods but provide the most enjoyment because the collector is actively engaged in the collection. Seines and other nets do not require the wearing of waders, so that high-quality sites can be enjoyed by wading in swimsuits.

COLLECTION BY ELECTROFISHING

Electrofishing is a technique that stuns and immobilizes individual fish. The use of electrofishing equipment has become the standard collection gear for many studies since the method is useful for drawing individuals from beneath banks, from deep waters, and from within dense cover. The principle of electrofishing is that a field is established between the anode and cathode. Usually, the collector stands within the middle of the field and the anode usually contains a net or ring wand that is directed into potential habitats where fish occur. Electrofishing includes two types of output, either alternating (AC) or direct (DC) current. Alternating current will immobilize fish "in place" and has the greatest potential of damaging muscle or tissue, while direct current is pulsed and causes the fish to be drawn to the anode due to the polarity of the medium and tissues. Direct current is typically pulsed to mimic the effects of alternating current.

The effectiveness of electrofishing is dependent on water quality. Electrofishing efficiency is determined by water conductivity, temperature, depth, and dissolved materials in the water. Since electrofishing requires visual observation of stunned fish, water clarity is important. Electrofishing is most efficient in shallow water where visual impairment is diminished but can be improved with increased power. Electrofishing operates on a power function based on voltage, amperage, frequency, and pulse width. All of these settings determine the effectiveness of the event. A variety of generator and battery systems are available. The greater the total wattage of the system increases the effectiveness of the equipment. Depending on the generator size, the system is either floated in a boat or barge, fished off a bridge or from alongside a bank, or carried on the collector's back on a frame. For small- to medium-sized streams, the backpack or bridge-applied long-line system is used. The choice of system is best determined if access to the stream location can be gained from a bridge or there is streamside access.

With increasing stream width and depth, greater power output is needed. The backpack system loses application with increasing stream size up to a maximum of 10 m wetted stream width. At stream widths greater than 10 m, the long-line or tote barge system should be used. The choice is determined by whether bridge access is available.

Non-wadeable systems are sampled using either a sport canoe or boat system. Sport canoe applications use the same system as the tote barge but facilitate the electrification of the anode so the collector has the ability to direct where fish are collected. This method allows the collectors to leave the canoe in shallow water and use the system like a tote barge but enter the canoe in deep water and navigate either by paddling or the use of a small outboard motor. Boat-mounted systems use either droppers or a stainless steel ball to evenly distribute the power across the anode. The boat-mounted system works well in a variety of boats but requires modification as water depth increases; thus, greater depths require long cathodes mounted to the boat frame that reach to the bottom and slower speeds so that fish can be drawn from the depths up the cathode to enter the field. Electrofishing systems are least precise for large non-wadeable rivers. Other approaches include electrified otter trawls, which are effectively large bag seines pulled by a boat in deep waters. This approach has significant application for species like Crystal darter and juvenile sturgeon, which occur in main channel habitats.

Other Collection Methods: Angling, minnow traps, or trot lines are common methods but less effective for most species than seining or electrofishing. Angling, that is, hook-and-line, is probably the most well-known method but requires experience and technique. The method is most useful for predators and some small non-game species. The choice of hook size, bait, or lures will determine method effectiveness.

Minnow traps include two inverted funnels that are attached to the end of a round or square holding area. Minnow traps are effective for the capture of small non-game species. The method efficiency is determined by the size of the funnel, entry point diameter, and the size of the holding area. Often if a female is first into the trap, males will congregate within the trap, while conversely a large dominant male will decrease the capture efficiency of other individuals.

Trot lines are long strings with large hooks that are baited and tied beneath logs, stumps, overhanging brush, and undercut banks. The gear is especially effective in capturing large catfish and other nocturnal predators. The gear is species selective and not useful for most survey applications.

Ichthyocides and Concussion Methods: The use of rotenone or other fish poisons is strictly regulated in Indiana and requires the appropriate permits and coordination with state agencies. It is commonly used in powdered or emulsified liquid form in fisheries management to remove unwanted fish species. Rotenone is derived from several plant roots, including derris root, hoary pea, and jicama plant. The method is effective since the extract binds with oxygen receptors in the gill epithelium and causes the individual to suffocate. The method is not species selective; however, mortality is often reversible if the individual is resuscitated.

Concussion methods were employed by early ichthyologists as an effective manner of sampling lakes. Dynamite or other explosives were detonated beneath the surface, effectively stunning the fish, causing them to float to the surface. For obvious reasons this method is not practiced and would be heavily regulated if it were.

Observing Fish: Unlike terrestrial habitats, aquatic habitats and the species occupying these areas are difficult to observe. With the increase in specialized diving equipment, qualitative and quantitative scuba and snorkeling studies have been developed to investigate feeding and breeding behaviors, observe species and habitat associations, and determine competition and predatory associations that would be impossible to duplicate in aquarium observations.

Collecting Permits: All collection of specimens for scientific purposes in Indiana and most other states must be accomplished through the procurement of a scientific purposes permit. The permit has an associated fee and requires an application including the locations where sampling will be conducted, purpose of sampling, disposition of specimens, and salvage of individuals that died during sampling. The collection of state endangered species is prohibited, unless specified by the permit.

DATA ACQUISITION, LABELING, AND DATA SHEET CAPTURE

Detailed notes are made at the time of each collection, which is one of the primary responsibilities of the crew. Portions of the data sheet can be completed prior to arrival at the site, including appropriate site identification information. In addition, appropriate habitat and ecological notes should be described. Important observations on species reproductive condition, breeding colors of fish encountered, and observations of spawning behaviors or other similar information should be written on the data sheet. Do not attempt to rely on memory. The headings for a sample data sheet for field notes are shown in Figure 3. The field data sheet is printed on the upper third of the data sheet of either medium-weight bond paper or on rite-in-the-rain paper. This preprinted format will ensure that minimum standard information is noted for each location. The bottom of the form can contain ecological observations and specific notes on individual species. Further information on species collected from the site may include the number collected, size range recorded in mm total length (TL), batch weight by species recorded to the nearest tenth of a gram, and presence of deformities, eroded fins, lesions, or tumors (DELT) anomalies. Individual lengths and weights can be recorded for each species. In addition, specific habitat information can be recorded for rare species and the number of individuals released back into the stream. All writing of labels and field notes should be completed with waterproof ink or #2 pencils. Although data can be recorded on a portable laptop computer, this is not recommended in the event of loss or exposure to wet surfaces. Locality information is geo-referenced using a global positioning system. Copies of the field sheets should be electronically stored where the collections are curated for study.

The following information is recommended for completion of the minimum location information:

COLLECTION NUMBER. The assignment of a unique number to each collection facilitates the identification of the specimens or container from a specific place or time. My normal number assignment includes the collector's initials, followed by the year of collection, and then a unique three-digit code. For example, a site number might be TPS-09-001. This number should be recorded on the top of the jar lid, while the label inside the jar should include the collection number, waterbody name, bridge, county, state, collectors, and date on rite-in-the-rain paper.

STATE AND COUNTY OR COUNTRY. The country of collection is listed first, followed by the state and county since records are often sorted or summarized by political jurisdictions. This

Coll. No. ____________

State or country: ____________ Country: ____________

Locality: ____________

Water: ____________

Vegetation: ____________

Bottom: ____________ Temp: ______ Air: ______

Shore: ____________ Current: ____________

Distance from shore or stream width: ____________ Tide: ____________

Depth of capture: ____________ Depth of water: ____________

Method of capture: ____________

Collected by: ____________ Date: ____________

Orig, preserve.: ____________ Time: ____________

Figure 3. Field sheet headings used in recording fish collection notes.

information is important for biological surveys and watershed information.

LOCALITY. The name of the waterbody of the stream or lake is recorded along with the bridge or access point. The distance to the nearest town is the direction in air miles to the largest nearby town. In addition, list latitude and longitude and township, range, and section or other standard geographic systems (i.e., land grant system). A good rule of thumb is to describe the location in general terms so that it can be easily located on a map and also may permit one to return to the site to repeat collection. To be able to document the site location, a variety of county or U.S. Geological Survey maps should be consulted. DeLorme atlases are an economical alternative to the quad or 7.5-minute individual topographic sheets that would be needed for complete coverage of an entire state.

The following is an example of proper locality data:

WABASH (EAST FORK WHITE) RIVER drainage,
IN, Monroe Co.
East Fork Jackson Creek, d/s Rogers Road bridge,
4.5 mi ESE Bloomington, Perry Twp., T 2S R 7W S 18, SE 1/4
Date: X:18:2008, lat. 38.0288889 N, lon. -86.7688722 W
T. P. Simon, C. C. Morris, T. P. Simon IV

This example includes the drainage and parenthetically the watershed within the drainage; state; county; stream name; two descriptions of the site including the bridge and distance in air miles from the center point of the nearest town; township name; bearings including township, range, section; date; geocoordinates based on global positioning system; and collectors.

Bottom. A description of the substrate composition may include an estimated percentage of each type. Common bottom types include bedrock, slab rock, cobble, gravel, sand, clay (i.e., hardpan), marl, silt, and detritus. In addition, other bottom materials such as woody debris, leaf packs, and sticks should be noted.

Temperature. A pocket or electronic thermometer is a minimum requirement for field sampling. Temperature gradients of lakes should be measured based on depth profiles. Temperature of air and water at the time of collection is useful for identifying cool- or coldwater springs or field tiles. Temperature is an important determinant of species occurrence of certain thermal guilds. For example, trout can only occur for short periods of time in streams that exceed 20°C, while coolwater streams are classified as those that never exceed 24°C, and warmwater streams are greater than 26°C. Temperature models are used to predict long-term effects and determine species requirements and potential impacts from global warming.

Turbidity. Record the water clarity and color of the water. Turbidity meters are available, but descriptions such as clear, slightly turbid, or turbid might be recorded. Turbidity is often expressed by the depth where a Secchi disc disappears from view. In other collecting, it is acceptable to note the bottom visibility or the depth where the bottom is barely seen.

Color. Color refers to the stain of the water itself, not to the apparent color imparted to it from suspended matter. Classification categories may include clear, light brown, or brown. The latter colors are mostly associated with tannin-stained waters from bogs or peat. Other colors are typically associated with various types of pollution.

Hardness. Hardness and alkalinity are measured variables and reflect the productivity of the water.

Dissolved Oxygen Concentration. The presence of oxygen is perhaps the most important variable determining the presence of aquatic life. Dissolved oxygen concentrations can be measured using electronic meters or by Winkler titration.

pH AND ALKALINITY. These are standard measures of productivity that determine the acidity or alkalinity of the site. Low or high pH values are representative of industrial impacts.

SHORE. Description of the immediate riparian corridor including the type of vegetation and presence of any emergent vegetation. Additional aquatic habitat description should include surrounding vegetation, topography, or development.

CURRENT. The current speed may be measured with a current meter or described by timing the distance an orange or rubber ball moves a measured distance over the course of a timed minute. Current speed should be recorded as meters per second. Current speeds should be classified as none, sluggish, slow, moderate, rapid, or torrential zones.

DISTANCE FROM SHORE OR STREAM WIDTH. When gill nets or hoop nets are set in open water or seining is accomplished from shore, the distance from the shore is recorded. In streams, the average, minimum, and maximum widths are recorded.

DEPTH OF CAPTURE AND DEPTH OF WATER. Depth of water is an important variable and is recorded along with the depth of capture as an independent entry.

METHOD OF CAPTURE. The method of collection determines in many situations the type of species captured. To evaluate the limitations of the sampling event or to compare future events with another, a description of all of the gear, settings, and operation should be noted, especially if any deviations are made.

COLLECTOR(S). The names of all personnel involved in the supervision, operation, and implementation of the sample collection are noted on the data sheet.

ORIGINAL PRESERVATIVE. The original preservative is recorded so that subsequent specimens may be handled properly. This is of particular importance if the specimen is to be used for histological, molecular, or morphological purposes.

DATE. The date is recorded with the month as a roman numeral, before the day and year (e.g., VI:18:2008).

TIME. The time interval from start of collecting to the termination of the sampling effort is recorded for estimating sampling effort. The time should be recorded using military time so that differentiation between day and night can be easily determined. The length of time can be summarized as the total number of seconds recorded on the electrofishing equipment time clock, which is the amount of time that electricity was applied to the unit.

NOTES. The species list for the locality should be recorded in phylogenetic sequence by family. For each species the following information should be recorded: (1) scientific name, (2) number of total individuals captured for that species, (3) life history stage classified as adult, juvenile, larvae, or various age groups. Additional notes may include (4) specific habitat information describing where the species was collected, (5) reproductive condition, (6) detailed color descriptions, especially of spawning fish, and (7) sources of pollution.

SAMPLE PRESERVATION, DISPOSITION, AND HANDLING REQUIREMENTS. Once sampling is completed, collections are put into appropriate-sized containers. Containers may be either plastic, glass, or polyethylene jars but should possess a tight sealing, non-leaking lid. Jar mouths should be wide enough to receive large, deep-bodied specimens such as sunfish and suckers. The wide-mouthed jar enables specimens to be preserved with their fins erect and easily removed. All jars used for sample preservation should be double labeled, so that an inside and external label is associated in each sample.

All sample jars, once appropriately labeled, are placed into large storage containers such as plastic totes or coolers for transport. When back at the vehicle, specimens are prepared for final disposition. Prior to fixation, tissues and DNA samples should be collected if appropriate. Tissue samples for protein analysis are placed in small foil packets on dry ice or liquid nitrogen; DNA samples may be placed in vials of 95 percent pure ethyl alcohol, dry ice, or liquid nitrogen. Fin clips are taken from the right side of the specimen.

Preservation of Fishes for Study

The long-term retention of specimens requires a two-step process so that individuals are first fixed and then preserved. The most widely used field fixative is the dilution of formaldehyde (1 part) with water (9 parts). This mixture is referred to as 10 percent formalin. The strength of formalin may be increased or decreased based on air temperature, fish size, or number of individuals in the jar. Large fish or significant numbers of fish require a stronger solution (8 parts water to 2 parts formaldehyde). Likewise, during the warmest summer months the concentration of formaldehyde should be increased to 20 percent formalin and increased in 5 percent increments with temperature increases of 3°C. The volume of formalin in the jar should be sufficient so that all individuals are covered with liquid in the jar. Fish should not be tightly packed into the jar and the jar should never be more than three-quarters full. Small specimens, including young, that is, larval and juvenile (less than 25 mm TL), should be preserved in lower dilutions, such as 5 percent formalin. Formalin can be buffered with household borax to reduce shrinkage of specimens and leaching of calcium from bone and otoliths. Borax should be added as 1 level teaspoon per quart of preserving solution. Animal care procedures require that fish be anesthetized with MS-222, carbon dioxide, clove oil, or similar product before being placed in formalin.

Specimens larger than 20 cm total length should have an incision on the right side of the abdomen to facilitate penetration of the fixative. The right side of the individual is cut, since the left side is the anatomical side and is used to take measurements, make counts, or for obtaining photographic images. The right side is where tissue is removed for genetic samples, scale samples for age and growth, or for access through the operculum to examine pharyngeal teeth. The incision on the abdomen should be half as long as the abdominal cavity and should be made with a sharp scalpel. Fish heavier than 1 kg should be prepared for preservation by making deep incisions into the muscle mass on either side of the vertebrae. The advantage of making slits into the body rather than injecting formalin is that the specimen can be soaked prior to study. Formaldehyde is toxic and can induce an allergic reaction with extended exposure over time. Formalin fumes should not be breathed or allowed to come in contact with skin. Latex gloves should be worn and specimens should be studied in a well-ventilated area, preferably beneath a fume hood.

Fixation of individuals takes 5 days to a week. Formalin is removed from the specimens after fixing by soaking them in water. Specimens should be soaked for 2 days and the water changed frequently or a minimum of once within the first 24 hours. Once formaldehyde is no longer smelled the specimens can be transferred to 70 percent ethyl alcohol, or if large, the specimen should be put through a series of increasing ethyl alcohol solutions from 45 percent, to 60 percent, and terminating in 70 percent ethyl alcohol. At least one change of 70 percent ethyl alcohol is recommended to complete the removal of formalin prior to permanent storage. Color fades less rapidly when specimens are maintained in darkness.

Fish may be readied for osteological preparation by either freezing or preserving in 75 percent ethyl alcohol. Individuals can be skeletonized with dermestid beetles or macerated in several changes of water. Never use chlorine bleach products since they will remain in the bones for months and slowly dissolve the bone. Osteological preparations involve the clearing of tissues and staining of bone and cartilage.

Otoliths can be removed for age determination from beneath the opercle and posterior the gills. Do not extract the otolith through the top of the head since this method will destroy the specimen. Otoliths are prepared by grinding one side flat on a piece of emery cloth while being held on the finger. The flat side of the otolith is then glued to a glass slide and the top ground down and polished on the emery cloth. The slide is finished by grinding with 1,000-grit powder to create a thin section of the otolith on the slide. The otolith rings can be counted similar to scales; however, otoliths are more accurate.

Tissues for DNA analysis usually involve either a fin clip from the right side including a portion of the pectoral shoulder or a tissue plug. Tissues should be placed in pure 99 percent ethyl alcohol or 200 proof Everclear. This will ensure that the tissues will be acceptable for later extraction of DNA.

Names of Fishes

Fish have both a common and scientific name that is used as a means to distinguish them from other forms. Unfortunately, common names vary across region despite the effort that has been expended to standardize names. Common names also change with much more frequency than scientific names. This becomes problematic especially when attempting to summarize literature since multiple names may be required for search. The scientific name differs from the common name in that they are working hypotheses that describe the systematics and phylogenetic relationships between terminal species. Changes in names reflect the advancement of our science, since this shows that progress is being made based on increasing knowledge of morphology and molecular and ecological relationships.

A scientific fish name is made up of two or three parts. Scientific names are printed in Latin or in a Latinized form of a Greek word and are written in italics. The first name is the generic name, which is capitalized and reflects the genus. The second is the species name. The species name can be divided into a series of related populations that make up the third name, which is the subspecies. The subspecies category recognizes important geographic differentiation within a species that makes it unique. A genus may have more than a single species within it, while a species does not necessarily contain more than a single form. Species are grouped into genera (plural). Examples of names for the fantail darter recognize a series of forms that range between northern and southern Indiana.

Genus	Species	Subspecies	Common Name
(capitalized)	*(lower case)*	*(lower case)*	(capitalized)
Etheostoma	*flabellare*	*flabellare,*	Barred fantail darter
Etheostoma	*flabellare*	*lineolatum,*	Striped fantail darter

A scientific name is first assigned to a species when it is described. The author of the description is considered the authority. This person is the one who first properly recognized and described the species or subspecies, and the author's name is placed after the scientific name. However, if another scientist moves the species into a genus other than the one it was originally described, then the name of the original person is placed in parentheses after the scientific name to raise attention to the movement of the species into another genus.

Alteration of the species name must follow the rules of the International Code of Zoological Nomenclature. The standardization of the rules applies to all faunal groups. Fishes have an added benefit in that considerable effort has been made to standardize the common names of fishes following the efforts of the American Society of Ichthyologists and Herpetologists and the American Fisheries Society. The names herein follow the convention of the sixth edition of the *Common and Scientific Names of Fishes from the United States and Canada* (Nelson et al. 2004). Several name deviations are recorded for species not known during the previous work. These names follow the protocols of Simon et al. (2002).

The recent changing of many genera and specific names, especially among the Cyprinidae, Salmonidae, and Percidae, has created a plethora of problems for students. These changes are the result of molecular studies that have revolutionized the study of phylogenetics and taxonomy. These studies are the result of extensive data collection efforts and the evaluation of hundreds of specimens. Current trends have been to raise subspecies to full species, while some species complexes have seen splitting of many species from groups that were thought to be a single taxon. For example, the splitting of the Spottail darter (*Etheostoma squamiceps*) into 5 cryptic species depends exclusively on molecular techniques. Further differentiation and recognition of additional species and unique genetic forms will progress with additional study. This study recognizes 4 new species and raises from synonymy another species.

Identification of Fishes

The accurate identification of fishes is important for professionals, amateurs, and anglers. The need to identify species with certainty is so that distribution, habitat, and ecological requirements can be determined for accomplishing conservation planning in light of anthropogenic disturbances that are a consistent problem in our watersheds.

The format for this book takes into consideration the need to identify an individual fish. The book is divided into a series of introductory chapters that summarize the purpose for this book, the field survey procedures, taxonomic measurements and collection protocols, and watersheds and zoogeographic distributions of species. The species accounts begin with a key to the adult and early life history stages of families of Indiana fishes. The family keys provide identifications so that the reader is then referred to additional species keys. Within each species account is a list of diagnostic attributes, distributions that show the geographic range of the species in Indiana watersheds, and a brief description of preferred habitat. Line drawings, photographs, and description of morphometric and meristic attributes will enable the reader to determine the direction for making counts of fin rays and scales and measurements of structures.

The distinguishing characteristics of the keys are based on facilitating the identification of species and other than placement in the text are not phylogenetic. In the species accounts, the species are arranged alphabetically and comparatively based on similarity. The species and subspecies are numbered throughout the text for ease of access to species accounts, illustrations, and photographs.

Although the keys have been made as simple as possible, additional help is provided in the included glossary and with the illustrations that accompany the family key. My goal was to enable anglers and professional biologists the ability to identify with certainty the species of interest. The keys in this text have been used by numerous students at both Purdue University and Indiana University, by professional biologists at the State of Indiana Department of Environmental Management, and by students and staff at the Indiana Biological Survey.

When using the key, the best approach is

1) Start with the family key and check the figures to ensure that the species account is accurate.

2) With the specimen in hand, follow the key to the individual family key. Check the figures, descriptions, and range maps to facilitate species identification. The range map should be used to validate the species identification; however, the individual fish may need to be looked at beneath a microscope or a hand lens.

3) Verify the lowest taxonomic identification using the following tools:
   a. The geographic range should include the locality that the species was collected from;
   b. The specimen form should be similar to the individual characteristics shown in the plate;
   c. Check against either a museum specimen or have a professional verify the identification if a new record outside of the documented range. The specimen in question is compared to the validated specimens.
   d. The specimen should correspond to adjacent states such as Ohio (Trautman 1981), Kentucky (Burr and Warren 1986), Michigan (Bailey et al. 2004), and Illinois (Smith 1979).

METHODS
FOR IDENTIFYING FISHES

Methods for Counting and Measuring Fish Traits

Correct identification sometimes requires the measurement of traits or the counting of structures in order to distinguish between 2 closely related species. Measurements have been adopted and changed between practitioners, but it is important to know how adapted methods change from standard measurements. The standard methods were first written by Carl Levitt Hubbs and Karl F. Lagler in their monumental work on the *Fishes of the Great Lakes Region*. The methods used here are based on these widely used procedures. Although these methods were proposed by Hubbs and Lagler (1964), they have their beginnings in the ichthyology laboratories of Louis Agassiz and David Starr Jordan.

The primary features of internal and external anatomy are shown on a hypothetical soft rayed and spinous rayed fish species (Figures 4–8). This section is divided into two parts, including methods for counting structures, that is, meristic features, including discrete variables such as fin rays and scales. The second part includes methods for measuring infinite variables such as length, depth, and width traits. These measurable traits are known as morphometric features.

METHODS FOR COUNTING FIN RAYS

NUMBER OF FIN RAYS (Figure 4)

Specific abbreviations are universal expressions that designate individual fins.

Dorsal fin rays—D   Pectoral fin rays—P1
Anal fin rays—A   Pelvic (ventral) fin rays—P2
Caudal fin rays—C

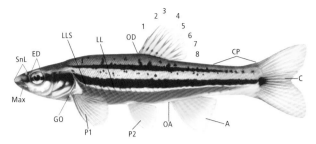

Figure 4. Fish morphology of a soft rayed fish (Southern redbelly dace, *Chrosomus erythrogaster*). A, anal fin; BD, body depth; C, caudal fin; CP, caudal peduncle; ED, eye diameter; GO, gill opening; LL, lateral line; LLS, lateral line scales; Max, maxillary barbel (in terminal position); OA, origin of anal fin; OD, origin of dorsal fin; P1, pectoral fin; P2, pelvic fin; SnL, snout length; 1–8 dorsal fin rays showing the method of counting (2 small rays at front of fin are not counted nor is the last ray since it is divided at its base).

SPINES

All spines (Figure 5, D1) are designated by roman numerals without respect to flexibility or development. As a practical matter, it may be desirable to treat as spines those morphologically hardened soft rays, such as those simple rays in Carp or the consolidation of rays as in catfishes. True spines are without segmentation and are not separable into 2 parts by connective tissue. Spines are found in the spinous dorsal fin (D1), pelvic fin (P2), and anal fin (A).

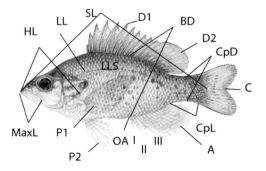

Figure 5. Anatomy of a spinous rayed fish (Orangespotted sunfish, *Lepomis humilis*). A, anal fin; BD, body depth at anus; C, caudal fin; CpD, caudal peduncle depth; CpL, caudal peduncle length; D1, spinous dorsal fin; D2, soft dorsal fin; HL, head length; LL, lateral line; LLS, lateral line scale; MaxL, maxillary length; OA, origin of anal fin; P1, pectoral fin; P2, pelvic fin; SL, standard length. Spinous rays are denoted by roman numerals and soft rays by arabic numerals.

Soft Rays

All soft rays (Figure 4) are designated by arabic numerals. Soft rays are usually branched, flexible, and segmented. The ray is branched and composed of 2 halves, although it is not required to be branched.

Principal and Branched Rays

In cypriniform fishes, such as minnows (Cyprinidae) and suckers (Catostomidae), the counts of rays are those of the principal rays. The secondary rays are often rudimentary or are too variable to count. The rule of counting is to include the branched rays plus 1 unbranched ray. This single unbranched ray reaches near the tip of the fin. If the count is to enumerate the branched rays, then these secondary rays are counted using lowercase roman numerals. This is particularly useful for counting caudal fin rays. The count is based on dividing the hypural plate in half along the midline and then counting the elongate branched rays in each half of the fin (Figure 6). For example, the convention for recording these values is upper half secondary rays first, then the principal rays, plus the lower half of the principal rays, and the secondary rays. Thus, the convention for writing the ray count shown in Figure 6 is v, 10 + 8, vi.

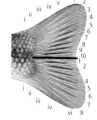

Figure 6. Method for counting caudal fin rays (Creek chub, *Semotilus atromaculatus*). Principal soft rays (denoted by arabic numerals) and secondary rays (lowercase roman numerals) in the caudal fin. Reporting convention for principal and secondary rays is v, 10 + 8, vi.

Rudimentary Rays

Members of the salmon and catfish families show a gradation of rays ranging from rudimentary in size to full rays. These rays exhibit a range of sizes and development. When counting, all these rays are included in the total ray counts (Figure 6). If only the principal rays are counted, then only those rays that have a branch or fork are included in the count. The maximum total count is included for all fins that possess either few or no branched rays.

Last Ray of Dorsal and Anal Fins (Figure 4)
For minnows, the last 2 rays of the dorsal and anal fins are considered a single ray for the purpose of count. These rays are connected and share a single pterigiophore so that they are the same terminal element despite appearing as 2 separate branched rays externally. Dissection beneath the tissue will reveal that these rays are shared branched rays.

Rays in Paired Fins
All rays in the paired fins are counted, including the smallest rays at the anterior and posterior edges of the fin. Counts of anal rays in minnows must be made beneath magnification for accurate identification. For other species, such as sculpin (Cottidae), the pelvic rays can best be viewed with magnification. The first ray may be bound to another small ray that can only be seen after dissection. In the cottids the pelvic fin spine may be represented by a bony splint that is connected in the membrane of the first soft ray. When recording spines and soft rays occurring in the same paired fin, the roman numeral spine number is recorded first followed by the soft ray arabic numeral. For example, the pelvic and anal fins of many perciform (i.e., percids, centrarchids, moronids) and scorpaniform (i.e., cottids) possess both spines and soft rays within the same fin. These would be recorded, for example, as P2—I/5, which refers to a single spine and 5 soft rays in the pelvic fin.

Rays in Median Fins
Counts in median fins, that is, single fins including the dorsal, anal, and caudal fins. For species that have both spines and rays in any of these fins, the counts are noted similarly to the paired fins. For example, anal fin counts are noted as II/8 or III/7. Some species may have a weakly divided dorsal fin (i.e., sunfish), but the fins are still reported as separate D1 and D2 counts. Rays are separated and counts are reported based on the presence of segmentation in the soft rays.

Scale Counts

The range of scale counts is usually expressed as the range of the majority of specimen with the outliers in parentheses. Counts are based on the entire scale row, including interpolated scales.

Lateral Line Scale Counts (Figure 7)

This scale count represents the number of pored scales horizontally along the midline of the individual, or in species without pored scales the count is made along the midline of the body in the area that would be occupied by a typical lateral line. The count starts at the gill cover and may include scales hidden from view without lifting the operculum. The count ends at the hypural plate or the caudal peduncle base. Scales that occur entirely on the caudal fin are not included in the count even if well developed or pored, nor are those scales that are beyond the crease of the fin bend.

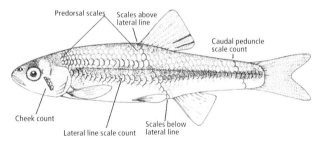

Figure 7. Various scale counts illustrated on a soft rayed fish (Spotfin shiner, *Cyprinella spiloptera*) showing hypothetical counts, including cheek, predorsal lateral line, scales above and below lateral line, and caudal peduncle scale counts.

Scales above Lateral Line (Figure 7)

The count includes scales above the lateral line from the origin of the dorsal fin (or from the origin of the spinous dorsal fin [D1] if more than a single fin) and counting posterior along the scale rows along a diagonal line, but not including lateral line row.

Scales below Lateral Line (Figure 7)

The count is similar to the previous count, except that the count starts at the anal fin origin. The count is made diagonally upward and anterior to the lateral line. All small scales are included in the count, but the lateral line is not included.

Predorsal Scales (Figure 7)
The number of scales before the dorsal fin is counted from the area near the nape to the origin of the dorsal fin. The count is made along the dorsal midline and usually is done on fish species that have a well-developed scaled nape that is separated from a naked or unscaled head. The number of scale rows before the dorsal is made from the dorsal fin origin and is usually fewer than the number of predorsal scales.

Cheek Scales (Figure 7)
The number of cheek scales is made by creating an imaginary line from the eye to the preopercular angle and counting the scale rows along that line.

Circumference Scale Count
This count is the number of scale rows crossing a line around the body just anterior to the dorsal fin origin. This count is used to separate several minnow species.

Caudal Peduncle Scale Count (Figure 7)
This count is similar to the circumference scale count, except the count is made around the narrowest portion of the peduncle where the lowest scale count is observed. The count is important in separating red-tailed redhorse species.

OTHER COUNTS
Branchiostegal Ray Counts
The branchiostegal rays include a series of bones that occur ventrally on the head, posterior of the jaws, and extend along the margins of the gills along the operculum. The count is made by extending the membranes and counting the rays that extend from the hyoid arch. The rays closer to the hyoid arch are usually small, short, slender, and more difficult to see. Both the left and right sides are counted and separated by a "+" sign. Typically in perciform fishes the number is symmetrical, but in the salmoniform fishes the number is usually high and assymetrical.

Pharyngeal Tooth Counts (Figure 8)

The throat teeth are the modified fifth gill arch of minnows and redhorse species. These structures are carefully dissected and cleaned so that the counts can be made. Each of these bones possesses 1 or 2 rows of teeth in minnows, with the exception of Carp, which have 3 rows. Sucker species possess a single row. A formula convention is used that shows the number of teeth from left to right representing the number of teeth in the minor (dorsal) row, separated from the number of teeth in the major row. For example, the formula 2,5—4,3 indicates that the pharyngeal bone on the left side has 2 small teeth on the minor row and 5 large teeth in the major row, while the right pharyngeal bone has 4 teeth in the major row and 3 small teeth in the minor row. A formula like 4—4 indicates that the species has no teeth in the minor row and 4 teeth in the major row (Figure 8).

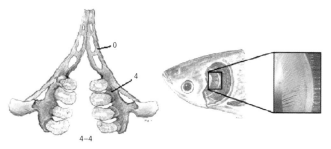

Figure 8. Pharyngeal gill arch showing upper limb with no teeth and lower limb with 4 teeth (left). Gill rakers of Bighead carp (left) (Schofield et al. 2005).

Gill Rakers (Figure 8)

The anterior row of gill rakers is counted on the first arch. This count is made on the back side of the first arch. All small or rudimentary rakers should be counted in the totals unless noted. A gill raker count is expressed as a single number that occurs along the entire row. The numbers on the upper and lower limbs if taken separately are separated by a "+" sign. The manner in which the count is made is noted, especially if made from the lower limb only. Another consideration is if a raker occurs between the angles of the upper and lower limb of the arch, then the raker is counted in the total for the lower limb.

Pyloric Caeca

These finger-like projections assist in processing food that enters the stomach. If the pyloric caeca is cut lengthwise from anterior to posterior, the pores of the caeca are arranged into a row and counted from inside. All tips are enumerated unless the branching is described.

Vertebral Counts

The count is usually described based on precaudal (trunk) and caudal vertebrae. The first caudal vertebrae is the first vertebrae possessing a hemal spine. The last precaudal (trunk) vertebrae may have complete hemal arches. The count includes the hypural plate, which is counted as a single vertebra. Distinct sutures along the vertebral axis delineate separate vertebrae, even if the sutures occur within the hypural complex. In heterocercal and internally heterocercal but externally nearly homocercal tails, all elements that are separated by definite sutures are counted.

Cephalic Pore Counts

The various head canals are illustrated in Figure 9. These canals are either complete or interrupted. The canal terminology developed by Hubbs and Cannon (1935) is used. The counts are expressed as complete numbers, that is, 9 operculomandibular pores; or if interrupted as 2 + 3 supraorbital canal pores, indicating that there are 2 anterior pores separated from 3 posterior pores. Only the coronal pore has a single pore. The lateral canal

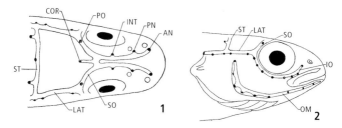

Figure 9. Head of a spiny rayed percid fish showing dorsal and lateral cephalic head canals structures used in identification. AN, anterior nasal pore; COR, coronal pore; INT, interorbital pore; IO, infraorbital canal; LAT, lateral canal; OM, preoperculomandibular canal; PN, posterior nasal pore; PO, postorbital canal; SO, supraorbital canal; ST, supratemporal canal (Hubbs and Cannon 1935).

connects the cephalic and includes counts of the pores or openings protruding from the sensory canal with the lateral line and the pored scales. The anterior and posterior nasal pores are associated with the supraorbital canal. Interrupted canal pores occur in the supraorbital and preoperculomandibular cephalic canals.

Scale Annuli (Figure 10)

Fish are indeterminate growers and continue to increase in size throughout their entire lives. Fish scales are similar to tree rings with daily rings being laid down on the scale. During periods of rapid daily growth the rings are widely spaced, while during slow growth periods the rings are tightly packed together. Each annuli can be counted to determine the age of the individual with each annulus representing a year. The focus is the center of the scale and the place to establish the point that the scale was formed, which is the equivalent of the age 0. As the scale increases in size by establishing radii or circuli there is a direct correlation with body size. The point where many radii or circuli come together is considered an annulus. Thus, prior to the first annulus formation age is considered age 0. It is necessary to calibrate one's eye to see the places where growth has slowed and an annulis has been established.

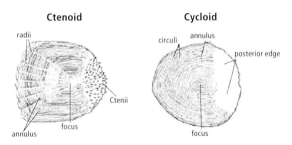

Figure 10. Scale morphology of spinous rayed and soft rayed fishes. Embedded portions of the scale are positioned to the right.

Morphometric Measurement Methods

Morphometric characters include aspects of length, depth, and width (Figure 11). These characters include all measureable attributes that are infinite, continuous variables. The best way to measure these characters is to use digital calipers. However,

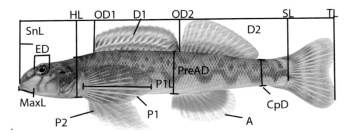

Figure 11. Morphometric measurements of spinous rayed fish (greenside darter, *Etheostoma blennioides*). A, anal fin; C, caudal fin; CPD, caudal peduncle depth; D1, spinous dorsal; D2, soft dorsal fin; ED, eye diameter; HD, head depth; HL, head length; MandL, mandibular length; OD1, origin spinous dorsal; OD2, origin soft dorsal; P1L, length of pectoral fin; P2L, length of pelvic fin; PreAD, preanal depth; SL, standard length; SnL snout length; TL, total length.

as with any method, good laboratory practices will include frequent and consistent calibration.

Morphometric measurements are made in a straight line rather than attempting to measure each character along the outline. Specimens that are curled, distorted, or deformed should be forced into normal position prior to measurement. This situation is a result of improper preservation.

Each fish trait is usually measured and then transformed into a proportion of standard length or total length. Many studies use standard length rather than total length because sometimes the caudal fin has been damaged or the caudal fin is missing. Smaller structures of the head are measured and related to the proportion of head length.

Length Measures

Standard length is measured from the tip of the snout to the posterior portion of the notochord. **Total length** extends from the tip of the snout to the tip of the caudal finfold. Morphometric measurements include **upper jaw length**—measured horizontally from the anterior snout or premaxillary to the posterior portion of the maxillary; **snout length**—from the tip of snout to anterior margin of the eye; **eye diameter**—anterior to posterior margin of the eye; **head length**—from the anterior snout to pectoral fin origin; **pectoral fin length**—horizontal distance from the origin of the pectoral fin to the tip of the depressed fin; **pelvic fin length**—horizontal distance from the origin of the pelvic bud or fin to the tip of the fin; **predorsal length**—anterior snout to origin of dorsal finfold or spinous dorsal fin; **spinous dorsal fin length**—basal fin length from the first to last dorsal spine; **spinous dorsal fin insertion** horizontal length from the snout to the attachment of the spinous dorsal fin to the body; **gap length**—distance between the spinous and soft dorsal fins; **soft dorsal fin origin**—horizontal distance from the anterior snout to the first ray of the soft dorsal fin; **soft dorsal fin length**—basal length of the soft dorsal fin from the first to last ray; **soft dorsal fin insertion**—horizontal distance from the snout to the attachment of the soft dorsal fin with the body; **preanal length**—snout to posterior margin of anus; and **postanal length**—posterior margin of the anus to the tip of the caudal finfold or fin.

Depth Measures

Head depth—vertical distance between the dorsum to ventrum of the head measured immediately posterior the eyes; **shoulder depth**—vertical distance measured at pectoral fin origin; **body depth**—vertical distance at anus; **mid-postanal depth**—vertical distance at the anterior apex of the mean myomere of the postanal series; and **caudal peduncle depth**—vertical distance at penultimate myomere. The yolk sac is measured along two planes, horizontally (**maximum yolk-sac length**) and vertically (**maximum yolk-sac depth**), at the greatest distance.

Width Measures

Head width—the distance between the exterior opercular margins immediately posterior the eye; **greatest body width**—the measurement is made at the point on the trunk where the greatest breadth is observed; **yolk-sac width**—the measure is made at the widest point across the yolk.

Osteology

Osteology is the study of bones, including the structure, development, and function. The jawless fishes (Agnathans) and the primitive species (i.e., Acipenseriformes, Lepisosteiformes, and Amiiformes) possess a variety of cartilaginous skeletal structures that reflect a primitive condition. Only the bony fishes possess ossification of skeletal elements. Ossification is the process of bone or bone-like tissue formation. During bone formation, connective tissues such as cartilage are invaginated by blood vessels. These blood vessels bring calcium and other minerals and deposit it in the ossifying tissues.

Osteology is a necessary study for any classification of higher level relationships. Thus, any study of family or higher level relationships is dependent on a skeletal collection, clearing and staining of a specimen series, or radiological photography (Gosline 1948). Most phylogenetic studies concentrate on the cranium and caudal fin skeleton (Figure 12). Position and shape of bones and the number of elements are important attributes of osteological studies.

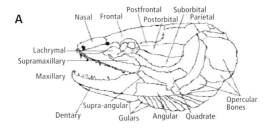

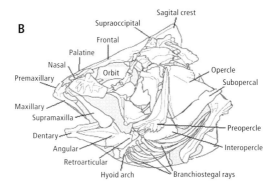

Figure 12. Head skeletal elements. (A) Bowfin (*Amia calva*) (Grande and Bemis 1998), and (B) perch (*Perca*). Illustration by Michel Couturea and B. Clavel (unpublished, 2005).

Distinguishing Characters and Pictorial Guide to Early Life History Stages of Fish Families

YOLK-SAC LARVAE

POST-YOLK-SAC LARVAE

ACIPENSERIDAE—STURGEONS

- Hatching size 7–12 mm TL
- No adhesive organ
- Large, dark yolk sac
- Anus posterior to midbody
- More than 50 total myomeres
- Preanal length of early, yolk-sac larvae about 65 percent TL
- Length from tip of snout to dorsal finfold origin about 25 percent TL for early, yolk-sac larvae

- Extended snout with 4 ventral barbels
- Ventral mouth
- Heterocercal tail

POLYODONTIDAE—PADDLEFISH

- Hatching size 8–9.5 mm TL
- Large, dark yolk sac
- More than 50 total myomeres
- No adhesive organ
- Anus posterior to midbody
- Small eye
- Preanal length of early, yolk-sac larvae about 60 percent TL
- Length from tip of snout to dorsal finfold origin about 35 percent TL for early, yolk-sac larvae

- Rostrum develops with 2 ventral barbels
- Numerous sensory patches on head and operculum
- Heterocercal tail

YOLK-SAC LARVAE	POST-YOLK-SAC LARVAE

LEPISOSTEIDAE—GAR

- Adhesive organ present
- Large, oval yolk sac. More than 50 total myomeres

- Elongate body
- Extended snout
- Anal fin origin anterior to dorsal fin origin
- Heterocercal tail

AMIIDAE—BOWFIN

- Hatching size 3–7 mm TL
- Adhesive organ present
- Total myomeres 60 or more

- Round, robust head
- Gular plate
- Long dorsal fin, origin above pectoral fins

ANGUILLIDAE—FRESHWATER EEL

- Larvae are absent from freshwaters of Indiana, but elvers with adult characteristics occur

CLUPEIDAE—HERRING

- Slender, little pigment, transparent
- Oil may or may not be visible
- Large oil globule, if present, will be located posteriorly
- Posterior vent
- Less than 10 postanal myomeres
- Dorsal finfold origin anterior, at mid–yolk sac early and just behind head later

- Slender, little pigment
- Posterior vent
- Anal fin posterior to dorsal fin

YOLK-SAC LARVAE   POST-YOLK-SAC LARVAE

HIODONTIDAE—MOONEYE

- Hatch at about 7 mm TL
- Large yolk sac
- Anterior oil globule
- Dorsal finfold origin near midbody

- Robust
- Large eye
- 17 or more postanal myomeres
- Dorsal fin insertion over anal fin

SALMONIDAE—TROUT

- Large, greater than 11 mm TL at hatching
- Large yolk, initially pendulus
- Advanced fin development prior to complete yolk absorption
- Vent about two-thirds back on body

- Robust
- Large, rounded head
- Adipose fin

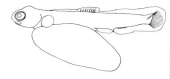

OSMERIDAE—SMELT

- Long, slender, herring-like
- Small head
- Yolk positioned well posterior to pectoral fins
- Single, anterior oil globule
- Vent about three-quarters back on body

- Elongate, slender, herring-like
- Adipose fin
- Anal fin posterior to dorsal fin

UMBRIDAE—MUDMINNOW

- Yolk with many oil globules
- Vent slightly posterior to midbody
- Urostyle extends to posterior margin of caudal finfold

- Robust
- Darkly pigmented
- Urostyle extends beyond margin of developing caudal fin

YOLK-SAC LARVAE	POST-YOLK-SAC LARVAE

ESOCIDAE—PIKE

- Darkly pigmented
- Vent about two-thirds back on body

- Elongate
- Extended, depressed, duck-like snout
- Posterior dorsal fin

CYPRINIDAE—CARPS AND MINNOWS

- Yolk long, cylindrical, initially bulbous anteriorly
- Pigmentation varies from light to heavy
- Vent usually slightly beyond midbody

- Pigmentation often in rows; dorsolaterally, midlaterally, along ventral margin of myomeres, and midventrally
- Air bladder obvious, becoming two-chambered, usually pigmented dorsally
- Single dorsal fin

CATOSTOMIDAE—SUCKERS

- Yolk long, cylindrical, initially more bulbous anteriorly
- Vent posterior, two-thirds to three-fourths back on body

- Mouth shape and position vary from interior (later in develop-ment) to terminal and oblique
- Pigment variable but often in three rows, dorsal, ventrally, and midventrally; dorsal pigment may also be in 1–3 rows
- Air bladder obvious
- Single dorsal fin

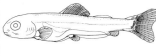

ICTALURIDAE—CATFISH

- Large bulbous yolk
- Barbels evident at hatching
- Advanced fin development before complete yolk absorption

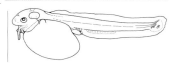

YOLK-SAC LARVAE	POST-YOLK-SAC LARVAE

AMBLYOPSIDAE—CAVEFISH

- Large, robust body
- Yolk sac large, truncate
- Precocious fin ray development
- Caudal fin rounded
- Pelvic fins lacking in all but single species (*Amblyopsis spelaea*)
- Eyes and pigment may be reduced or lacking in all genera except *Chologaster*

APHREDODERIDAE—PIRATE PERCH

- Small, about 3 mm TL at hatching, yolk absorbed between 4 and 5 mm TL
- Usually less than 30 total myomeres
- Anterior oil globule

- Head and body robust
- Usually less than 30 total myomeres
- Anus begins to migrate toward gular region at about 9 mm TL

PERCOPSIDAE—TROUT-PERCH

- Hatching size 5.3–6 mm TL
- More than 30 total myomeres
- Large head
- Pointed snout with inferior mouth
- Vent slightly anterior

- Large head
- Adipose fin
- Long snout
- Air bladder obvious

LOTIDAE—BURBOT

- More than 50 total myomeres
- Large head
- Short gut
- Anterior vent opens laterally on finfold

- Single barbel on chin
- Second dorsal fin and anal fin long
- Isocercal tail
- Pelvic fins positioned under pectoral fin

Distinguishing Characters and Pictorial Guide   75

YOLK-SAC LARVAE	**POST-YOLK-SAC LARVAE**

FUNDULIDAE—KILLIFISH

- Stubby, robust
- Caudal fin with rays at hatching
- Vent anterior, near posterior margin of yolk

- Large head
- Superior mouth
- Rounded caudal fin
- Stocky caudal peduncle
- 10 or more dorsal rays

POECILIIDAE—LIVEBEARERS

- Development occurs inside female

- Scales present at birth
- Rays in all fins at birth
- Superior mouth
- Dorsal fin short, 7–8 rays

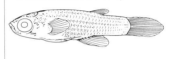

ATHERINOPSIDAE—SILVERSIDES

- Elongate, slender
- Anterior vent (about one-quarter back on body), immediately behind yolk sac
- Preanal myomeres 6–9
- Preanal finfold absent or vestigial

- Elongate, slender
- Mouth small, terminal
- Two dorsal fins
- Anterior vent

GASTEROSTEIDAE—STICKLEBACK

- Short (5–6 mm TL), stubby
- Vent at midbody or slightly posterior
- Vitelline vessel over yolk networked
- Small oil globules present

- Sloping head, superior mouth
- Narrow caudal peduncle

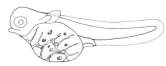 

YOLK-SAC LARVAE   POST-YOLK-SAC LARVAE

MORONIDAE—TEMPERATE BASS

- Vent slightly posterior to midbody
- Single, large, anterior oil globule
- Low total myomere count less than 25

- S-shaped gut
- Low myomere count
- Late larvae with well-developed mouth with teeth
- Spinous dorsal fin develops secondarily

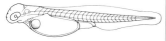   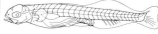

CENTRARCHIDAE—SUNFISH

- Large, oval yolk sac at hatching
- Position of oil globule variable, but usually posterior
- Vent anterior to midbody

- Usually robust with large head
- Air bladder distinct
- Gut short, coils with increasing growth
- Spinous and soft dorsal fins continuous

PERCIDAE—PERCH

- Vent near midbody
- Large anterior oil globule
- Pectoral fins usually well developed at hatching
- Total myomere counts higher in moronids or centrarchids

- Large pectoral fins
- Spinous dorsal separate from soft dorsal fins

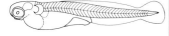   

SCIAENIDAE—DRUM

- Small, 3–5 mm TL
- Large posterior oil globule
- About 25 total myomeres

- Heavy, truncate body
- Large, deep head
- Spinous and soft dorsal fins continuous
- Soft dorsal fin long with greater than 24 rays

YOLK-SAC LARVAE	POST-YOLK-SAC LARVAE

COTTIDAE—SCULPIN

- Robust with large head and large, round yolk sac
- Fins well developed before yolk absorption is complete
- Anterior vent

- Large pectoral fins
- Two dorsal fins
- Second dorsal fin and anal fin long
- Caudal fin spatulate

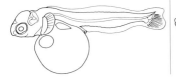

Key to the Families of Indiana Fishes

1 a) Pectoral and pelvic fins absent; mouth a sucking disc or hood-like, without jaws; 7 external gill openings; a single nostril.............................**LAMPREYS**—*Petromyzontidae*

b) Paired fins present (at least a single pair); without a sucking disc or hood, jaws present; a single external gill opening; paired nostril...2

2 a) Tail deeply forked, with caudal fin asymmetrical in lateral view, that is, either heterocercal or modified heterocercal (see figure below)..3

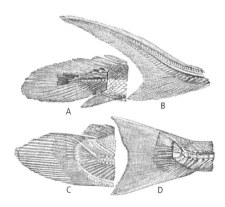

Caudal fin types. (A) diphycercal, (B) heterocercal, (C) modified heterocercal, and (D) homocercal (Kingsley 1899).

b) Caudal fin homocercal 6

3 a) Snout having a long paddle-like structure; opercular flap long; 2 small barbels on ventral surface of paddle; skin of body naked without bony plates ....
PADDLEFISHES—*Polyodontidae*

   b) Snout lacking a paddle-like structure; opercular flap short; skin of body with bony plates 4

4 a) Snout shovel-shaped or conical; with 4 large barbels on lower surface; body with 5 rows of bony plates; mouth ventral................................. **STURGEONS**—*Acipenseridae*

   b) Snout not shovel-shaped or conical; without barbels; lacking large bony plates; mouth terminal (see figure below) 5

A   B   C

Typical mouth shapes of fishes: (A) subterminal, (B) terminal, and (C) superior.

5 a) Body with a continous sheath of hard, plate-like scales; no gular plate; snout an elongate, beak-like structure ...
.... **GARS**—*Lepisosteidae*

b) Snout rounded and short; gular plate present; scales cycloid overlapping as in ordinary fishes; dorsal fin of more than 45 rays, beginning anterior of anal fin insertion ... .**BOWFINS**—*Amiidae*

6 a) Pelvic fins absent; dorsal, anal, and caudal fins continuous; body lamprey-shaped; scales small appearing to be scaleless..**EEL**—*Anguillidae*

b) Pelvic fins present; dorsal, anal, and caudal fins separated...7

7 a) Adipose fin present 8

b) Adipose fin absent..11

8 a) Barbels present, usually 4 pair around mouth; body naked; each pectoral spine with a strong sharp spine at front of ray..............................**CATFISHES**—*Ictaluridae*

b) Barbels absent; scales present..9

9 a) Auxiliary process present at base of pelvic fin (may be small and blunt in *Salvelinus*); scales minute, usually with 100 or more in lateral series, with mouth large and strong, or scales fewer than 100 in lateral series and mouth small; the posterior end of maxillary not extending beyond middle of eye; the teeth absent or very weak...... **TROUT AND WHITEFISHES**—*Salmonidae*

   b) Auxiliary process lacking at base of pelvic fin; scales relatively large, about 40–75 in lateral series 10

10 a) Scales ctenoid; dorsal fin with 2 weak spines; pelvic and anal fins with 1 weak spine; dorsal fin origin more anterior, much nearer snout than caudal fin; lateral line present............................**TROUT-PERCH**—*Percopsidae*

   b) Dorsal fin origin at about midbody, approximately equidistant between snout and base of caudal fin; scales cycloid; less than 75 scales in lateral series; lateral line absent .... **SMELT**—*Osmeridae*

11 a) A single prominent barbel on tip of chin ....
.... **BURBOT**—*Lotidae*

b) No prominent barbel on tip of chin 12

12 a) Anus under throat (usually anterior of anal fin, anterior of pelvic fins except in young); dorsal fin with 3 anterior spines.......................**PIRATE PERCH**—*Aphredoderidae*

b) Anus immediately anterior anal fin 13

13 a) Eyes absent; body pale and nearly colorless.....................
.... **CAVEFISHES**—*Amblyopsidae*

b) Eyes present; body normally pigmented 14

14 a) Three to 11 dorsal spines not connected to one another by a membrane; pelvic fin a single prominent spine and possessing 1–2 rudimentary rays ....
....................................**STICKLEBACKS**—*Gasterosteidae*

b) Dorsal fin with or without spines; when spines are present they are connected to one another by membrane ....
.... 15

15 a) A single continuous dorsal fin without spines or with a single stout spine at the anterior insertion of the dorsal fin; no pelvic spines... 16

b) Either 2 separated dorsal fins possessing spines, or if a single fin, then the first contains stiff spines................25

16 a) Dorsal and anal fin with a single stout spine that is saw-toothed on posterior edge..
.... **CARP AND GOLDFISH**—*Cyprinidae*

b) Dorsal and anal fins without stout, sawtoothed spine 17

17 a) Upper lip with 3 large barbels; body slender and snake-like; depth less than 12.5 times into SL ....
....**LOACHES**—*Cobitidae*

b) Upper lip with no barbels or with a single small barbel; body deeper; depth 16.6–33.3 times into SL 18

18 a) Head scaleless 19

b) Head partly scaled, the cheek either partly or entirely scaled..22

19 a) Pelvic auxiliary process present; gill opening extending forward on throat to beneath eye; principal rays of anal fin 17 or more 20

b) Pelvic auxiliary process absent; gill opening not extending forward on throat to beneath eye; lower margins of gill covers not overlapping on midline of throat; principal rays of anal fin 16 or fewer 21

20 a) Keel on midline of belly with sharp, sawtoothed projections; dorsal fin anterior of anal fin; lateral line absent; teeth if present on tongue are small and feeble; gill rakers many, long and slender........... **HERRINGS**—*Clupeidae*

b) Keel on midline of belly without sharp, sawtoothed projections; dorsal fin situated over anal fin; lateral line complete or well developed; stout, sharp teeth on tongue; gill rakers few, short and knob-like ....
.... **MOONEYES**—*Hiodontidae*

21 a) Dorsal fin with 8 (9 in *Opsoepoedeus emilae*) principal rays; throat teeth in 1 or 2 rows, with 6 or fewer teeth in primary row; mouth not sucker-like (except in *Phenacobius mirabilis*); anal fin forward; distance from front of anal fin to base of caudal fin (B) contained less than 2.5 times distance from front of anal fin to tip of snout (A) ....**NATIVE MINNOWS**—*Cyprinidae*

b) Dorsal fin with either 10 or more principal rays, or if only 9 (exception genus *Erimyzon*), then lateral line is absent or reduced to a few pores; mouth inferior, sucker-like, and with striated and papillose lips; throat teeth in a single row of 20 or more teeth; anal fin placed far back; distance from (B) contained more than 2.5 times (A)....
.... **SUCKERS**—*Catostomidae*

22 a) Caudal fin deeply forked; snout duck-shaped, with large canine teeth; more than 100 scales in lateral series; branchiostegal rays 11–19............................. **PIKES**—*Esocidae*

b) Tail rounded; snout not duck-shaped, rather jaws short, with villiform teeth; fewer than 50 transverse scales in lateral series; branchiostegal rays less than 10 23

23 a) Mouth not protractile (possessing a frenum)..................
.... **MUDMINNOWS**—*Umbridae*

b) Mouth protractile (frenum absent) 24

24 a) Dorsal fin base almost entirely over anal fin; scales in lateral series usually more than 30; anal fin of males not slender and rod-like, third anal fin ray branched...........
.... **TOPMINNOWS**—*Fundulidae*

b) Dorsal fin base almost entirely behind anal fin base; scales in lateral series usually 30 or fewer; anal fin of male modified into a slender, rod-like fin (gonopodium); third ray of anal fin unbranched.. .... **LIVEBEARERS**—*Poeciliidae*

25 a) Body naked...32
   b) Body scaled 26

26 a) Distance from rear margin of gill cover to base of pelvic fin (A) much greater than distance from base of pelvic fin to front of anal fin (B); base of pectoral fin near upper edge of gill opening; spinous dorsal separate from soft dorsal and with 3–5 thin spines.....................................27
   b) Distance from rear of gill cover to base of pelvic fin (A) much less than distance from base of pelvic fin to front of anal fin (B); base of pectoral fin far below upper edge of gill opening; spinous dorsal separate or not from soft dorsal, but if separate with 6 or more spines 28

27 a) Anal spine single; eye near middle of head; adipose eyelid absent...................... **SILVERSIDES**—*Atherinopsidae*

   b) Anal fin with 2 (young) or 3 spines; eye distinctly anterior to middle of head; adipose eyelid present................. .... **MULLETS**—*Mugilidae*

28 a) Dorsal fin soft rays 24 or more; caudal fin bluntly pointed; central rays moderately elongated; lateral line extends onto caudal fin ....**DRUM**—*Sciaenidae*

b) Dorsal fin soft rays with 15 or fewer; caudal fin either forked, truncate (square), or rounded; lateral line either not extending or barely extending onto caudal fin.....29

29 a) Total dorsal spines and rays 15 or fewer (IV–V, 9–10); lateral line absent, maximum length usually less than 45 mm .... **PYGMY SUNFISHES**—*Elassomatidae*

b) Total dorsal spines and rays 16 or more; lateral line may be incomplete, but typically with several pored scales along lateral line...30

30 a) Anal spines 1 or 2............................**PERCHES**—*Percidae*

b) Anal spines 3 or more..31

31 a) Dorsal fins separated by a deep notch or only slightly connected; a sharp spine near posterior of gill cover; margin of preopercle (bone anterior of gill cover) strongly sawtoothed (serrate) ....
.... **TEMPERATE BASSES**—*Moronidae*

b) Spinous dorsal and soft dorsal well connected, with at most a deep notch between; no sharp spine at edge of gill cover; margin of preopercle usually smooth, weakly sawtoothed in a few species..
.... **SUNFISHES**—*Centrarchidae*

32 a) Pelvic fin with 1 thin spine and 3–5 soft rays; pelvic fin not modified into a suction cup; anal fin spines absent.
....**SCULPINS**—*Cottidae*

b) Pelvic spines with a modified suction cup ....
....**GOBIES**—*Gobiidae*

FAMILY AND SPECIES
ACCOUNTS OF INDIANA FISHES
INCLUDING KEYS

LAMPREY FAMILY—PETROMYZONTIDAE
(SPECIES PLATES 1–7)

The Agnatha are jawless vertebrates that lack paired fins and possess a single median nostril. They are the most primitive fish group (Nelson 2006). The order Petromyzontiformes includes the single family Petromyzontidae, but some authorities place the Southern Hemisphere species in either Petromyzontidae or separate families Geotriidae and Mordaciidae (Hubbs and Potter 1971; Hardisty and Potter 1971a, 1982; Potter 1980). These 3 families differ in the number of oral fimbriae (Khirdir and Renaud 2003). The family includes both freshwater and marine representatives. Few reliable fossil representatives exist other than *Maxomyzon pieckoensis,* which is from the Pennsylvanian period about 280 millions years ago (Bardack and Zangerl 1972). The lamprey include about 40 species in 8 genera. Five genera, *Caspiomyzon, Entosphenus, Ichthyomyzon, Lampetra,* and *Petromyzon,* inhabit the northern hemisphere, while *Exomegas, Geotria,* and *Mordacia* occur in the southern hemisphere (Bailey 1980; Nelson 2006).

The Petromyzontidae has a naked body, with round, suctorial mouth possessing horny teeth, often sharp, on funnel and tongue (Figure 13). A long dorsal fin, often of 2 parts; no paired fins and no paired fin girdles. No bone in the skeleton; skull cartilaginous; vertebra without centra. A single median nasal opening between the eyes, not connected to the pharynx. Seven pairs of gill pouches, each pouch opening externally through an opening. Muscle blocks or myotomes not divided by a horizontal septum into dorsal and ventral parts (Figure

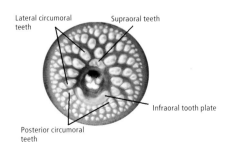

Figure 13. Sea lamprey oral hood showing teeth patterns and names.

Figure 14. Trunk myomere count from first complete myomere posterior gill slit to full myomere anterior anus. Evolutionary stem parasitic species have usually given rise to either 1 or more non-parasitic satellite species (Vladykov and Kott 1979). These stem and satellite species are called paired species (Hardisty and Potter 1971b).

14). Characteristic metamorphosis from blind, toothless larva or ammocoete to toothed, sighted adult in 1–4 years (Nelson 2006). The larval period may last 4–6 years.

Seven species in 3 genera are known from Indiana. All adult lamprey exhibit sexual dimorphism, with females possessing a well-developed anal finfold with the caudal fin turning upward, while the male anal finfold is barely developed and the tail bends downward. The lumen of the intestinal tract becomes non-functional and closes in fully mature individuals. Length and weight of adults diminish with development and spawning (Vladykov 1951).

KEY TO THE LAMPREY OF INDIANA

1   a) One continuous dorsal fin sometimes shallowly notched. Trunk myomeres 62 or fewer 2

    b) Two distinct dorsal fins either close together or well separated. Trunk myomeres 65 or more 5

2   a) Innermost teeth of radial series (circumoral teeth) all unicuspid (single pointed). Myomeres from the last gill opening to anus, 47–56, rarely more than 55 3

    b) Usually 6–10 (range 1–11) circumoral teeth bicuspid. Myomeres 53–62, rarely less than 55.. 4

3   a) Teeth large and sharply pointed. Snout long; the sucking disc may be expanded wider than body width. Parasitic upon fishes. Alimentary canal functional until ready to spawn, when it begins to atrophy. Total length of spawning adult 254–356 mm TL....................................**SILVER LAMPREY**— ....*Ichthyomyzon unicuspis*

    b) Teeth small and bluntly pointed, many covered by skin. Snout short; sucking disc cannot be expanded wider than

body width. Non-parasitic. During transformation from ammocoete to adult, the alimentary tract becomes shriveled into a non-functional, thread-like strand. Total length of spawning adults 130–180 mm ....
NORTHERN BROOK LAMPREY—*Ichthyomyzon fossor*

4 a) Usually 51–56 myomeres, transverse lingual lamina linear to weakly bilobed; disc large, its length usually contained fewer than 13.3 times in total length...
............**CHESTNUT LAMPREY**—*Ichthyomyzon castaneus*

b) Usually 55–59 myomeres, transverse lingual lamina moderately to strongly bilobed; disc relatively small, its length usually contained more than 13.3 times in total length.........
..........................**OHIO LAMPREY**—*Ichthyomyzon bdellium*

5 a) Teeth radiating in series from throat outward. Teeth large and sharply pointed. Base of supraoral not as wide as throat opening; cusps close together. Myomeres 65–76, rarely less than 64. Sides of body heavily mottled with darker shades. Parasitic on fishes. Alimentary tract functional until ready to spawn. Spawning adults 330–762 mm...................................

...................................**SEA LAMPREY**—*Petromyzon marinus*

b) Teeth in clusters, not in radiating series. Teeth blunt and many partially or entirely hidden by skin. Base of supraoral as wide as, or wider than, throat opening; the cusps widely separated. Myomeres 53–74. Sides of body bicolored or unicolored; not mottled. Non-parasitic. After transforming, alimentary tract becomes a thread-like strand. Length of spawning adult 130–200 mm .... *Lampetra*

6 a) Myomeres fewer than 62, usually less than 60; a pair of widely separated supraoral teeth and row of infraoral teeth, all other teeth reduced to absent; oral disc distinctly smaller than body width ....
..............**LEAST BROOK LAMPREY**—*Lampetra aepyptera*

b) Myomeres more than 62; some teeth in marginal fields of funnel well developed, usually 3 pairs of lateral bicuspids; oral disc almost as wide as body..
.... **AMERICAN BROOK LAMPREY**—
....*Lampetra appendix*

1   OHIO LAMPREY—*Ichthyomyzon bdellium* (Jordan). Large, sharp, well-developed disc teeth, oral disc wide or wider than head, supraoral teeth 2-3, circumoral teeth 2-2-2-2; single, slightly notched dorsal fin. Usually 56–62 trunk myomeres; black lateral line organs. Blue or gray above, white to slightly mottled below; gray fins. Ohio River basin from SW NY to northern IN and eastern IL, south to northern AL. Large rivers and moderate-sized streams. Rare. Ammocoetes occur in silt pools and backwaters. Adult parasitic, ammocoete detrital filter feeder. Brood hiding, lithophil (A.2.3). Maximum size 272 mm TL.

2   CHESTNUT LAMPREY—*Ichthyomyzon castaneus* Girard. Large, sharp disc teeth, supraoral teeth, usually 2-3, 2-2-2-2-2 circumoral teeth; oral disc expanded, wide or wider than head; single, slightly notched dorsal fin. Usually 51–56 trunk myomeres; black lateral line organs. Grayish-brown to yellowish-tan above, white or yellowish-olive below; yellow fins. Lake Michigan MI, WI, MN throughout Ohio and Mississippi River basins to LA and eastern TN west to central KS and OK to Gulf Coastal Plain. Large rivers, lakes, and reservoirs. Common. Ammocoetes found in sand pools and backwaters. Adult parasitic, ammocoete detrital filter feeder. Brood hiding, lithophil (A.2.3). Maximum size 310 mm TL.

3   NORTHERN BROOK LAMPREY—*Ichthyomyzon fossor* Reighard and Cummins. Small, blunt disc teeth, usually 2 supraoral teeth and 1-1 or 1-1-1 circumoral teeth; expanded oral disc smaller than head; single, slightly notched dorsal fin. Usually 50–52 trunk myomeres. Lateral line unpigmented. Dark gray or brown above, pale gray, yellowish, or silvery-white below. Great Lakes and northern Mississippi River basins to Hudson Bay, northern IN to western WV, eastern KY, and central OH. Moderate-sized rivers and streams. Ammocoetes found in still pools buried in sand, debris, and silt. Rare to occasional. Adult and ammocoete non-parasitic, detrital filter feeder. Brood hiding, lithophil (A.2.3). Maximum size 163 mm TL.

4   SILVER LAMPREY—*Ichthyomyzon unicuspis* Hubbs and Trautman. Large, sharp disc teeth, usually 2 supraoral teeth and 1-1-1 or 1-1-1-1 circumoral teeth; expanded oral disc as wide or wider than head; single, slightly notched dorsal fin. Usually 49–52 trunk myomeres. Black lateral line organs. Grayish-brown to yellowish-tan above, light yellow or tan below; yellowish fins. Great Lakes and Mississippi River basins from QC west to MB south to NE and MS including TN. Large rivers, lakes, and reservoirs. Ammocoetes found in muck pools and backwaters. Occasional to common. Adult parasitic, ammocoete detrital filter feeder. Brood hiding, lithophil (A.2.3). Maximum size 370 mm TL.

1 OHIO LAMPREY—
Ichthyomyzon bdellium

2 CHESTNUT LAMPREY—
Ichthyomyzon castaneus

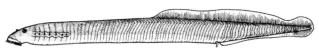

3 NORTHERN BROOK LAMPREY—
Ichthyomyzon fossor

4 SILVER LAMPREY—
Ichthyomyzon unicuspis

5 LEAST BROOK LAMPREY—*Lampetra aepyptera* (Abbott). Disc teeth blunt and degenerate; 2 widely separate supraoral teeth, usually 1-2-1 or 1-1-1 lateral circumoral teeth, without posterior circumoral teeth (range: 0–22), and 7–12 infraoral teeth. Expanded oral disc narrower than head width. Two dorsal fins. Usually 52–59 trunk myomeres. Unpigmented lateral line organs. Light tan to silverish-gray above, yellow or white below; yellow or gray fins. Spawning males mottled grayish-brown above with black lateral stripe from eye to base of first dorsal fin. Edges of dorsal fins black, golden stripe from middle of dorsal fins to caudal fin. Range from Atlantic Slope to Mobile Bay, AL, and MS, to south-central MO and AR, in Mississippi River. Creeks and small rivers, ammocoetes in pools and backwaters buried in sand. Occasional to common. Adult and ammocoete non-parasitic, detrital filter feeder. Brood hiding, lithophil (A.2.3). Maximum size 180 mm TL.

6 AMERICAN BROOK LAMPREY—*Lampetra appendix wilderi* (DeKay). Disc teeth blunt; 2 supraoral teeth, usually 2-2-2 lateral circumoral teeth, usually 19–26 posterior circumoral teeth and 7–8 infraoral teeth. Expanded oral disc narrower than head width. Two dorsal fins. Usually 67–73 trunk myomeres. Unpigmented lateral line organs. Gray to slate-blue above, white or silver-white below; yellow fins. Dark gray to black blotch on tail. Spawning males olive-green or pinkish-purple to shiny black above with black stripe at base of dorsal fins. Range from Great Lakes basin throughout Mississippi River basin. Common. Creeks and small rivers, ammocoetes buried in sand substrates in pools. Adult and ammocoete non-parasitic, detrital filter feeder. Brood hiding, lithophil (A.2.3). Maximum size 220 mm TL.

7 SEA LAMPREY—*Petromyzon marinus* Linnaeus. Large, sharp disc teeth, supraoral teeth 2, usually 2-2-2-2 lateral circumoral teeth, 8–10 posterior circumoral teeth. Expanded oral disc wide or wider than head width. Two dorsal fins. Usually 66–75 trunk myomeres. Unpigmented lateral line organs. Mottled black with either bluish-gray or olive-brown above, cream or yellowish-white below; olive-brown fins. Great Lakes and coastal areas from Atlantic Coast to Gulf of Mexico. Adults in Great Lakes, large rivers, and creeks, ammocoetes buried in large particle substrates. Rare to occasional. Adult parasitic, ammocoete detrital filter feeder. Brood hiding, lithophil (A.2.3). Maximum size 558 mm TL.

5   LEAST BROOK LAMPREY—
Lampetra aepyptera

6   AMERICAN BROOK LAMPREY—
Lampetra appendix

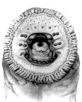

7   SEA LAMPREY—
Petromyzon marinus

PADDLEFISH FAMILY—POLYODONTIDAE
(SPECIES PLATE 8)

The Paddlefish are survivors of an ancient fish fauna. The large, elongate oar-shaped snout is used for stability during swimming and feeding (Figure 15). The earliest fossils may date to the late Cretaceous about 70–75 million years ago (Grande 1980). Five species are known, 3 are extinct from western North America (Grande and Bemis 1991).

Paddlefish can attain large sizes, including a 2.16 m (85 in) specimen. Their extinct Chondrostei relatives occurred during the Devonian about 350 million years ago. These extinct Chondrostei are considered the closest relative to the sturgeon (Patterson 1982; Lauder and Liem 1983), while Paddlefish are considered the sister species by others (Nelson 1969). The extinct *Paleopsephurus* (Cretaceous, Montana), thought to be a Paddlefish, is considered the nearest relative to sturgeon and chondrosteids and Paddlefish more distant relatives (Gardiner 1984). *Acipenser* fossils occur in the upper Cretaceous strata of western North America (Gardiner 1984; Cavender 1986).

The American and Chinese paddlefish are members of very different trophic guilds. The American species is a planktivore with a non-protrusible mouth. The Chinese species has a protrusible jaw, lacks long gill rakers, and is highly predaceous on fishes and macroinvertebrates (Vasetskiy 1971; Chenhan and Yongjun 1988; Grande and Bemis 1991).

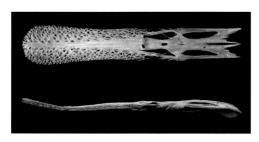

Figure 15. Skeletonized snout or paddle of the Paddlefish.

STURGEON FAMILY—ACIPENSERIDAE
(*SPECIES PLATES 9–10*)

The sturgeons and the paddlefish are considered the most primitive bony fishes. Their extinct relatives, the Chondrostei, occurred during the Devonian about 350 million years ago. The Acipenseridae comprise about 23 living species within two subfamilies, Scaphirhynchinae (Shovelnose sturgeon) and Acipenserinae (typical sturgeon). In sturgeon and paddlefish the posterior vertebrae continue far into the dorsal lobe of the caudal fin (heterocercal type), branchiostegal rays are absent or inconspicuous, and the skeleton is primitive cartilage, with the exception of ossified bones on the head; the intestine has a spiral valve. Sturgeon have a protrusible mouth, toothless in adults, with fleshy lips. The prominent snout has 4 barbels located between the mouth and the snout tip. A lateral line and typical scales are absent, instead 5 rows of bony scutes along the body are very sharp in young fish but become smooth with age. Molecular relationships support a polytomy including *Huso* and *Acipenser* (Artyukhin 2006).

The sturgeons are northern hemisphere fishes; some are freshwater and others are anadromous. The genus *Acipenser* is Holarctic with 5 species in North America and about 11 in Europe and Asia. The genus *Scaphirhynchus* contains 4 species that are found in central and southern North America. Two additional genera—*Huso* has 2 species and *Psuedoscaphirhynchus* has 3 species—occur in Europe and Asia. Sturgeons are the largest freshwater fishes and life spans of larger species may exceed 150 years. *Huso* the Beluga inhabits the Black and Caspian seas and tributaries and is the largest freshwater fish, with weights of 1,300 kg (2,800 lbs) and lengths of 8 m (26 ft) (Berra 2001).

1   a) Snout pointed, conical; barbels smooth; caudal peduncle
        short distance from base of anal fin (A) insertion to base
        of notochord origin is less than from origin of pelvic fin
        to origin of anal fin origin (B). Lower lip with 2 posterior
        lobes weakly to strongly papillose. Dorsal lobe of caudal fin
        without a long filament. Spiracle present at anterior end of
        the groove continuous with gilt slit ....
        ....**LAKE STURGEON**—*Acipenser fulvescens*

    b) Snout flattened and shovel-shaped; barbels fringed; distance
        from insertion of anal fin to ventral margin of caudal fin
        origin (A) is greater than the distance from origin of pelvic
        fin to origin of anal fin (B). Caudal peduncle covered with
        bony plates; dorsal lobe of caudal fin with a long filament
        (sometimes broken off). Spiracles absent.................................
        .... **SHOVELNOSE STURGEON**—
        ....*Scaphirhynchus platorynchus*

GAR FAMILY—LEPISOSTEIDAE
(*Species plates 11–14*)

The gar are a group of primitive neopterygian fishes that swam
in the warm shallow waters of the late Cretaceous. Two genera
include *Lepisosteus* and *Atractosteus,* which evolved during
the Early Jurassic about 200 million years ago (Wiley 1976).

The gars are primitive predators and they possess an at-
tenuated, needle-like snout (Figure 16) with numerous teeth, a
tubular and elongate body protected by overlapping, diamond-
shaped ganoid scales, an abbreviated heterocercal caudal fin,
and a primitive lung (swim bladder connected to the esophagus), which allows breathing of atmospheric air. The basic jaw
mechanism is adapted to biting. Fins exhibit an apomorphic

Figure 16. Comparative snout morphologies of Alligator gar
(far left), Longnose gar, Spotted gar, and Shortnose gar (far
right) (Smith 1979).

character over Acipenseridae and Polyodontidae; each dorsal and anal ray has a bone support and the caudal fin has the abbreviate heterocercal (hemicercal) condition. Gar have a rudimentary spiral valve in the intestine and a large, vascularized bilobed swim bladder. The swim bladder is used as an accessory lung during periods of low dissolved oxygen concentration; it also provides buoyancy (Renfro and Hill 1970).

Of the living gar in North America, four are present in Indiana, including the Alligator gar, *Atractosteus spatula,* Spotted gar, *Lepisosteus oculatus,* Longnose gar, *Lepisosteus osseus,* and Shortnose gar, *Lepisosteus platostomus.*

KEY TO THE GAR OF INDIANA

1 a) Snout long and narrow, least width of snout (A) going more than 10 times into length (B). Caudal peduncle length at least twice its height........**LONGNOSE GAR**—*Lepisosteus osseus*

  b) Snout short and broad, least width of snout (A) going less than 10 times into length (B). Caudal peduncle length less than twice its height.. 2

2 a) Snout short and broad, distance from tip of snout to corner of mouth (A) less than rest of head (B). Width at nostrils 1.5 or more times eye diameter .... **ALLIGATOR GAR**—*Atractosteus spatula*

  b) Snout moderate in length and width; distance from tip of snout to corner of mouth (A) longer than rest of head (B); snout width at nostrils 1.0–1.5 times eye diameter 3

3 a) Top of head and pectoral and pelvic fins with dark, round spots; predorsal scale rows usually 50 or fewer (45–54); scales in lateral series (including small scales at base of tail fin) usually 54–58 .... **SPOTTED GAR**—*Lepisosteus oculatus*

  b) Top of head and pectoral and pelvic fins without dark, round spots; predorsal scale rows usually 51 or more; scales in lateral series usually 60–64 (59–65) ....**SHORTNOSE GAR**—*Lepisosteus platostomus*

8 PADDLEFISH—*Polyodon spathula* (Walbaum). Large oar-like paddle, with elongate body shape like a shark. Snout about a third of TL. Mouth large, jaws without teeth. Unscaled except on caudal peduncle. Gill cover with large fleshy, pointed flap on posterior edge. Eye tiny. Grayish-blue to nearly black, sometimes mottled above, and white below. Mississippi River basin from NY to LA, including Gulf Slope from TX to AL. Extirpated from Lakes Erie and possibly Michigan. Rare to occasional. Large rivers including shoals and deep waters. Planktivore drift feeder. Open subtrate, lithopelagophil (A.1.2). Maximum size 1,505 mm TL.

9 LAKE STURGEON—*Acipenser fulvescens* Rafinesque. Cone-shaped snout; spiracle present; upper lobe of caudal fin without long filament. Anal fin origin behind dorsal fin origin. Caudal peduncle long but thick; tip of anal fin extending to anterior edge of fulcral caudal scute. Olive-brown to gray above, white below; dark gray or brown fins. Anal rays 24–30, gill rakers 32–35; scutes on back 9–17; lateral scutes 29–42. Great Lakes and Hudson Bay basins throughout Mississippi River. Rare to occasional. Large rivers occupying benthic habitats over sand, gravel, and muck. Benthic invertivore feeder. Open subtrate, lithopelagophil (A.1.2). Maximum size 1,400 mm FL (distance to fork in caudal fin).

10 SHOVELNOSE STURGEON—*Scaphirhynchus platorynchus* (Rafinesque). Snout flat and shovel-shaped. Fleshy lobes on lower lip 4, with 4 fringed barbels. Caudal peduncle long and slender and covered with bony scutes. Caudal fin with elongate filament. No spiracle. Scutes on belly except in small juveniles. Bases of outer barbel in line or anterior of inner barbels. Light brown or tan above, white below; brown or tan fins. Anal rays 18–23. Mississippi River basin from PA to MT, south to LA. Common. Large rivers in main channel over sand, gravel, or woody debris snags. Benthic invertivore feeder. Open subtrate, lithopelagophil (A.1.2). Maximum size 605 mm FL (distance to fork in caudal fin).

11 ALLIGATOR GAR—*Atractosteus spatula* (Lacepede). Short, broad, duck-shaped snout; upper jaw length shorter than distance from mouth edge to gill opening; 2 rows of teeth on upper jaw. Dark olive-brown or black above, white to yellow below; fins dark brown with spots on median fins. Juveniles black with white dorso-median arrow from dorsal fin to snout. Predorsal scales 48–54, gill rakers 59–66. Mississippi River basin from OH and IL to Gulf of Mexico; from Esconfina River, FL, to Veracruz, Mexico. Extremely rare; previously considered extirpated. Large rivers in pool habitat associated with large trees and woody debris; previously found in riverine wetland habitats. Ambush carnivore. Open subtrate, phytophil (A.1.5). Maximum size 3,048 mm TL.

8 PADDLEFISH—
Polyodon spathula

9 LAKE STURGEON—
Acipenser fulvescens

10 SHOVELNOSE STURGEON—
Scaphirhynchus platorynchus

11 ALLIGATOR GAR—
Atractosteus spatula

Family and Species Accounts of Indiana Fishes 105

 12 SPOTTED GAR—*Lepisosteus oculatus* Winchell. Moderately long snout; upper jaw longer than distance from mouth to gill cover. Head with many large olive-brown to black spots on head, body, and fins. Lateral scales 53–59; predorsal scales 45–54; gill rakers 15–24. Olive-brown to black above, white to yellow below; fins spotted. Great Lakes including Erie and southern MI throughout Mississippi River basin to Gulf Coast; Gulf Coastal drainage from Apalachicola River, FL, to Nueces River, TX. Common in inland lakes and common to occasional in large rivers. Small to large rivers, creek mouths, and lakes including sloughs and marshes. Ambush carnivore. Open substrate, phytophil (A.1.5). Maximum size 910 mm TL.

 13 LONGNOSE GAR—*Lepisosteus osseus* Linnaeus. Long, narrow snout, more than twice as long as the distance from mouth to gill cover; single row of sharp needle-like teeth on upper jaw. Lateral scales 57–63; predorsal scales 47–55; gill rakers 14–31. Olive-brown above, white below; dark spots on median fins. Atlantic Slope from NJ to central FL, Great Lakes basin and Mississippi River basin to Gulf Coast; Gulf Coast from FL to Rio Grande, TX, and Mexico. Common. Small to large rivers, moderate-sized streams, inland lakes and reservoirs, and slough and marshes. Ambush carnivore. Open substrate, phytolithophil (A.1.4). Maximum size 2000 mm TL.

 14 SHORTNOSE GAR—*Lepisosteus platostomus* Rafinesque. Short, broad snout; upper jaw longer than distance from mouth to gill opening; single row of teeth on upper jaw. Lateral scales 59–65; predorsal scales 50–60; gill rakers 16–25. Olive or brown above, white below; median fins with spots and paired fins without spots. Mississippi River basin from central OH to MT, south to northern AL and LA; Lake Michigan basin; Gulf Coast along LA shore. Occasional to common. Creeks, small rivers to large rivers, lakes, marshes, and sloughs. Ambush carnivore. Open substrate, phytophil (A.1.5). Maximum size 800 mm TL.

12 SPOTTED GAR—
Lepisosteus oculatus

13 LONGNOSE GAR—
Lepisosteus osseus

14 SHORTNOSE GAR—
Lepisosteus platostomus

BOWFIN FAMILY—AMIIDAE
(*Species plate 15*)

The family consists of a single extant species and several extirpated species that date to more than 208 million years ago. This
primitive fish possesses many pleisiomorphic traits, including
a gular plate (Figure 17), a non-protrusile bite, an abbreviate
heterocercal (hemicercal) caudal fin, a heavily vascularized
and subdivided air bladder that functions as a lung, and a
rudimentary intestinal spiral valve. The dorsal fin is long and
each ray articulates with a bony support. Scales are uniquely
surfaced. The ontogenetic development includes the presence
of an adhesive organ and a highly vascularized yolk sac, and
the fish possesses more than 60 total myomeres and lacks
barbels or other sensory structures (Simon 1990).

Bowfin are considered an undesirable sport fish because of
their predatory habits and poor taste. The flesh is considered
soft and has been described as tasting like "cotton." Bowfin
were stocked into many farm ponds around the middle of the
twentieth century as a tool to manage sport fish populations
and relieve stunting problems among sunfish populations.

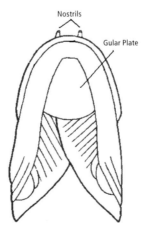

Figure 17. Location of gular plate on ventral side of head in
Amia calva.

MOONEYE FAMILY—HIODONTIDAE
(*SPECIES PLATES 16–17*)

The mooneyes or "toothed herrings" are confined to large water bodies of central North America. Greenwood (1973) considered hiodontids and their relatives to be closely related to clupeiform fishes, with their groups together forming the sister group to all other bony fishes above the level of primitive fishes.

Hiodontids have adipose eyelids, an auxiliary process above the pelvic fin base, cycloid scales, well-developed lateral lines, and prominent teeth on jaws and tongue, and the belly midline is keeled but lacks the row of spiny scutes. The dorsal fin is immediately above the base of the anal fin rather than far forward as in herrings. They lack an oviduct and eggs are extruded directly through the body cavity rather than through oviducts prior to spawning.

KEY TO THE MOONEYES OF INDIANA

1 a) Origin of dorsal fin slightly behind front of anal fin; dorsal fin with 9 or 10 principal rays; iris golden in live specimens; keel on midline of belly extending forward from vent nearly to pectoral fin bases; pectoral fins usually extending posteriorly to origin of pelvic fins...........**GOLDEYE**—*Hiodon alosoides*

   b) Origin of dorsal fin distinctly forward of front of anal fin; dorsal fin with 11 or 12 principal rays; iris silvery; keel on midline of belly extending forward from vent only as far as pelvic fin bases.......................**MOONEYE**—*Hiodon tergisus*

AMERICAN EEL FAMILY—ANGUILLIDAE
(*SPECIES PLATE 18*)

The American eel, order Anguilliformes, is a freshwater species, but the group is large and diverse, including 21 families and 720 species (Castle 1984). Almost all species are marine and many inhabit the deep sea. Anguilliformes have very elongate, serpentine bodies, lack pelvic fins (some also lack pectoral fins), and have scales absent or small and embedded. The eel-like form has apparently evolved independently several times, and there are several groups of eels that are not related to true eels and are included in other orders.

15 BOWFIN—*Amia calva* Linnaeus. Elongate, nearly cylindrical body. Long dorsal fin extending more than half of back. Nostrils tube-like, mouth large with many teeth; upper jaw extends beyond eye. Round pectoral, pelvic, and caudal fins. Large bony gular plate. Dorsal fin rays 42–53. Mottled olive above, creamy yellow to pale green below; black bands on dark green dorsal and caudal fins, pelvic fins green, yellow to orange halo around prominent black spot near base of upper caudal fin. Brilliant green on lips, throat, belly, and pelvic fins. Great Lakes and Mississippi River basins from QC to MN south to Gulf of Mexico, and Atlantic and Gulf Coastal Plain. Common. Marshes, lakes, and backwater habitats of large rivers associated with vegetation. Ambush carnivore. Nest spawning, phytophil (B.2.5). Maximum size 870 mm TL.

16 GOLDEYE—*Hiodon alosoides* (Rafinesque). Deep, laterally compressed, silver-sided body. Dorsal fin origin opposite or behind anal fin origin. Fleshy keel along belly extends from pectoral fin base to anal fin origin. Large mouth; maxillary extends beyond eye. Dorsal rays 9–10, anal rays 29–34, lateral scales 57–62. Bluish-green above with silver reflection, silvery-white below; clear to dusky fins; iris golden. Wide ranging from Hudson Bay, Mississippi and Missouri river basins, south to LA. Rare. Deep pools and main channel of large rivers, lakes, and reservoirs. Drift invertivore. Open substrate, lithopelagophil (A.1.2). Maximum size 500 mm TL.

17 MOONEYE—*Hiodon tergisus* Lesueur. Deep, laterally compressed, silver-sided body. Dorsal fin origin in front of anal fin origin. Fleshy keel along belly from pelvic fin base to anal fin origin. Mouth moderate; maxillary extends to front of eye. Dorsal rays 11–12, anal rays 26–29, lateral scales 52–57. Silver above and below; iris silver. Great Lakes and Hudson Bay to Mississippi River, south to Gulf of Mexico, Gulf Slope from Mobile Bay, AL, to Lake Pontchartrain, LA. Rare to occasional. Deep pools and main channel of large rivers, lakes, and reservoirs. Drift invertivore. Open substrate, lithopelagophil (A.1.2). Maximum size 445 mm TL.

18 AMERICAN EEL—*Anguilla rostrata* (Lesueur). Elongate, serpentine lamprey-like body; small, pointed head. Dorsal fin extends more than half of body, continuous with caudal and anal fins. Lower jaw extends beyond upper jaw. Olive-brown to yellow above, white to yellow below; fins similarly colored as body. Catadromous species, spawning in Atlantic Ocean–ascending streams and rivers to spawn. Great Lakes, Mississippi River, and Gulf Coast basins from NF to SD. Rare. Large streams and moderate-sized rivers to large rivers. Carnivore. Marine-spawning species. Maximum size 1,200 mm TL.

15 BOWFIN—
Amia calva

16 GOLDEYE—
Hiodon alosoides

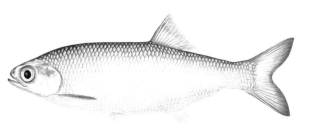

17 MOONEYE—
Hiodon tergisus

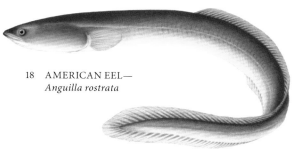

18 AMERICAN EEL—
Anguilla rostrata

HERRING FAMILY—CLUPEIDAE
(*Species plates 19–23*)

The herring, order Clupeiformes, is a large group of mostly marine and anadromous species that comprise 63 genera and 174 species (McGowan and Berry 1984; Grande 1985). They are important forage and commercial fishes (Nelson 1984).

Herring are silvery, deep-bodied fishes with adipose eyelids, pelvic axillary processes, and a midventral keel composed of modified scales (scutes). Teeth are small or absent; gill rakers are long, slender, and numerous; pyloric caeca are numerous, adipose fin and lateral line are absent; scales are cycloid. Most are pelagic marine species, some are anadromous, and a few live permanently in freshwater.

KEY TO THE HERRING OF INDIANA

1. a) Mouth subterminal; last ray of dorsal fin elongated into a long, slender filament; predorsal midline naked; principal rays of dorsal fin usually 14 or fewer; a dark spot behind upper end of gill opening (spot sometimes absent in large adults). Stomach muscular and like the gizzard of a chicken 2

   b) Last ray of dorsal fin not elongated into a long, slender filament; predorsal midline scaled; principal rays of dorsal fin usually 16 or more; no dark spot behind upper end of gill opening. Stomach not muscular like that of a chicken gizzard 3

19   ALABAMA SHAD—*Alosa alabamae* Jordan and Evermann. Mouth oblique, lower jaw equal to or projecting only slightly beyond snout. Jaw teeth lacking. Gill rakers 42–48 on first gill arch. Gray-green above, gradually shading to silver side, white to silver below; clear fins. Gulf Coastal Plain from FL to LA, north to Mississippi River basin including Cumberland, Tennessee, Missouri, Arkansas, Ouachita, and Red rivers. Previously considered extirpated, possibly rare. Open water of moderate to large rivers. Filter-feeding planktivore. Open substrate, phytolithophil (A.1.4). Maximum size 449 mm TL, males smaller, reaching 401 mm TL.

2 a) Lower jaw extends past tip of snout; rays of anal fin usually 20–25; scales in lateral series usually 50 or fewer; caudal fin bright yellow in live specimens; anterior origin of dorsal fin over pelvic insertion; lateral line scales fewer than 50, usually 40–43; dark spot behind end of gill opening smaller than eye diameter.........**THREADFIN SHAD**—*Dorosoma petenense*

b) Lower jaw not projecting beyond tip of snout; rays of anal fin usually 29–35; scales in lateral series usually 55 or more; tail fin gray or dusky-colored in live specimens; anterior origin of dorsal insertion distinctly behind pelvic insertion; lateral line scales greater than 52, usually 58–65 (range 52–70); dark spot behind end of gill opening as equivalent or larger than eye .... **GIZZARD SHAD**—*Dorosoma cepedianum*

3 a) Posterior end of maxillary beneath the front of eye; mouth smaller, nearly vertical, not reaching to middle of eye. Common in Lake Michigan drainage and select tributaries. Lateral line scales 42–50; dorsal rays usually 13 or 14; body depth in adult usually less than head length ....
....**ALEWIFE**—*Alosa psuedoharengus*

b) Posterior end of maxillary extends to middle of eye or farther posterior; mouth larger, oblique. Common in Ohio River drainage. Lateral line scales 36–60; dorsal rays usually 15 or more; body depth in adult usually less than head length... 4

4 a) Tip of lower jaw extending well beyond upper jaw; eye diameter less than snout length; jaws with teeth; lateral line scales 36–50 ....**SKIPJACK HERRING**—*Alosa chrysochloris*

b) Tip of lower jaw only slightly beyond upper jaw; eye diameter equal to snout length; jaws without teeth; lateral line scales 55–60 ....**ALABAMA SHAD**—*Alosa alabamae*

19 ALABAMA SHAD—
    Alosa alabamae

20   SKIPJACK HERRING—*Alosa chrysochloris* (Rafinesque). Mouth strongly oblique, lower jaw extends beyond upper jaw. Gill rakers 20–24, rakers on lower limb of first gill arch. Bluish-green above ending abruptly, silver sided, silver below; clear to dusky fins. Red River of the North to Mississippi River basin south to Gulf of Mexico from FL to TX. Occasional to locally common. Open water of clear to turbid large rivers and reservoirs. Intentionally introduced into Lake Michigan. Schooling species, occurs over sand and gravel substrates. Filter-feeding planktivore. Open substrate, phytolithophil (A.1.4). Maximum size 460 mm TL.

21   ALEWIFE—*Alosa pseudoharengus* (Wilson). Strongly oblique mouth, about 45° to horizontal; large eye, diameter greater than snout length; deep bodied. Usually gill rakers 39–41 on first gill arch. Bluish-green above, silver sided above, silver sided below; clear to dusky fins. Great Lakes to Atlantic Coast, south to SC. Introduced into Lake Michigan. Common to abundant, relative abundance experiences wide fluctuations. Schooling species, occurs over all bottom types. Particulate-feeding planktivore. Open substrate, phytolithophil (A.1.4). Maximum size 350 mm TL.

22   GIZZARD SHAD—*Dorosoma cepedianum* (Lesueur). Elongate last dorsal ray, snout blunt, distinctly subterminal mouth; deep notch at center of upper jaw. No scales on nape. Dorsal fin origin above or behind pelvic fin origin. Silvery-blue above, becoming silvery-white, with bluish-green reflections on head and body. Large purple-blue spot near upper edge of gill cover in young and small adults, white to silver below; gray or dusky fins. No black pigment on chin or inside mouth. Dorsal rays 10–13, anal rays 25–36, lateral scales 52–70. Ubiquitous, found throughout the Great Lakes and eastern United States in Mississippi, Atlantic, and Gulf Coast. Abundant. Schooling species occurs over all bottom types. Filter-feeding herbivore. Open substrate, lithopelagophil (A.1.2). Maximum size 350 mm TL.

23   THREADFIN SHAD—*Dorosoma petenense* (Guenther). Snout more pointed than Gizzard shad, black pigment on chin and inside mouth. Dorsal rays 11–14, anal rays 17–27, lateral scales 40–48. Purple shoulder spot near upper edge of gill cover fading in adults. Purple to dusky gray above, grading to silver side, white to silver below; yellow anal and caudal fins remaining clear to dusky. Ohio and Mississippi rivers south to Gulf of Mexico and Atlantic Slope. Introduced widely into inland lakes. Abundant to locally common. Occurs in lakes, reservoirs, and pools of large rivers in open water over sand, mud, and woody debris. Filter-feeding planktivore. Open substrate, phytophil (A.1.5). Maximum size 178 mm TL.

20 SKIPJACK HERRING—
Alosa chrysochloris

21 ALEWIFE—
Alosa pseudoharengus

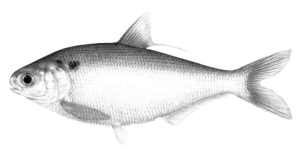

22 GIZZARD SHAD—
Dorosoma cepedianum

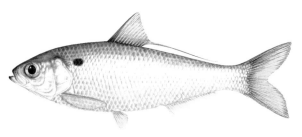

23 THREADFIN SHAD—
Dorosoma petenense

SUCKER FAMILY—CATOSTOMIDAE
(SPECIES PLATES 24–44)

The Catostomidae is a North American family with 11 genera and 59 species in the United States and Canada (Nelson 2006). The Harelip sucker had been reclassified as a member of the genus *Moxostoma,* rather than *Lagochila* (Nelson et al. 2004). The species is considered extinct (Simon et al. 2002).

The suckers are diagnosed by a subterminal mouth; fleshy protractile lips and premaxillaries; posteriorly positioned anal fin with less than 11 rays; pharyngeal arch with 20 or more teeth in a single row; a Weberian apparatus; cycloid scales; and a head without scales (Nelson 2006). Dorsal fin morphology varies from a short fin base with 8–17 soft rays, such as in the genera *Catostomus, Erimyzon, Hypentelium, Minytrema,* and *Moxostoma,* to a long fin base with 22–35 rays, such as in *Cycleptus, Ictiobus,* and *Carpiodes.* All suckers possess a minimum of 10 dorsal rays.

Size range in suckers is from minnow-sized lengths of 102–229 mm TL to the large *Ictiobus cyprinellus,* which may exceed 914 mm TL and weigh up to 36 kg. Suckers biomass support an important commercial fishery in some parts of the country (Emery et al. 1999). Small individuals are important prey items for game species. Habitats range from small headwater streams to large rivers and reservoirs. Spawning runs occur in the spring when adults ascend streams and rivers and concentrate in riffles and below dams (Kay et al. 1994). Spawning occurs over gravel substrates (Kay et al. 1994; Simon 1999). Most suckers are benthic species that feed on aquatic insects (Goldstein and Simon 1999). Some species that possess a more terminal mouth strain crustaceans from the water column. Varying sensitivities are known among sucker species to anthropogenic stress. The genera *Moxostoma, Erimyzon,* and *Minytrema* are among the most sensitive (Emery et al. 1999).

KEY TO THE SUCKERS OF INDIANA

1 a) Mouth with non-protractile upper lip and split lower lip (status: extinct) .... **HARELIP SUCKER**—*Moxostoma lacerum*

   b) Mouth with protractile upper lip and lower lip with either striated or papillose lower lip that may be divided into equal parts.. 2

2 a) Dorsal fin with more than 20 rays; length of its base into SL less than 4.0 3

   b) Dorsal fin with 18 or fewer rays; length of its base into SL greater than 4.0.. 9

3 a) Lateral line scales more than 50. Eye closer to posterior edge of opercular membrane than to tip of snout. Body depth into SL 4.0–4.4 .... **BLUE SUCKER**—*Cycleptus elongatus*

   b) Lateral line scales fewer than 50. Eye closer to tip of snout than to posterior edge of opercular membrane. Body depth into SL less than 4.0 .... *Carpiodes* spp. or *Ictiobus* spp., 4

4 a) Subopercle broadest below middle. Distance A is about equal to B. Anterior fontanelle (located by probing dorsal surface of head between notrils) present. Lower fins cream-colored, colorless, or clear, almost lacking in pigment. Anterior lobe of dorsal fin essentially filamentous. Intestinal configuration of circular loops.......... **CARPSUCKERS**—*Carpiodes* spp., 5

   b) Subopercle broadest at middle. Distance A is less than B. Anterior fontanelle much reduced or lacking. Lower fins darkly pigmented. Anterior lobe of dorsal fin rounded or pointed but not filamentous. Intestinal configuration of elongated loops .... **BUFFALOES**—*Ictiobus* spp., 7

5 a) No nipple on tip of lower lip. Posterior edge of lower lip forming an acute angle. Tip of lower lip clearly in advance of anterior nostril. Snout in lateral view usually notched. Scales in lateral line usually 36–40. Body depth into SL 2.6–3.2. Head length into SL 3.2–3.8 .... **QUILLBACK**—*Carpiodes cyprinus*

   b) Light nipple on tip of lower lip. Posterior edge of lower lip usually forming an obtuse angle. Tip of lower lip scarcely or not at all in advance of anterior nostril. Snout in lateral view usually rounded and not notched. Scales in lateral line usually 33–37. Body depth into SL 2.2–3.1. Head length into SL 3.5–4.3... 6

6 a) Body depth into SL 2.5–3.1. Length of anterior rays of depressed dorsal fin usually less than 0.33 length of dorsal fin base ....**RIVER CARPSUCKER**—*Carpiodes carpio*

b) Body depth into SL 2.2–2.6. Length of anterior rays of depressed dorsal fin usually greater than length of dorsal fin base ....**HIGHFIN CARPSUCKER**—*Carpiodes velifer*

7 a) Mouth large, terminal, and extremely oblique. Tip of upper lip about level with lower margin of eye. Lips thin and shallowly grooved. Length of upper jaw nearly equal to snout length ....**BIGMOUTH BUFFALO**—*Ictiobus cyprinellus*

b) Mouth smaller, subterminal, and almost horizontal. Tip of upper lip at a level far below lower margin of eye. Lips thick and deeply grooved. Length of upper jaw much less than snout length.. 8

8 a) Body depth into SL 2.4–2.8. Back highly arched and compressed into mid-dorsal ridge (appearing humpbacked in combination with small head). Head small, its length into SL 3.4–4.1. Length of anterior rays of dorsal fin base about 1.6. Length of upper jaw into snout length 1.5–2.0. Head thickness at operculum bulge into SL 5.2–6.1 ....
..................**SMALLMOUTH BUFFALO**—*Ictiobus bulbalus*

b) Body depth into SL 2.9–3.5. Back not highly arched or ridged but rounded over top from side to side. Head large, its length into SL 2.9–3.8. Length of anterior rays of dorsal fin into dorsal fin base 2.2–2.5. Length of upper jaw into snout length 2.0–2.5. Head thickness at opercular bulge into SL 4.7–5.4 ...
.... **BLACK BUFFALO**—*Ictiobus niger*

9 a) Lateral line incomplete (developed anteriorly in adult spotted suckers) or absent 10

b) Lateral line complete and well developed 12

10 a) Lateral series scales 42–46. Distinct blackish spots present on each scale base, resulting in series of longitudinal stripes that are most distinct (except in the smallest young where the faint spots and stripes may be restricted to region above anal fin base). Body depth into SL usually greater than 4.0. Lateral line somewhat developed anteriorly in adults ....
..........................**SPOTTED SUCKER**—*Minytrema melanops*

b) Lateral series scales 35–41 (33–45). Blackish spots absent on each scale base. Body depth into SL usually less than 3.5. Lateral line lacking at all ages ....
....**CHUBSUCKERS**—*Erimyzon* spp., 11

11 a) Dorsal rays 11–12 (10–13). Lateral series scales 35–37 (33–40). Body depth into SL 3.3 or less. Unbroken, blackish lateral stripe very distinct in young, least distinct in large adults (Lake Michigan drainage) ....**LAKE CHUBSUCKER**—*Erimyzon sucetta*

b) Dorsal rays 9–10 (8–11). Lateral series scales 39–41 (37–45). Body depth into SL usually 3.3 or more. Dusky lateral stripe broken into series of more or less confluent blotches (these blotches sometimes very faint or absent in large adults) .... **CREEK CHUBSUCKER**—*Erimyzon oblongus*

12 a) Lateral line scales 55 or more ....*Catostomus* spp., 13

b) Lateral line scales fewer than 54 14

13 a) Lateral line scales 55–85. Snout short, scarcely protruding beyond upper lip.................................... **WHITE SUCKER**— ....*Catostomus commersonii*

b) Lateral line scales more than 90. Snout elongated, protruding well beyond upper lip ....**LONGNOSE SUCKER**—*Catostomus catostomus*

14 a) Top of head between eyes concave. Body with 5 (4–6) dark, usually prominent oblique bars. Lips heavily papillose......... .... **NORTHERN HOGSUCKER**—*Hypentelium nigricans*

b) Top of head between eyes usually convex. Body not marked with dark oblique bars. Lips primarily plicate but may be papillose posteriorly and in corners.. ....*Moxostoma* spp. (Redhorses), 15

15 a) Body scales, principally above lateral line, with distinct, dark spots at the base. Tail always pink, red, or carmine in life; color soon fades in preserved specimens 16

b) Body scales without dark spots at their bases. Tail always slate-colored in life..19

16 a) Scales around caudal peduncle 16 (7 above and below the 2 lateral line scales). Lower lip plicate with few papillae at corners. Dorsal fin slightly concave in young to convex adults. Pharyngeal teeth heavy, comb-like .... **GREATER REDHORSE**—*Moxostoma valenciennesi*

b) Scales around caudal peduncle 12 (5 above and below the 2 lateral lines). Lower lip either entirely plicate or partially papillose, especially along the posterior half. Dorsal fin falcate to straight. Pharyngeal teeth thin, comb-like, or thick, molar-like 17

17 a) Head small and short, its length into SL usually 4.3–5.4 times in young-of-the-year and adults, 3.5–4.0 times in young less than 76 mm TL. Mouth small. Folds of lower lip transversely divided into large papillae; lower lip appearing swollen; posterior edge forming a straight line, rarely an obtuse angle. Pharyngeal teeth about 53 per arch, thin and comb-like. Dorsal fin falcate 18

b) Head bulky and long, its length into SL usually less than 4.3 times in young-of-the-year and adults, 3.0–3.8 in young less than 76 mm TL. Mouth large. Folds of lower lip almost always smooth; papillae absent; lower halves nearly straight along posterior margin, which may be weakly scalloped. Pharyngeal teeth 33–45 per arch, large and molar-like. Dorsal fin straight or slightly concave in large young and adults .... **RIVER REDHORSE**—*Moxostoma carinatum*

18 a) Dorsal fin straight; caudal fin equal; back not elevated but symmetrical with body; dorsal rays 13; pelvic fin rays 9; lips large in size........................... **SHORTHEAD REDHORSE**—..*Moxostoma macrolepidotum*

b) Dorsal fin concave or falcate; upper lobe of caudal fin greater than lower lobe in size; back elevated anterior dorsal fin origin; dorsal fin rays 12, pelvic fin rays 10; lips smaller in size. ....**SMALLMOUTH REDHORSE**—*Moxostoma breviceps*

19 a) Dorsal fin rays 15 (14–17). Length of dorsal fin base equal or almost equal to distance from back of head to dorsal fin origin. Lower lip folds partly or entirely dissected into fine, irregular-shaped papillae; lower lip halves forming an angle of about 90°. Dorsal fin slightly concave to convex ....
.......................**SILVER REDHORSE**—*Moxostoma anisurum*

b) Dorsal fin rays 12–13 (10–15). Length of dorsal fin base 0.67–0.75 the distance from back of head to dorsal fin origin. Lower lip folds not dissected into papillae; lower lip halves in an almost straight line or broad obtuse angle, usually over 100°. Dorsal fin slightly falcate 20

20 a) Lateral line scales 40–42 (37–45). Rays of pelvic fins usually 9, rarely 8 or 10. Least depth of caudal peduncle into its length usually less than 1.6. Snout blunt to rounded but not overhanging mouth. Head length into SL 3.9–4.3 ....
...............**GOLDEN REDHORSE**—*Moxostoma erythrurum*

b) Lateral line scales 44–47 (43–51). Rays of 1 or both pelvic fins usually 10 (8–11). Least depth of caudal peduncle into its length greater than 1.7. Snout rounded and swollen, slightly overhanging mouth ventrally. Head length into SL 4.1–4.8..
......................**BLACK REDHORSE**—*Moxostoma duquesnei*

24 RIVER CARPSUCKER—*Carpiodes carpio* (Rafinesque). Deep bodied, with small conical head. Nipple present in middle of lower lip. Snout short, rounded and bullet-shaped, snout length less than distance from back of eye to upper margin of gill opening. Upper jaw extends past anterior eye. First dorsal fin ray short, usually not extending past middle of dorsal fin when depressed. Lateral scales 33–36. Olive-green, dusky gray, or bronze above grading into silver on side, white below; dusky gray, white, or pink to clear fins. Mississippi River drainage from PA to MT south to Gulf Coast. Introduced into Lake Erie. Common. Backwaters and deep pools of small to large rivers, lakes, and reservoirs. Filter-feeding detritivore. Open substrate, lithopelagophil (A.1.2). Maximum size 380 mm TL.

25 QUILLBACK—*Carpiodes cyprinus* (Lesueur). Deep bodied, with small conical head. Nipple absent in middle of lower lip. Snout long, equal to distance from back of eye to upper margin of gill opening. Upper jaw does not extend past anterior of eye. First dorsal fin long but does not extend past rear margin of dorsal fin when depressed. Lateral scales 36–37. Olive to gray above with silver or bluish-green reflections, with silver sides, median fins gray or dusky, paired fins either orange or white. Great Lakes, Hudson Bay, and Mississippi River basins from QC to AB, south to LA, Atlantic Slope from NY to NC, Gulf Coast from FL to LA. Common. Backwaters and deep pools of small to large rivers, lakes, and reservoirs. Benthic-feeding detritivore. Open substrate, lithopelagophil (A.1.2). Maximum size 800 mm TL.

26 HIGHFIN CARPSUCKER—*Carpiodes velifer* (Rafinesque). Deep bodied, with small conical head. Nipple present in middle of lower lip. Snout short, rounded, snout length less than distance from back to eye to upper margin of gill opening. Upper jaw extends past anterior of eye. First dorsal fin long, extending past posterior margin of dorsal fin when depressed. Lateral line scales 33–36. Olive to gray above with silver sides, clear or dusky fins. Lake Michigan and Mississippi River basins from PA to MN, south to LA and Gulf Coastal Plain to FL, and Atlantic Slope from NC. Occasional. Backwaters and deep pool of small to large rivers, lakes, and reservoirs. Filter-feeding detritivore. Open substrate, lithopelagophil (A.1.2). Maximum size 305 mm TL.

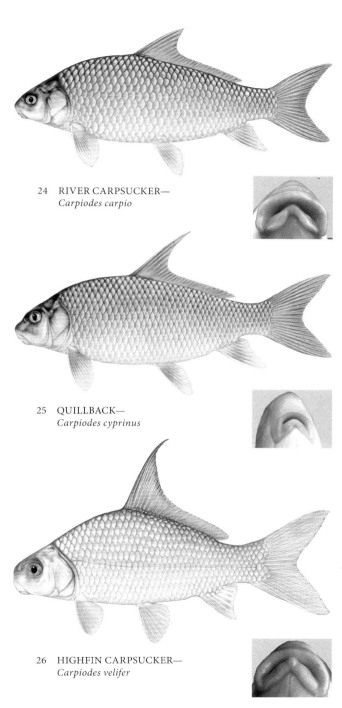

24 RIVER CARPSUCKER—
Carpiodes carpio

25 QUILLBACK—
Carpiodes cyprinus

26 HIGHFIN CARPSUCKER—
Carpiodes velifer

27 LONGNOSE SUCKER—*Catostomus catostomus* (Forster). Round bodied, with elongate snout. Deep median notch in lower lip, 0–1 row of papillae at middle of lower lip, 2 rows of papillae on upper lip. Usually dorsal rays 9–11, pectoral rays 16–18; lateral scales 95–120, caudal peduncle scales 26–34. Dark olive or gray to bluish with greenish-gold to copper brown grading into white, yellow, orange below, with red to rust-colored stripe on side; median fins dusky, amber or pink paired fins. Great Lakes, Atlantic, Arctic, Pacific, and upper Ohio River basins. Rare. Deep, clear, cold water of Lake Michigan and tributary streams over gravel and cobble substrates. Invertivore. Open substrate, lithopelagophil (A.1.2). Maximum size 643 mm TL.

28 WHITE SUCKER—*Catostomus commersonii* (Lacepede). Round bodied, with short snout. Deep median notch in lower lip, 0–3 rows of papillae at middle of lower lip, 2–6 rows of papillae on upper lip, lower lip twice as thick as upper lip. Usually dorsal rays 10–12, lateral scales 53–74, scale rows above lateral line 8–11. Olive-brown to tan above with dusky-edged scales giving a mottled appearance; clear, yellowish, or orange fins. Widespread, occurring in Great Lakes, Atlantic, Arctic, and Mississippi River basins. Common to abundant. Ubiquitous, occurring in all size streams from small headwater streams to large rivers, lakes, marshes, swamps, and Lake Michigan, occurring over muck, sand, and gravel substrates. Benthic-feeding detritivore. Open substrate, lithopelagophil (A.1.2). Maximum size 635 mm TL.

29 BLUE SUCKER—*Cycleptus elongatus* (Lesueur). Round bodied, with small head (length going 5 times into SL). Snout blunt overhanging small, horizontal mouth. Lips papillose. Dorsal fin long, falcate. Long caudal peduncle; deeply forked caudal fin. Dorsal fin rays 28–37, anal rays 7, lateral scales 51–59. Blue or gray above, blue to white below. Dark blue to gray fins. Spawning males are blue to black with minute white tubercles covering head, body, and fins. Large females pallid to light blue with fewer tubercles. Mississippi River drainage from PA to MT, south to LA. Occasional to common. Large rivers in fast current or in deep, fast runs over sand, gravel, cobble, boulder, or bedrock substrates. Invertivore. Open substrate, lithopelagophil (A.1.2). Maximum size 930 mm TL.

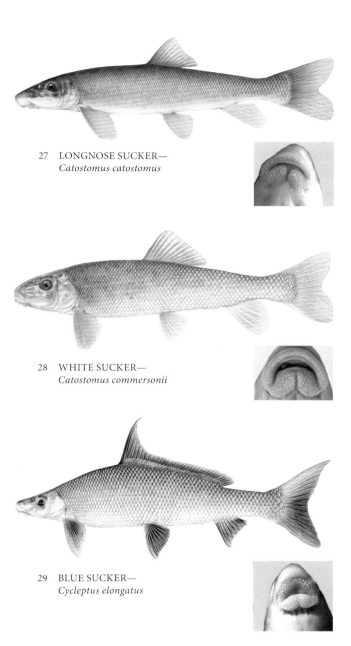

27 LONGNOSE SUCKER—
Catostomus catostomus

28 WHITE SUCKER—
Catostomus commersonii

29 BLUE SUCKER—
Cycleptus elongatus

 30 CREEK CHUBSUCKER—*Erimyzon oblongus* (Mitchill). Thicker round bodied. Small mouth, nearly straight; plicate lips, with lips meeting at nearly right angle. No lateral line. Dorsal fin rounded. Caudal peduncle narrow. Dorsal rays 10, anal rays 7 and bilobed, lateral line scales 40–45. Olive to brown above, dark-edged scales, with 5–8 large dark blotches along side, white to yellow below; yellow-orange to olive-gray fins. Spawning males dark brown above, pink to yellow below; orange paired fins, yellow median fins; with 3 large tubercles on each side of snout. Young with faint yellow stripe above black stripe extending from snout to caudal fin base. Atlantic Slope, Great Lakes to Gulf Coast and occurring throughout the Mississippi River basin. Common. Headwater creeks, streams, riverine wetlands, and small rivers over sand and gravel substrates. Found associated with submerged vegetation. Invertivore. Open substrate, lithopelagophil (A.1.2). Maximum size 345 mm TL.

 31 LAKE CHUBSUCKER—*Erimyzon sucetta* (Lacepede). Thicker round bodied, body depth greater than Creek chubsucker. Small mouth, nearly straight; plicate lips, with lips meeting at nearly right angle. No lateral line. Dorsal fin rounded. Caudal peduncle narrow. Dorsal rays 10, anal rays 7 and bilobed, lateral line scales 34–39. Olive to brown above, dark-edged scales, without large dark blotches along side; possessing lateral stripe, white to yellow below; yellow-orange to olive-gray fins. Spawning males dark above and below often with brassy appearance, orange to yellow fins. Great Lakes and Mississippi River lowlands to Gulf Coast from FL to TX, occurring along Atlantic Slope from VA to FL. Occasional. Inland lakes, swamps, marshes, ponds, pannes, and reservoirs over sand, fine silt-covered substrates, and woody debris and leaf packs. Associated with submerged vegetation. Invertivore. Open substrate, phytophil (A.1.4). Maximum size 463 mm TL.

 32 NORTHERN HOGSUCKER—*Hypentelium nigricans* (Lesueur). Round-bodied sucker. Large, rectangular head with concave depression between eyes in adults. Body wide in front of dorsal fin and tapering posteriorly. Long, blunt snout, horizontal mouth; large fleshy lips, many papillae on lips; 2 halves of lower lips broadly joined in middle. Large fan-shaped pectoral fins. Lateral line complete. Dorsal rays 11, pectoral rays (both fins together) 32–38, lateral line scales 44–54. Dark olive or brown to reddish-brown above, with light stripes and dark mottling along scale rows, snout blue or black, pale yellow or white below; orange to yellow fins, with black edges on dorsal and caudal fins. Widely distributed from Hudson Bay and Great Lakes to Mississippi River basins, south to AL, AR, and LA, east along Atlantic Slope from NY to GA, and Gulf Slope from FL to AL. Common. Rock riffles, runs, and pools from moderate-sized creeks and small rivers, not as common in large rivers, seldom in reservoirs. Invertivore. Open substrate, lithophil (A.1.3). Maximum size 610 mm TL.

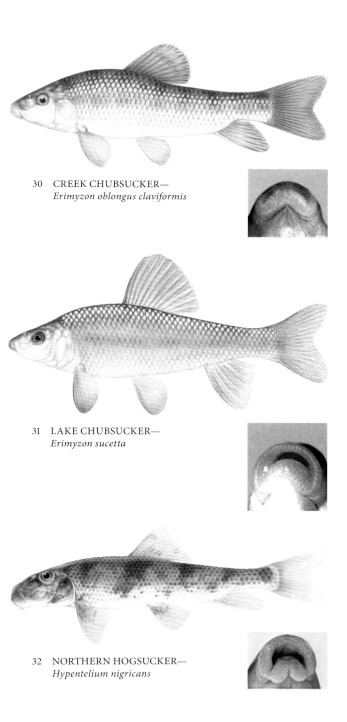

30 CREEK CHUBSUCKER—
Erimyzon oblongus claviformis

31 LAKE CHUBSUCKER—
Erimyzon sucetta

32 NORTHERN HOGSUCKER—
Hypentelium nigricans

33 SMALLMOUTH BUFFALO—*Ictiobus bubalus* (Rafinesque). Deep bodied; small conical head; small, subterminal mouth, with distinct grooves on thick upper lip; front of lip below lower edge of eye. Upper jaw length less than snout length. Eye large. Nape with strong keel. Anal rays 9, pelvic rays 10, lateral line scales 36–37. Gray, olive, or dark gray above with either dark blue or olive reflections, side gray or dusky with black flecks, white to gray below; pelvic fins gray or black, remaining fins olive or black. Lake Michigan and Mississippi River basin from PA to MT, south to Gulf of Mexico from AL to TX, and introduced in AZ reservoirs. Common. Small and large rivers in pools, backwaters, and main channel borders associated with trees and woody debris. Detritivore. Open substrate, lithopelagophil (A.1.2). Maximum size 780 mm TL.

34 BIGMOUTH BUFFALO—*Ictiobus cyprinellus* (Valenciennes). Deep bodied, large oval eye, mouth terminal but obliquely shaped. Upper lip equal to front lower edge of eye. Upper jaw length equal to snout length. Upper lip with faint groove, upper lip smaller in thickness than lower lip. Anal rays 8–9, pelvic rays 10–11, lateral line scales 35–36. Gray to olive above, with green or copper reflection, black to olive side, white to pale yellow below; brown or black fins. Hudson Bay, lower Great Lakes, and Mississippi River basins from ON to SK, south to LA; introduced into reservoirs in AZ and CA. Occasional. Large rivers and reservoirs, occurring in pools and backwaters; associated with sand and fine substrates. Detritivore. Open substrate, lithopelagophil (A.1.2). Maximum size 889 mm TL.

35 BLACK BUFFALO—*Ictiobus niger* (Rafinesque). Deep bodied; small eye that is less than distance from tip of lower jaw to end of maxillary; mouth terminal, slightly oblique in shape. Upper lip thickness equal in size to lower lip; lip without distinct grooves. Upper lip less than lower edge of eye. Upper jaw length equal to snout length. Nape rounded or only weakly keeled. Anal rays 8–9, lateral line scales 37–39. Lower Great Lakes and Mississippi River basins from MI to SD, south to LA, along Gulf Slope, and west from LA to NM; introduced into reservoirs in AZ. Rare. Small and large rivers, reservoirs, and backwaters in deep pools commonly associated with woody debris. Detritivore. Open substrate, lithopelagophil (A.1.2). Maximum size 1,000 mm TL.

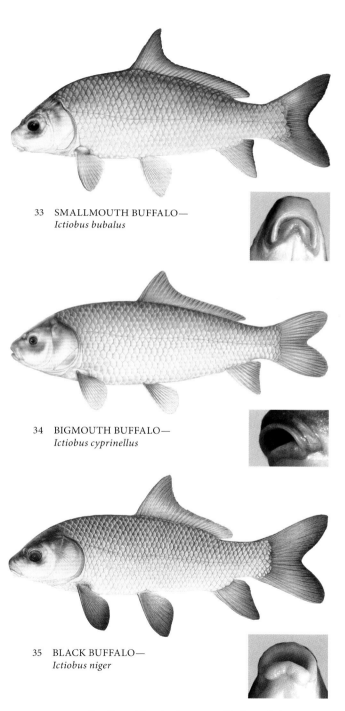

33 SMALLMOUTH BUFFALO—
Ictiobus bubalus

34 BIGMOUTH BUFFALO—
Ictiobus cyprinellus

35 BLACK BUFFALO—
Ictiobus niger

36 SPOTTED SUCKER—*Minytrema melanops* (Rafinesque). Round bodied; small horizontal mouth; thin plicate lips, U-shaped lower lip edge. No lateral line (if present rarely developed on more than a few scales). Dorsal fin edge either straight or concave. Dorsal rays 12, anal rays 7, lateral scales 42–47. Dark green or olive-brown above, 8–12 parallel rows of dark spots at scale bases on back and side, white below; black edges on dorsal and caudal fins, light yellow-orange to slate-olive median fins. Lower Great Lakes and Mississippi River basins from PA to MN and south to Gulf of Mexico, and Atlantic Slope from NC to TX. Common. Pools of creeks, small and large rivers associated with submerged vegetation over clay, sand, or gravel. Invertivore. Open substrate, lithopelagophil (A.1.2). Maximum size 495 mm TL.

37 SILVER REDHORSE—*Moxostoma anisurum* (Rafinesque). Round bodied; acutely V-shaped posterior edge on deeply divided lower lip; many small papillae on upper and lower lips. Dorsal fin slightly convex. Large, moderately forked caudal fin; equal, usually pointed lobes. Dorsal rays 14–16, lateral line scales 40–42, scales around caudal peduncle 12. Blue-green or brown above, pale yellow–silver to brassy sides; no dark spots on scale bases; pale yellow to red anal and paired fins. Great Lakes, Hudson Bay, and Mississippi River basin from QC to AB, south to AL, Atlantic Slope from VA to GA. Common. Pools and runs of small and moderate-sized rivers, reservoirs, and inland lakes over muck to cobble rock substrates. Invertivore. Open substrate, lithophil (A.1.3). Maximum size 570 mm TL.

38 SMALLMOUTH REDHORSE—*Moxostoma breviceps* (Cope). Round bodied, head small. Plicate lips smaller with large papillae on lower lip, nearly straight rear edge on lower lip. Back elevated anterior dorsal fin origin. Moderately concave to falcate dorsal fin. Large unequally forked caudal fin, upper lobe larger than lower lobe. Dorsal fin rays 12, pelvic rays 10 (rarely 9). Olive to tan above, copper to silver-colored sides, crescent-shaped dark spots on scales and back and side, white or yellow below; yellow to red fins. Great Lakes and Ohio River basins. Common. Pools, riffles, and runs of moderate and large rivers over gravel, cobble, and boulder substrates. Invertivore. Open substrate, lithophil (A.1.3). Maximum size 600 mm TL.

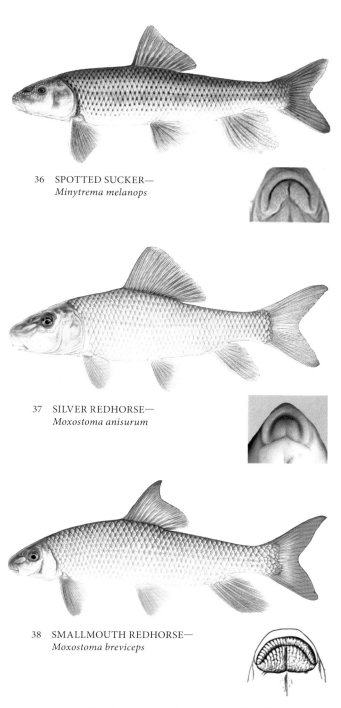

36 SPOTTED SUCKER—
Minytrema melanops

37 SILVER REDHORSE—
Moxostoma anisurum

38 SMALLMOUTH REDHORSE—
Moxostoma breviceps

39 RIVER REDHORSE—*Moxostoma carinatum* (Cope). Round bodied, head large, 25 percent SL. Large plicate lip, slightly V-shaped near posterior edge lower lip. Molar-like teeth on pharyngeal arch. Dorsal fin concave. Large caudal fin with pointed upper lobe and smaller rounded lower lobe. Dorsal rays 12–14, lateral scales 42–44, scales around caudal peduncle 12–13. Olive-bronze above, gold reflections; crescent-shaped dark spots on scales on back and side, yellow to bronze below; deep yellow or orange anal and paired fins, caudal fin red. Great Lakes and Mississippi River basin from QC to IA, south to AL and west to OK, south to Gulf Coast from FL to LA. Occasional. Pools and swift runs of small to large rivers and reservoirs. Benthic invertivore. Open substrate, lithophil (A.1.3). Maximum size 600 mm TL.

40 BLACK REDHORSE—*Moxostoma duquesnei* (Lesueur). Round bodied, slender caudal peduncle. Plicate lips, broadly V-shaped rear edge on lower lip. Many blade-like teeth on slender pharyngeal arch. Dorsal fin concave. Caudal fin moderately forked, usually equal with pointed lobes. Dorsal fin rays 12–14, pelvic fin rays 10, lateral scales 44–47, caudal peduncle scales 12–14. Dusky silver or gray above, gold to brassy side, green reflections, white or yellow below; orange fins. Lower Great Lakes and Mississippi River basins from ON and NY, south to AL, and west to OK. Common. Rock substrates of pools and swift riffles in creeks, and small to moderate-sized rivers. Invertivore. Open substrate, lithophil (A.1.3). Maximum size 480 mm TL.

41 GOLDEN REDHORSE—*Moxostoma erythrurum* (Rafinesque). Round bodied, stout caudal peduncle. Plicate lips, V- or U-shaped on posterior margin on lower lip. Many blade-like teeth on slender pharyngeal arch. Dorsal fin concave. Large moderately forked caudal fin has equal pointed lobes. Dorsal fin rays 12–14, pelvic rays 9, lateral scales 40–42, scales around caudal peduncle 12. Olive to brassy above; dark-edged scales on back and anterior half of side; yellow to brassy sides, pale green reflections, yellow or white below; yellow to orange anal and paired fins, gray dorsal fin. Spawning male with dark stripe along side and bright salmon-colored anal fins, large tubercles on snout. Great Lakes, Hudson Bay, and Mississippi River basins from NY to ND, south to AL and OK, isolated in MS; Atlantic Slope from MD to NC, and Mobile Bay from AL and southeast TN. Common. Rock substrate pools, runs, and riffles in creeks, small and moderate-sized rivers, sometimes lakes and reservoirs. Invertivore. Open substrate, lithophil (A.1.3). Maximum size 660 mm TL.

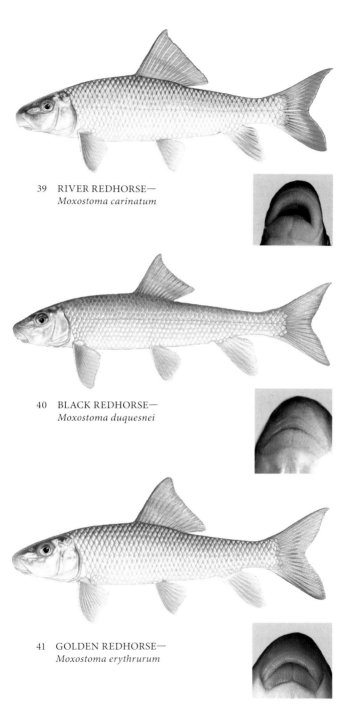

39 RIVER REDHORSE—
Moxostoma carinatum

40 BLACK REDHORSE—
Moxostoma duquesnei

41 GOLDEN REDHORSE—
Moxostoma erythrurum

42   HARELIP SUCKER—*Moxostoma lacerum* Jordan and Brayton. Round bodied, mouth distinct without non-protractile upper lip and split lower lip. Mississippi River and Lake Erie basin from IN east to OH, south to TN and west to AR. Small to moderate-sized rivers in clear streams over gravel and cobble in runs and slow pools. Extinct, not observed since 1893. Invertivore. Open substrate, lithophil (A.1.3). Maximum size 375 mm TL.

43   SHORTHEAD REDHORSE—*Moxostoma macrolepidotum* (Lesueur). Round bodied, head small (about 20% SL); plicate lips, large papillae on lower lip, nearly straight along posterior edge on lower lip. Blade-like teeth on slender pharyngeal arch. Body without large body depth in front of dorsal fin origin. Dorsal fin moderately concave. Large, moderately forked caudal fin with equal-sized lobes. Dorsal fin 12–13, lateral line scales 42–44, scales around caudal peduncle 12–13. Olive to tan above, copper or silver on yellowish side, crescent-shaped dark spots on scales on side and back, white or yellow fins, caudal fin red. Great Lakes, Hudson Bay, and Mississippi River drainage from QC to AB south to northern AL and OK, Atlantic Slope drainage from NY to SC. Abundant. Pools, riffles, and runs in creeks, small to moderately sized rivers, lakes, and reservoirs over gravel, cobble, and boulder substrates. Invertivore. Open substrate, lithophil (A.1.3). Maximum size 720 mm TL.

44   GREATER REDHORSE—*Moxostoma valenciennesi* Jordan. Round bodied, head large (about 25% SL), plicate lips, thick V-shaped posterior edge on lower lip. Blade-like teeth on slender pharyngeal arch. Dorsal fin convex. Pointed lobes on large, forked caudal fin. Dorsal fin rays 13–14, lateral scales 42–45, scales around caudal peduncle 15–16, scales over back (at dorsal fin origin) 12–13. Bronze or copper above, dark spots on scales on back and side, silver-yellow or white below; yellow to red fins, caudal fin red. Great Lakes, Hudson Bay, and Mississippi River from QC and VT to ON and MN, south to Ohio River. Rare. Pools and runs of moderate to large rivers and lakes over sand, gravel, and cobble substrates. Benthic invertivore. Open subtrate, lithophil (A.1.3). Maximum size 744 mm TL.

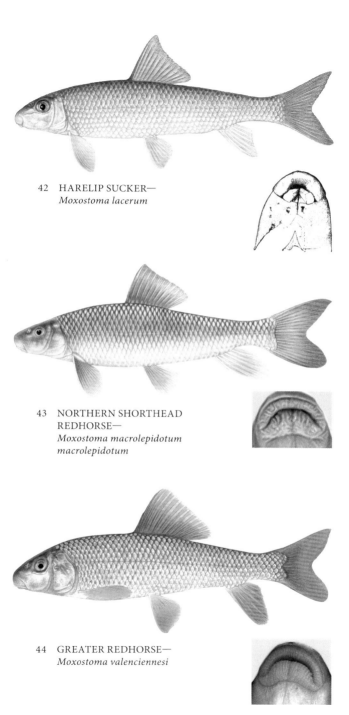

42 HARELIP SUCKER—
Moxostoma lacerum

43 NORTHERN SHORTHEAD
REDHORSE—
*Moxostoma macrolepidotum
macrolepidotum*

44 GREATER REDHORSE—
Moxostoma valenciennesi

MINNOW FAMILY—CYPRINIDAE
(SPECIES PLATES 45–106)

The Cyprinidae is the largest freshwater family with 220 genera and over 2,420 species globally (Nelson 2006). There are 61 genera and 428 known or undescribed species in North America (Scharpf 2009). The species richness of minnows in Indiana includes 25 genera and 61 species (Simon et al. 2002). The minnow fauna in Indiana is most diverse in the Ohio River basin, followed by the Mississippi River and Lake Michigan basins (Table 3).

The minnows are diagnosed by pharyngeal teeth in 1–3 rows with never more than 8 teeth in any row; lips thin, not with plicae or papillae; barbels present or absent; upper jaw bordered

TABLE 3. BASIN DISTRIBUTION OF FAMILY
CYPRINIDAE IN INDIANA

Species/Basin	Lake Michigan	Lake Erie	Ohio River	Mississippi River
Campostoma anomalum anomalum			X	
Campostoma pullum		X	X	
Campostoma oligolepis	X			X
Carassius auratus	X	X	X	X
Chrosomus eos	X			
Chrosomus erythrogaster			X	
Clinostomus elongatus			X	
Couesius plumbeus plumbeus	X			
Ctenopharyngodon idella	X	X	X	X
Cyprinella lutrensis lutrensis			X	X
Cyprinella spiloptera	X	X	X	X
Cyprinella cf. spiloptera			X	X
Cyprinella whipplei			X	X
Cyprinus carpio	X	X	X	X
Ericymba buccata	X	X	X	X
Erimystax dissimilis			X	
Erimystax x-punctata trautmani			X	
Hybognathus hayi			X	
Hybognathus nuchalis			X	
Hybopsis amblops		X	X	X
Hybopsis amnis	X		X	
Hypophthalmichthys molitrix			X	
Hypophthalmichthys nobilis			X	
Luxilus chrysocephalus chrysocephalus	X	X	X	X
Luxilus cornutus frontalis	X	X		
Lythrurus fasciolaris			X	
Lythrurus fumeus			X	
Lythrurus umbratilis cyanocephalus	X	X	X	X
Lythrurus cf. umbratilis			X	
Macrhybopsis hyostoma			X	
Macrhybopsis storeriana			X	

only by premaxillary, usually protrusible; spine-like rays in dorsal fin (bundled soft ray elements that fused embryonically); a Weberian apparatus; cycloid scales; and a head without scales (Nelson 2006). Dorsal fin morphology varies from a short fin base with 8–10 soft rays, such as in the genera *Campostoma, Chrosomus, Clinostomus, Couesius, Cyprinella, Erycimba, Erimystax, Hybopsis, Hybognathus, Notemigonus, Luxilus, Lythrurus, Macrhybopsis, Nocomis, Notropis, Opsopoeodus, Phenacobius, Pimephales, Rhinichthys, Scardinius*, and *Semotilus*, to a long fin base with 15–22 rays, such as in *Cyprinus, Carassius, Ctenophyarngodon, Hypophthalmichthys*, and *Mylopharyngodon*. All minnows possess a minimum of 8 dorsal rays.

The smallest minnow matures at the size of 10 mm, but most range from 50–130 mm TL, while the largest individuals

Species/Basin	Lake Michigan	Lake Erie	Ohio River	Mississippi River
Nocomis biguttatus	X	X	X	X
Nocomis micropogon		X	X	
Notemigonus crysoleucas	X	X	X	X
Notropis anogenus	X	X	X	
Notropis ariommus			X	
Notropis atherinoides atherinoides	X	X	X	X
Notropis blennius			X	
Notropis boops			X	
Notropis buchanani			X	
Notropis chalybaeus	X			X
Notropis dorsalis dorsalis				X
Notropis heterodon	X		X	X
Notropis heterolepis heterolepis	X		X	X
Notropis hudsonius	X		X	X
Notropis percobromus			X	X
Notropis photogenis		X	X	
Notropis rubellus	X	X	X	
Notropis shumardi			X	
Notropis stramineus stramineus	X	X	X	X
Notropis texanus	X			X
Notropis volucellus	X	X	X	X
Notropis wickliffi			X	
Opsopoeodus emiliae emiliae	X		X	X
Phenacobius mirabilis		X	X	X
Pimephales notatus	X	X	X	X
Pimephales promelas promelas	X	X	X	X
Pimephales vigilax vigilax			X	
Rhinichthys cataractae cataractae	X			
Rhinichthys obtusus	X	X	X	X
Scardinius erythrophthalmus	X			
Semotilus atromaculatus	X	X	X	X

may weigh up to 45.4 kg (100 lbs). Introduced species, such as *Cyprinus carpio,* support an important commercial fishery in some parts of the country (Becker 1983). Small individuals are important prey items for game species. Habitats range from small springs and headwater streams to large rivers and reservoirs. Spawning periods are prolonged and occur from spring until summer (Simon 1999). Spawning occurs over gravel substrates, within nests, beneath stones, over submerged aquatic vegetation, in crevices, or may be broadcast (Simon 1999). Most minnows are representatives of specialized feeding guilds that ingest a variety of algae or aquatic insects or are predators (Goldstein and Simon 1999). Some species possess a more terminal mouth that is used to strain crustaceans from the water column. Varying sensitivities are known among minnow species to anthropogenic stress.

KEY TO THE MINNOWS OF INDIANA

1 a) Stout, sawtoothed spine at origin of dorsal and anal fins; dorsal fin long with greater than 15 rays 2

    b) No stout, sawtoothed spine at origin of dorsal or anal fins; dorsal fin short, with less than 15 rays....................................3

2 a) Upper jaw with two barbels on each side; lateral line scales greater than 31 (except in mirror or leather carp, which are partially scaled or scaleless); first gill arch rakers less than 28; pharyngeal teeth in 3 rows (1,1,3—3,1,1) and those in main row heavy and with flattened grinding surfaces..................... ....**CARP**—*Cyprinus carpio*

    b) Upper jaw without barbels; lateral line scales less than 31; first arch gill rakers greater than 28; pharyngeal teeth in 1 row (4—4) and not heavy and without flattened grinding surfaces .... **GOLDFISH**—*Carassius auratus*

3 a) Distance from anal fin origin to base of caudal fin going 3 times or more into distance from anal fin origin to tip of snout 4

    b) Distance from anal fin origin to base of caudal fin going 2.5 times or less into distance from anal fin origin to tip of snout 5

4 a) Pharyngeal teeth in 2 rows with prominent parallel grooves; lateral line scales less than 39.. ....**GRASS CARP**—*Ctenopharynogdon idella*

b) Pharyngeal teeth in 1 or 2 rows without prominent parallel grooves; lateral line scales greater than 39 .... **BLACK CARP**—*Mylopharyngodon piceus*

5 a) Belly behind pelvic fins with a fleshy keel; anal fin rays greater than 11 (rarely 10); anterior part of lateral line strongly curved downward 6

b) Belly behind pelvic fins without a fleshy keel; anal fin rays less than 10 (rarely higher); anterior part of lateral line only slightly curved downward 9

6 a) Eyes located about midway between top and bottom margins of head; lateral line scales less than 60 7

b) Eyes located closer to bottom margin of head; lateral line scales greater than 60 8

7 a) Keel on belly behind pelvic fins not crossed by scales; dorsal fin rays usually 8 (occasionally 7 or 9); median fins not bright red in live individuals; scale rows around body directly in front of dorsal fin greater than 30; lateral line scales greater than 41 .... **GOLDEN SHINER**—*Notemigonus crysoleucas*

b) Keel on belly behind pelvic fins crossed by scales; dorsal fin rays 10 or 11 (occasionally 9); median fins bright red in live individuals over 75 mm TL; scale rows around body directly in front of dorsal fin less than 30; lateral line scales less than 41 .... **RUDD**—*Scardinius erythrophthalmus*

8 a) Keel on belly extending from anus to origin of pelvic fins; gill rakers of first gill arch long, slender, and separate .... **BIGHEAD CARP**—*Hypophthalmichthys nobilis*

b) Keel on belly extending from anus to near origin of pectoral fins; gill rakers of first gill arch fused into sponge-like apparatus .... **SILVER CARP**—*Hypophthalmichthys molitrix*

9 a) Dorsal fin rays 9; mouth very small and nearly vertical .... **PUGNOSE MINNOW**—*Opsopoeodus emiliae*

b) Dorsal fin rays 8; mouth larger and more horizontal 10

10 a) Small conical barbel at corner of mouth 11

b) No barbel at corner of mouth 20

11 a) Upper lip connected to snout by broad frenum (no groove between upper lip and tip of snout) 12

b) Upper lip not connected to snout by broad frenum (groove between upper lip and tip of snout) 13

12 a) Eye diameter greater than distance from tip of snout to anterior tip of lower jaw; snout projecting beyond lower lip less than 1 mm .... **WESTERN BLACKNOSE DACE**— .... *Rhinichthys obtusus*

b) Eye diameter less than or equal to distance from tip of snout to anterior tip of lower jaw; snout projecting beyond lower lip 1–3 mm; mouth slightly oblique .... **LONGNOSE DACE**—*Rhinichthys cataractae*

13 a) Distance from nostril to front dorsal fin origin nearly equal to distance from front of dorsal fin to base of caudal fin 14

b) Distance from nostril to front of dorsal fin much less than distance from front of dorsal fin to base of caudal fin 16

14 a) Lateral line scales greater than 57; anal fin rays 8; dorsal fin origin slightly behind pelvic fin origin .... **LAKE CHUB**—*Couesius plumbeus*

b) Lateral line scales less than 46; anal fin rays 7; dorsal fin origin about equal to or slightly in front of pelvic fin origin 15

15 a) Spot at caudal fin base large and prominent (fades in large adults); distance from tip of snout to front of eye 1.3 times or more into distance from front of eye to posterior edge of gill cover; nuptial male with tubercles confined to top of head; prominent red spot behind eye (not in young) .... **HORNYHEAD CHUB**—*Nocomis biguttatus*

b) Spot at caudal fin base faint or absent; distance from tip of snout to front of eye 1.2 times or less into distance from front of eye to posterior edge of gill cover; nuptial male with tubercles extending onto snout; no prominent red spot behind eye .... **RIVER CHUB**—*Nocomis micropogon*

16 a) Side with continuous dark stripe from caudal fin base to tip of snout, or side uniformly pigmented 17

b) Side with a row of dark blotches, numerous dark X-shaped markings or speckles 18

17 a) Stripe along midlateral dark and well developed; distance from tip of snout to dorsal fin origin equal to or slightly greater than distance from dorsal fin origin to caudal fin base .... **BIGEYE CHUB**—*Hybopsis amblops*

b) No stripe along midlateral; distance from tip of snout to dorsal fin origin much less than distance from dorsal fin

origin to caudal fin base...
.... **SILVER CHUB**—*Macrhybopsis storeriana*

18 a) Upper jaw extending past front of eye; eye diameter less than distance from back of eye to upper end of gill opening; side with numerous small, round (punctate), dark speckles; snout bulbous and extending past mouth...
.... **SHOAL CHUB**—*Macrhybopsis hyostoma*

   b) Upper jaw not extending past front of eye; eye diameter about equal to distance from back of eye to upper end of gill opening; side with numerous X-shaped markings or a row of dark blotches; snout not bulbous and only moderately overhangs mouth..19

19 a) Midlateral with a broken lateral band of 7–11 oblong, dark blotches; lateral line scales greater than 43; preorbital head length less than postorbital length..
.......................**STREAMLINE CHUB**—*Erimystax dissimilis*

   b) Midlateral without a broken lateral band of dark blotches; lateral line scales less than 43; preorbital head length greater than postorbital length...
............**GRAVEL CHUB**—*Erimystax x-punctata trautmani*

20 a) Snout blunt, half-ray in front of dorsal fin that is distinctly separated from first principal ray, although connected by a membrane; scale flattened, predorsal area crowded and smaller than scales on sides; adults with dark spot at anterior edge in middle of dorsal fin, not at base................................21

   b) Half-ray at front of dorsal fin slender and tightly bound to first principal ray; scales predorsal region not flattened or crowded, or smaller than scales on side 23

21 a) Lining of visceral cavity silver; crescent-shaped mark on snout between nostril and upper lip; intestine short, with a single S-shaped loop ....
.......................**BULLHEAD MINNOW**—*Pimephales vigilax*

   b) Lining of visceral cavity black; no crescent-shaped mark on snout between nostril and upper lip; intestine long, with several loops.. 22

22 a) Lateral line complete; dusky stripe along midlateral and spot at base of caudal fin usually indistinct; mouth terminal and oblique......**BLUNTNOSE MINNOW**—*Pimephales notatus*

   b) Lateral line incomplete, not extending past anal fin; dusky stripe along midlateral and spot at base of caudal fin usually

indistinct; mouth terminal and oblique.................................
.....**FATHEAD MINNOW**—*Pimephales promelas promelas*

23 a) Lower jaw with a hard, shelf-like, cartilaginous ridge, separated from lower lip by groove... 24

   b) Lower jaw without a hard, shelf-like, cartilaginous ridge.....
.... 26

24 a) Number of scale rows around body just in front of dorsal fin less than 39; distance between eyes on top of head equal to distance from back of eye to upper end of gill opening; breeding males without black pigment in anal fin; breeding males without tubercles beside each nostril...........................
LARGESCALE STONEROLLER—*Campostoma oligolepis*

   b) Number of scale rows around body just in front of dorsal fin greater than 40; distance between eyes on top of head less than distance from back of eye to upper end of gill opening; breeding males with black pigment in anal fin.................. 25

25 a) Body barely compressed laterally, crescent-shaped row of 1–3 large tubercles on inside margin of nostril, tubercles on nape and body, body strongly arched at nape. Complete lateral line, lateral scales 42–54, scales around body at dorsal fin origin 32–44, scale rows from lateral line to lateral line 15–17, pectoral fin rays 15–16, gill rakers on first arch 21–33, pharyngeal teeth 0,4—4,0 or 1,4—4,1. Spawning male with black band on orange dorsal and anal fins ....
....**COMMON STONEROLLER**—*Campostoma anomalum*

   b) Body barely compressed laterally, without crescent-shaped row of 1–3 tubercles on inside margin of nostril, fewer tubercles on nape and body, body not strongly arched at nape. Complete lateral line, lateral scales 49–55, scales around body at dorsal fin origin 36–46, scale rows from lateral line to lateral line 18–20, pectoral fin rays 16–19, gill rakers on first arch 21–33, pharyngeal teeth 0,4—4,0 or 1,4—4,1. Spawning male without black band on orange dorsal and anal fins......
...........**CENTRAL STONEROLLER**—*Campostoma pullum*

26 a) Lateral line scales greater than 50 27

   b) Lateral line scales less than 50 30

27 a) Small flap-like barbel in groove above upper lip near corner of mouth; upper lip much wider at midline than on either side.................... **CREEK CHUB**—*Semotilus atromaculatus*

b) No barbel in groove above upper lip near corner of mouth; upper lip uniform in width.. 28

28 a) Lateral line scales less than 70; lining of visceral cavity silver; lower jaw protruding beyond upper jaw; anal fin rays 9; single dusky, horizontal stripe on each side... ....**REDSIDE DACE**—*Clinostomus elongatus*

b) Lateral line scale greater than 70; lining of visceral cavity black; lower jaw not protruding beyond upper jaw (mouth terminal); anal rays 8; two dusky, horizontal stripes on each side.. 29

29 a) Chin slightly anterior to upper lip; mouth sharply oblique, usually more than 45° with horizontal, and more curved; length of upper jaw less than, equal, or slightly more than 25 percent HL............... **NORTHERN REDBELLY DACE**— .... *Chrosomus eos*

b) Upper lip anterior to lower lip and chin; mouth slightly oblique, usually less than 45° with horizontal, and little curved; length of upper jaw greater than 25 percent HL....... ....**SOUTHERN REDBELLY DACE**— .... *Chrosomus erythrogaster*

30 a) Mouth sucker-like; lower lip with a prominent lobe on each side......................................**SUCKERMOUTH MINNOW**— ....*Phenacobius mirabilis*

b) Mouth not sucker-like; lower lip without a prominent lobe on each side 31

31 a) Undersurface of head distinctly flattened; lateral length of upper jaw greater than eye diameter.....................................32

b) Undersurface of head not distinctly flattened; lateral length of upper jaw less than or equal to eye diameter 33

32 a) Honeycomb-like pearl organs, cavernous spaces along lower jaw...................**SILVERJAW MINNOW**—*Ericymba buccata*

b) No honeycomb-like pearl organ, cavernous spaces along lower jaw ....**EASTERN BIGMOUTH SHINER**— ....*Notropis dorsalis*

33 a) Intestine long, greater than twice standard length, with several loops.. 34

b) Intestine short, less than twice standard length, with a single S-shaped loop...35

34 a) Snout length less than or equal to eye diameter; scales on upper side darkly edged, forming a distinct diamond-shaped pattern; front of lip equal with or above bottom of eye ....
............................**CYPRESS MINNOW**—*Hybognathus hayi*

b) Snout length greater than eye diameter; scales on upper side not darkly edged, not forming distinct diamond-shaped pattern; front of upper lip below bottom of eye............................
.... **MISSISSIPPI SILVERY MINNOW**—
.... *Hybognathus nuchalis*

35 a) Caudal fin base with prominent black spot, as large or larger than pupil of eye and outline either round or square ....
...........................**SPOTTAIL SHINER**—*Notropis hudsonius*

b) Caudal fin base without prominent black spot, or if spot present, much smaller than pupil of eye 36

36 a) All dorsal fin membranes with dark pigment or specks of pigment confined to posterior membranes of fin 37

b) Dorsal fin membranes without dark pigment, or if pigment is present, it is not distributed throughout fin or confined to posterior membranes of fin 40

37 a) Body depth usually going less than 3.5 times into SL; dark pigment uniformly distributed on dorsal fin membranes, not forming a distinct blotch in posterior dorsal fin ....
.... **RED SHINER**—*Cyprinella lutrensis*

b) Body depth usually going more than 3.5 times into SL; dark pigment concentrated on dorsal fin membranes in posterior dorsal fin, forming a distinct blotch in adults.................... 38

38 a) Anal rays 9; dark pigment present in first few dorsal fin membranes, except in small young; dark stripe on side or caudal peduncle broad and faint, poorly defined above and centered on lateral line pores ....
.....................**STEELCOLOR SHINER**—*Cyprinella whipplei*

b) Anal rays 8; dark pigment faint or absent from first few dorsal fin membranes, except in breeding male 39

39 a) Head depth at anterior eyes greater than 10 percent HL; dark stripe on side of caudal peduncle narrow and prominent, sharply defined above and centered below lateral line pores, prominent from anus to caudal base ....
............................**SPOTFIN SHINER**—*Cyprinella spiloptera*

b) Head depth at anterior eyes less than 10 percent HL; dark stripe on side or caudal peduncle sharply defined extending

from head to caudal base ....
TIPPECANOE SHINER—*Cyprinella* cf. *spiloptera* nov. sp.

40 a) Anal fin rays greater than 9 41

b) Anal fin rays less than 9 52

41 a) Visceral cavity black 42

b) Visceral cavity silver (may have black specks) 44

42 a) Eye width going into head length more than 2.5 times; eye width more than 1.5 times into snout length...........................
.... **POPEYE SHINER**—*Notropis ariommus*

b) Eye width going into head length less than 2.5 times; eye width less than 1.5 times into snout length......................... 43

43 a) Scales between head and dorsal fin origin less than or equal to 12–16; pigment present on anterior third of chin; scales around body in front of dorsal fin less than or equal to 29; dark lines running parallel along upper sides, converging into V-shaped pattern behind dorsal fin ....
....**STRIPED SHINER**—
....................................*Luxilus chrysocephalus chrysocephalus*

b) Scales between head and dorsal fin origin greater than 16; pigment absent from anterior third of chin; scale around body in front of dorsal fin greater than 29; upper sides without dark lines that converge behind dorsal fin (except in breeding males) .... **COMMON SHINER**—
.... *Luxilus cornutus frontinalis*

44 a) Scales between head and dorsal fin origin small and crowded; scales between head and dorsal fin origin greater than 21; scales between head and dorsal fin distinctly smaller than scales behind dorsal fin... 45

b) Scales between head and dorsal fin origin not small and crowded; scales between head and dorsal fin origin less than 20; scales between head and dorsal fin not distinctly smaller than scales behind dorsal fin... 48

45 a) No distinct spot at base of anterior dorsal rays and membranes.......................**RIBBON SHINER**—*Lythrurus fumeus*

b) Black pigment at anterior base of dorsal fin extending onto rays and membranes, appears as a distinct black spot...... 46

46 a) Anal fin rays 9–10 (sometimes 11); body depth contained 4.5 or more times into SL; body appears round; head length usually greater than greatest body depth; 8–11 saddle bands

across back; breeding males without tubercles on cheek; mouth horizontal .... **SCARLETFIN SHINER**— ....*Lythrurus fasciolaris*

b) Anal fin rays 11–13 (sometimes 10); body depth contained fewer than 4.5 times into SL; body laterally compressed, slab-sided in appearance; head length usually less than body depth; saddle bands across back faint or absent; breeding males with tubercles on cheeks; mouth oblique 47

47 a) Anal fin rays 11–12 (sometimes 10); body depth contained less than 4.0 into TL; no saddles across upper side of body with vertical bands; tubercles limited to fins and snout................. ....**REDFIN SHINER**—*Lythrurus umbratilis*

b) Anal fin rays 10; body depth contained greater than 4.0 into SL; saddles across upper side of body with vertical bands; tubercles on head and nape .... **SILVER CREEK SHINER**— ....*Lythrurus* cf. *umbratilis* nov. sp.

48 a) Dorsal fin origin well behind pelvic fin origin; pelvic fin rays 8 49

b) Dorsal fin origin even with or just slightly behind pelvic fin origin; pelvic fin rays 9 51

49 a) Snout short and rounded, length usually contained more than 1.5 times in postorbital head length; no distinct black streak along side; body deepest at dorsal fin origin ....**EMERALD SHINER**—*Notropis atherinoides*

b) Snout longer and pointed, length usually contained less than 1.5 times in postorbital head length; distinct black streak above silver stripe along side; body deepest midway between head and dorsal fin origin... 50

50 a) Long, sharply pointed snout longer than eye diameter, eye moderate. Dorsal fin origin well behind pelvic fin origin (about middle of pelvic fin). Lateral line complete, lateral line scales 36–45, anal rays 9–11. Pharyngeal teeth 2,4—4,2 or 1,4—4,1. Olive above, often with a narrow dusky stripe along back, black streak just above silver stripe along side, iridescent blue along side, silver below; fins clear with faint red at base of dorsal fin. Breeding male blue above, with orange to bright rosy red head, front half of body, and fin bases ....**ROSYFACE SHINER**—*Notropis rubellus*

b) Slender, elongate, laterally compressed body. Narrow, conical snout (equal to eye diameter), large eye. Dorsal fin origin behind pelvic fin origin. Lateral line complete, lateral line scales 36–45, anal rays 9–11. Pharyngeal teeth 0,4—4,0, gill rakers on lower limb short 5–7. Olive above, silver side with punctate lateral line, cheek and operculum pink, silver below; fins clear. Breeding males with red snout, crimson on operculum and cheek, along pectoral girdle and fins, and along base of paired and median fins .... **CARMINE SHINER**—*Notropis percobromus*

51 a) Paired black, crescent-shaped areas between nostrils; anal fin rays 10–12; tall, pointed dorsal fin, anterior dorsal fin rays extend well beyond posterior rays when fin depressed.......... .... **SILVER SHINER**—*Notropis photogenis*

   b) No distinct, black, crescent-shaped areas between nostrils; anal fin rays 9; shorter dorsal fin, anterior dorsal fin rays do not extend well beyond posterior rays when fin depressed... ....**SILVERBAND SHINER**—*Notropis shumardi*

52 a) Black lateral band, continues forward through eye and around snout..53

   b) Dusky or indistinct lateral band, not continuing forward through eye and around snout.. 58

53 a) Visceral cavity black; lateral line complete......................... 54

   b) Visceral cavity silver (may have black specks); lateral line incomplete...55

54 a) Mouth vertical, nearly 80° with horizontal; mouth small, upper jaw extending only to below anterior nostril; upper jaw contained more than 4 times into HL ....**PUGNOSE SHINER**—*Notropis anogenus*

   b) Mouth oblique, about 45° with horizontal; mouth large, upper jaw extending to below posterior nostril; upper jaw length contained less than 4 times into HL............................. .... **BIGEYE SHINER**—*Notropis boops*

55 a) Lower lip and chin without black pigment; dark borders to lateral line pores form crescent-shaped black cross-hatches along scale edges .... **BLACKNOSE SHINER**— .... *Notropis heterolepis*

   b) Lower lip and chin with black pigment; dark borders to lateral line pores do not form crescent-shaped black cross-bars; mouth making an angle greater than 30° with horizontal.... 56

56 a) Dark stripe on midline of back poorly defined anterior dorsal fin origin; breast scaled; scales of row above lateral line with dark bars that produce zigzag appearance while alternating with black marks on lateral line scales ....**BLACKCHIN SHINER**—*Notropis heterodon*

b) Dark stripe on midline of back sharply defined anterior dorsal fin origin; breast without scales; scales in row above lateral line without dark bars 57

57 a) Anal fin rays 8; inside of mouth with black pigment; unpored lateral line scales greater than 10 .... **IRONCOLOR SHINER**—*Notropis chalybaeus*

b) Anal fin rays 7; inside of mouth without black pigment; unpored lateral line scales less than 10 .... **WEED SHINER**—*Notropis texanus*

58 a) Anal fin rays 7 59

b) Anal fin rays 8 60

59 a) Stripe along back expanded just in front of dorsal fin and interrupted along dorsal fin base; scales on back and upper side forming a cross-hatched pattern; lateral line pores bounded above and below by dark paired chromatophores . ... **SAND SHINER**—*Notropis stramineus*

b) Stripe along back uniform in width and surrounding dorsal fin base; scales of back and upper side not forming a definite cross-hatched pattern; lateral line pores bounded irregularly by dark chromatophores or not at all; mouth large, length of upper jaw greater than or equal to eye diameter .... **RIVER SHINER**—*Notropis blennius*

60 a) Width of anterior lateral line scales going 2 times or less into their depth.................**PALLID SHINER**—*Hybopsis amnis*

b) Width of anterior lateral line scales going 2 times into their depth 61

61 a) Sides of body without pigment; infraorbital canal short or underdeveloped; visceral cavity silver; tips of pelvic fin reaching to or beyond anal fin origin; dorsal and anal fins more falcate, first rays noticeably longer than last; upper lip extends nearly to center of eye ....
.................................**GHOST SHINER**—*Notropis buchanani*

b) Sides of body with pigment; infraorbital canal complete; visceral cavity silver with black flecks; tips of pelvic fin not reaching to anal fin origin; dorsal and anal fins less falcate, first rays not noticeably longer than last; upper lip extends to bottom third of eye... 62

62 a) Body depth usually contained more than 4.5 times into SL; caudal peduncle depth usually contained more than 2.5 times in HL; postdorsal fin streak absent or faint; color dark, marking usually prominent; lateral scale line 35–37..............
...................................**MIMIC SHINER**—*Notropis volucellus*

b) Body depth usually contained less than 4.5 times into SL; caudal peduncle depth usually contained less than 2.5 times in HL; postdorsal streak dark and well developed; color moderately dark, markings usually not as prominent; lateral line scales 33–35................................**CHANNEL SHINER**—
.... *Notropis wickliffi*

45 COMMON STONEROLLER—*Campostoma anomalum* (Rafinesque). Hard cartilaginous ridge on lower jaw with subterminal mouth. Body barely compressed laterally, crescent-shaped row of 1–3 large tubercles on inside margin of nostril, tubercles on nape and body, body strongly arched at nape. Complete lateral line, lateral scales 42–54, scales around body at dorsal fin origin 32–44, scale rows from lateral line to lateral line 15–17, pectoral fin rays 15–16, gill rakers on first arch 21–33, pharyngeal teeth 0,4—4,0 or 1,4—4,1. Spawning male with black band on orange dorsal and anal fins. Distributed throughout the Ohio River and upper Atlantic Slope basins. Abundant. Rocky riffles, runs, and pools of headwaters, creeks, and small and medium rivers. Particulate-feeding herbivore. Brood-hiding lithophil (A.2.3). Maximum size 276 mm TL.

46 CENTRAL STONEROLLER—*Campostoma pullum* (Agassiz). Hard cartilaginous ridge on lower jaw with subterminal mouth. Body barely compressed laterally, without crescent-shaped row of 1–3 tubercles on inside margin of nostril, fewer tubercles on nape and body, body not strongly arched at nape. Complete lateral line, lateral scales 49–55, scales around body at dorsal fin origin 36–46, scale rows from lateral line to lateral line 18–20, pectoral fin rays 16–19, gill rakers on first arch 21–33, pharyngeal teeth 0,4—4,0 or 1,4—4,1. Spawning male without black band on orange dorsal and anal fins. Distributed throughout the Mississippi, Wabash, Hudson Bay, and Gulf Coast from TX to Mexico. Abundant. Rocky riffles, runs, and pools of headwaters, creeks, and small and medium rivers. Particulate-feeding herbivore. Brood-hiding lithophil (A.2.3). Maximum size 250 mm TL.

47 LARGESCALE STONEROLLER—*Campostoma oligolepis* Hubbs and Greene. Hard cartilaginous ridge on lower jaw with subterminal mouth. Body barely compressed laterally, without crescent-shaped row of 1–3 tubercles on inside margin of nostril, fewer tubercles on nape and body, body deepest at dorsal fin origin. Complete lateral line, lateral scales 43–47, scales around body at dorsal fin origin 31–36, scale rows from lateral line to lateral line 16–19, pectoral fin rays 17–19, gill rakers on first arch 20–28, pharyngeal teeth 0,4—4,0 or 1,4—4,1. Spawning male with either no or weak black band on orange dorsal and anal fins. Distributed in upper Mississippi River and Lake Michigan basins from WI and MN to Ozarks in northeastern OK, south to Mobile Bay. Abundant. Rocky riffles, runs, and pools of headwaters, creeks, and small and medium rivers. Particulate-feeding herbivore. Brood-hiding lithophil (A.2.3). Maximum size 289 mm TL.

45 COMMON STONEROLLER—
Campostoma anomalum

46 CENTRAL STONEROLLER—
Campostoma pullum

47 LARGESCALE STONEROLLER—
Campostoma oligolepis

48   GOLDFISH—*Carassius auratus* (Linnaeus). Deep, thick body, terminal mouth. No barbels present. Stout, sawtoothed spine (and 2 smaller spines) at front of dorsal and anal fins. Large caudal fin. Scales large, lateral line scales 25–31, long dorsal fin 15–21 rays, anal rays 5–6, and pharyngeal teeth 0,4—4,0. Grayish-green above, brassy sheen on back and sides; white to yellow below; gray to brown dorsal and caudal fins. Exotic, introduced from Asia in early 1600s and distributed throughout most of United States, ON, AB, and BC. Occasional to locally common. Shallow, turbid pools and backwaters, usually associated with submerged aquatic vegetation in rivers, ponds, and lakes. Detritivore. Open substrate phytophil (A.1.5). Maximum size 360 mm TL.

49   NORTHERN REDBELLY DACE—*Chrosomus eos* (Cope). Slender compressed body. Round, short snout equal to eye diameter, mouth upturned, chin extends past upper lip. Dorsal fin origin behind pelvic fin origin. Lateral line incomplete, lateral line scales 70–90, dorsal rays 8, anal rays 7–8. Scales are so small that they appear to be absent. Olive above, two lateral stripes separated by golden metallic stripe in between, bottom stripe extends from snout to caudal fin base terminating in large black spot, red below; fins dusky on membranes. Atlantic, Hudson Bay, upper Mississippi and Great Lakes. Extirpated from northern IN where formerly occurred in wetland pannes. Lakes, ponds, bogs and pools of headwater creeks and streams associated with silt and submerged vegetation. Invertivore/planktivore. Open substrate lithopelagophil (A.1.2). Maximum size 73 mm TL.

50   SOUTHERN REDBELLY DACE—*Chrosomus erythrogaster* (Rafinesque). Slender, compressed body. Moderately pointed snout, longer than eye in adults, oblique, slightly subterminal mouth ending anterior eye. Dorsal fin origin behind pelvic fin origin. Lateral line incomplete, lateral line scales 67–95, anal fin rays 8. Pharyngeal teeth 0,5—5,0. Scales so small that they appear to be absent. Olive above, with 2 black stripes along side, upper 1 thin, broken into spots posteriorly, lower stripe wide, becoming thin on caudal peduncle, black spots on side often in a row, silver-yellow side, black wedge-shaped caudal spot, white, yellow, or red below; red at base of dorsal fin with rest of fins yellow. Great Lakes and Mississippi River basins from NY south to TN. Isolated populations in MS, KS, CO, and NM. Occasional. Spring-fed creeks and headwater streams in pools over rock substrates. Particulate-feeding invertivore. Open substrate lithopelagophil (A.1.2). Maximum size 78 mm TL.

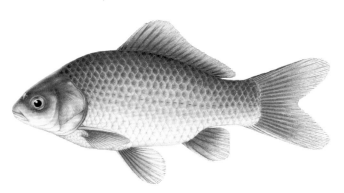

48 GOLDFISH—
Carassius auratus

49 NORTHERN REDBELLY DACE—
Chrosomus eos

50 SOUTHERN REDBELLY DACE—
Chrosomus erythrogaster

 51   REDSIDE DACE—*Clinostomus elongatus* (Kirtland). Body slender, laterally compressed. Large oblique mouth; long, pointed snout; dorsal fin origin behind pelvic fin origin. Complete, decurved lateral lines. Small scales, lateral scales 59–75, anal rays 9, pharyngeal teeth 2,5—4,2. Spawning male steel blue above, yellow-gold stripe along side, bright red on lower side; white below. Upper Susquehanna River basin, Great Lakes (not including Lake Superior), and Mississippi River from NY and ON to MN south to WV. Rare. Gravel, cobble, and sand pools of headwater streams and creeks to small rivers in clear coolwater streams. Benthic and drift insectivore. Brood-hiding lithophil (A.2.3). Maximum size 96 mm TL.

 52   LAKE CHUB—*Couesius plumbeus* (Agassiz). Moderately compressed, slender body, head flattened above and below, moderately pointed snout. Barbel at corner of mouth, mouth barely subterminal. Dorsal fin origin over or slightly behind pelvic fin origin. Complete lateral line; lateral scales 53–70, anal rays 8, pharyngeal teeth 2,4—4,2. Brown to green above, dark stripe along silver-gray side and belly, dusky caudal spot. Male may have a red pectoral and pelvic fin origins and corners of mouth. Distributed from Yukon River, AK, throughout most of Canada and northern United States to NY and southern end of Lake Michigan, west to NE and WA. Rare. Occurs in lake proper and tributaries over gravel substrates in pools and runs of streams along rock lake margins. Insectivore. Open substrate lithopelagophil (A.1.2). Maximum size 227 mm TL.

 53   GRASS CARP—*Ctenopharyngodon idella* Valenciennes. Round, laterally compressed slightly, reduced head length but wide, terminal mouth. Dorsal fin origin in front of pelvic fin origin. Large lateral scales 34–45, dark edged with black spot at base. Dorsal rays 7, anal rays 8, pharyngeal teeth 2,5—4,2 or 2,4—4,2. Gray to green above with brassy reflection, white to yellow below, clear to gray-brown fins. Exotic, native to eastern Asia and introduced in AR by mid-1960s. Found throughout Mississippi River basin and intentionally stocked into farm ponds for vegetation control. Occasional. Occurs in lakes, large rivers, and backwaters over a variety of substrates. Particulate-feeding herbivore. Open substrate pelagophils (A.1.1). Maximum size 1,250 mm TL.

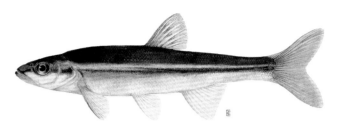

51   REDSIDE DACE—
Clinostomus elongatus

52   LAKE CHUB—
Couesius plumbeus

53   GRASS CARP—
Ctenopharyngodon idella

54   RED SHINER—*Cyprinella lutrensis* (Baird and Girard). Deep, laterally compressed body. Terminal mouth, rounded snout. Dusky dorsal fin, no black blotch on posterior half of fin. Diamond-shaped scales, lateral scales 32–36, scales around body 26, scales around caudal peduncle 14. Anal fin rays 9, pectoral rays 14, pharyngeal teeth 0,4—4,0. Dusky olive above, with blue to black upper side, black stripe along back, diffuse dark stripe along rear half of silver side. Spawning males with red fins (except dorsal), blue back and side, dark blue bar before pink bar behind head on side. Mississippi River from WI and western IN and SD and WY, south to LA; Gulf Coast from Mississippi River to TX. Widely introduced. Occasional. Creeks and small rivers over sand, silt, and rock pools and runs. Benthic insectivore. Brood-hiding speleophil (A.2.4). Maximum size 90 mm TL.

55   SPOTFIN SHINER—*Cyprinella spiloptera* Cope. Moderate, laterally compressed body. Terminal mouth, rounded snout. Dusky dorsal fin, with black blotch on posterior half of fin. Dorsal fin origin slightly behind anal fin origin. Diamond-shaped scales, lateral scales 35–39, scales around body 26, scales around caudal peduncle 14. Anal fin rays 8, pectoral rays 14, pharyngeal teeth 1,4—4,1. Dusky olive above, black median stripe along back; sometimes a dusky bar on side behind head, diffuse dark stripe along rear half of silver side. Spawning males with blue back and side, yellow-white fins, dusky dorsal fins. Atlantic Slope from QC to VA, Great Lakes, Hudson Bay, and Mississippi River from NY and ON to OK and AL. Abundant. Sand and gravel creeks to nearshore areas of small rivers. Particulate-feeding insectivore. Brood-hiding speleophil (A.2.4). Maximum size 106 mm TL.

56   TIPPECANOE SHINER—*Cyprinella* cf. *spiloptera* nov. sp. Moderate, laterally compressed body. Terminal mouth, rounded snout. Head elongate and slightly compressed. Dusky dorsal fin, with black blotch on posterior half of fin. Dorsal fin origin over pelvic fin origin. Diamond-shaped scales, lateral scales 35–39, scales around body less than 26, scales around caudal peduncle 14. Anal rays 9, pectoral rays 14, pharyngeal teeth 1,4—4,1. Dusky olive above, black median stripe along back; sometimes a dusky bar on side behind head, diffuse dark stripe along body from pectoral fin to caudal peduncle base on silver side. Spawning males with blue back and white fins. Endemic. Tippecanoe and middle Wabash River, IN and IL. Abundant. Sand and gravel creeks to nearshore areas of small rivers. Particulate-feeding insectivore. Brood-hiding speleophil (A.2.4). Maximum size 110 mm TL.

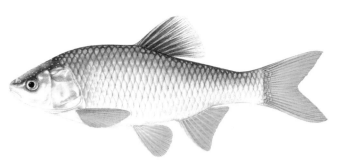

54   RED SHINER—
Cyprinella lutrensis

55   SPOTFIN SHINER—
Cyprinella spiloptera

56   TIPPECANOE SHINER—
Cyprinella cf. *spiloptera*

57   STEELCOLOR SHINER—*Cyprinella whipplei* Girard. Fairly deep bodied, pointed snout, terminal mouth. Enlarged dorsal fin. Dusky dorsal fin with black blotches on all membranes. Diamond-shaped scales, lateral scales 36–(37–38)–40, scales around body 26, scales around caudal peduncle 14. Anal rays 9, pectoral rays 15, pharyngeal teeth 1,4—4,1. Dusky olive above with blue reflections, dark midline stripe along back; diffuse dark stripe along rear half of silver side. Spawning male has blue back and side, reddish snout, white-edged yellow fins. Mississippi River basin from OH to AR, south to AL and LA. Common. Runs and pools of creeks and small to medium-sized rivers over sand and gravel substrates. Drift invertivore. Brood-hiding speleophil (A.2.4). Maximum size 135 mm TL.

58   CARP—*Cyprinus carpio* Linnaeus. Deep, thick bodied, strongly arched at dorsal fin origin, flattened below. Mouth terminal to subterminal, with two barbels, larger on each side of upper jaw. Long dorsal fin with 17–21 rays. Stout, sawtoothed spine (and 2 smaller spines) at front of dorsal and anal fins. Large scales 32–38, anal rays 5–6, pharyngeal teeth 1,1,3—3,1,1. Gray to brassy green above, scales on back and upper side dark edged, with black spot at base, white to yellow below; clear to dusky fins with red-orange caudal and anal fins. Exotic, native to Eurasia and introduced in 1831. Ubiquitous, widely distributed throughout Canada and United States. Abundant. Lakes, ponds, reservoirs, and backwaters of small to moderate-sized rivers and slow-flowing streams with excessive amounts of productivity. Benthic-filter-feeding, grazing-suction-feeding detritivore. Open substrate phytolithophil (A.1.4). Maximum size 1,220 mm TL.

59   SILVERJAW MINNOW—*Ericymba buccata* Cope. Slightly compressed body. Head dorsally flattened, large "pearl organs" (silver-white chambers) along jaw margin. Body deepest at nape, long snout, subterminal mouth. Dorsal fin origin over pelvic fin origin. Complete lateral line, lateral scales 31–36, anal rays 8, pharyngeal teeth 1,4—4,1 or 0,4—4,0. Straw or light tan to olive-yellow above, dark median stripe along back, darkest in front of dorsal fin; scales may be darkly outlined, silver sides, rarely with a dark stripe, white below. Atlantic Slope, Mississippi, and Great Lakes basins from NY, PA, and MD to eastern MO. Common. Shallow sandy streams, creeks, and small rivers in riffles. Benthic-drift-feeding invertivore. Open substrate lithopelagophil (A.1.2). Maximum size 80 mm TL.

57 STEELCOLOR SHINER—
Cyprinella whipplei

58 CARP—
Cyprinus carpio

59 SILVERJAW MINNOW—
Ericymba buccata

60   STREAMLINE CHUB—*Erimystax dissimilis* (Kirtland). Long slender body, deepest at nape, flattened below; dorsal fin origin in front of pelvic fin origin. Barbel at corner of subterminal mouth; long, rounded snout, large eyes, pectoral fin horizontal with respect to body plane. Complete lateral line, lateral line scales 43–51. Anal fin rays 7, pharyngeal teeth 0,4–4,0. Dark olive above, scales darkly outlined, series of dark dashes along back, often with dark spots on back and upper side, often with a gray stripe along silver side, 7–15 horizontal oval or round dark gray blotches along side, white below; white to gold spot at front and back of dorsal fin, other fins clear. Ohio River basin from NY to IN, south to St. Francis and White River, AL and AR. Rare. Small to large rivers in runs and riffle habitats over cobble, gravel, boulder substrates. Benthic-hunting invertivore. Open substrate lithophil (A.1.3). Maximum size 138 mm TL.

61   GRAVEL CHUB—*Erimystax x-punctata trautmani* Hubbs and Crowe. Long, slender body (less slender than streamline chub), deepest at nape, flattened below; dorsal fin origin in front of pelvic fin origin. Barbel at corner of subterminal mouth; long, rounded snout, large eyes, pectoral fin horizontal with respect to body plane. Complete lateral line, lateral line scales 38–45, caudal peduncle scales 12. Anal fin rays 7, pharyngeal teeth 0,4–4,0. Dark olive above, lacking dark gray blotches along side, dark dashes along back, with many dark Xs on back and side, with blue reflection along side, white below; clear fins. Great Lakes from ON, Ohio River, and Mississippi River basins from NY to IL, south to KY, north to WI, and west to AR and OK. Rare. Small to large rivers in runs and riffle habitats over cobble, gravel, boulder substrates. Benthic-hunting invertivore. Open substrate lithophil (A.1.3). Maximum size 120 mm TL.

62   CYPRESS MINNOW—*Hybognathus hayi* Jordan. Compressed body, deepest and widest at dorsal fin origin. Small, slightly subterminal mouth (rear edge of mouth in front of eye). Moderately large eyes, about 33 percent HL. Pointed dorsal fin. Deep caudal peduncle. Scales on back and upper side darkly outlined with black. Basioccipital process broad and straight to slightly concave posteriorly. Complete lateral line, lateral scales 34–41. Anal fin rays 8, pectoral fin rays 14–16, pharyngeal teeth 0,4–4,0. Long, coiled gut, black peritoneum. Light to dark olive above, thin dusky to yellowish-green stripe along back, silver along side, with a dusky stripe on caudal peduncle. Spawning males with yellow stripe along side and lower fins. Ohio and Mississippi river basins from southwest IN to MO, south to Gulf Coast from FL to TX. Rare. Swamps, oxbows, and backwaters of low-gradient streams and large rivers, usually associated with muck and detritus. Detritivore. Open substrate lithophil (A.1.3). Maximum size 105 mm TL

60   STREAMLINE CHUB—
      Erimystax dissimilis

61   EASTERN GRAVEL CHUB—
      Erimystax x-punctata

62   CYPRESS MINNOW—
      Hybognathus hayi

63 MISSISSIPPI SILVERY MINNOW—*Hybognathus nuchalis* Agassiz. Compressed body, deepest and widest at dorsal fin origin. Small, slightly subterminal mouth (rear edge of mouth in front of eye). Moderately small eyes, about 25 percent HL. Pointed dorsal fin. Deep caudal peduncle. Scales on back and upper side not darkly outlined with black. Basioccipital process broad and distinctly concave posteriorly. Complete lateral line, lateral scales 34–41. Anal fin rays 8, pectoral fin rays 15–16, pharyngeal teeth 0,4—4,0. Long, coiled gut, black peritoneum. Light brown to yellowish-olive above, wide dusky to yellowish-green stripe along back, silver side, with a dusky stripe extending from pectoral fin origin to caudal peduncle. Spawning males with yellow stripe along side and lower fins. Mississippi River basins south to Gulf of Mexico from AL to TX, west to NM. Common. Low-gradient streams to large river backwaters and pools, usually associated with muck and detritus. Particulate-feeding detritivore. Open substrate lithopelagophil (A.1.2). Maximum size 180 mm TL

64 BIGEYE CHUB—*Hybopsis amblops* (Rafinesque). Slender, slightly compressed body. Large elliptical eye, about equal to length of snout, directed upward. Small mouth, projecting well beyond upper lip. Dorsal fin origin over or slightly behind pelvic fin origin. Complete lateral line, lateral scales 33–38, anal fin rays 8, pharyngeal teeth 1,4—4,1. Light yellow or straw-tan above, dark stripe along back in front of dorsal fin, scales darkly outlined—producing wavy continuous lines, may have a dark caudal spot. Spawning male with small scattered tubercles over head and heavily distributed on nape. Lake Erie, Ohio River, and Ozarks basins from NY to eastern IL south to GA, west to OK. Common. Small to large-sized rivers and moderate-sized streams of moderate gradient in riffles with sand or gravel substrates. Benthic-hunting invertivore. Open substrate lithopelagophil (A.1.2). Maximum size 88 mm TL.

65 PALLID SHINER—*Hybopsis amnis* (Hubbs and Greene). Slender, fairly compressed body. Large eye, about to length of snout, directed upward. Small mouth, snout projecting beyond upper lip. Barbel rarely at corner of mouth. Dorsal origin over or in front of pelvic fin origin. Complete lateral line, lateral scales 33–38, anal rays 8, pharyngeal teeth 1,4—4,1. Straw-yellow above, scales usually dark edged, black stripe along silver side and around snout (stripe darkest at rear), may possess a caudal spot, white below; clear fins. Spawning male with small scattered tubercles over head and mostly absent from nape. Mississippi River, Cumberland River, and Gulf Coast basin from WI south to LA to eastern KY, west to OK, and along Gulf Coast from LA to TX. Rare. Medium to large rivers in sand and silt-covered pools. Benthic-hunting invertivore. Reproductive guild unknown. Maximum size 84 mm TL.

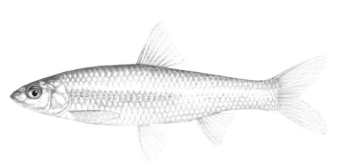

63   MISSISSIPPI SILVERY MINNOW—
Hybognathus nuchalis

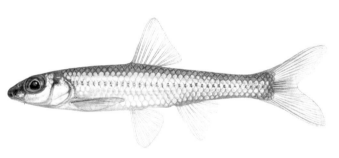

64   BIGEYE CHUB—
Hybopsis amblops

65   PALLID SHINER—
Hybopsis amnis

66   SILVER CARP—*Hypophthalmichthys molitrix* (Valenciennes). Deep bodied, laterally compressed. Eye set far forward on head, directed downward. Large head; mouth upturned without teeth on jaws. Stout spine on anal, pectoral, and dorsal fins with heavy serration on posterior edge of pectoral fin only. Dorsal fin origin posterior pelvic fin origin. Head and opercle scaleless. Scales tiny, resembling a trout. Smooth ventral keel extends from isthmus at the base of the gills to base of anal fin. Lateral scales 95–103. Dorsal rays 8, pectoral fin 15–19, anal fin falcate, rays 12–13, pharyngeal teeth 4—4, moderately long and bluntly rounded. Gill rakers numerous, fused or covered with a net-like, porous matrix. Intestine long and looped, 3–6 times TL. Gray to olive-green above, silver on side, white below; clear fins. Exotic, widely introduced into Mississippi River basin from IL south to Gulf Coast from AL to LA, west to CO and NV. Occasional. Large rivers in pools and runs associated with woody debris and soft substrates. Filter-feeding herbivore/detritivore. Open substrate pelagophil (A.1.1). Maximum size 1260 mm TL.

67   BIGHEAD CARP—*Hypophthalmichthys nobilis* (Richardson). Deep bodied, laterally compressed. Eye far forward on head, directed downward. Large head, mouth upturned without teeth on jaws, lower jaw projecting beyond upper jaw. Stout spine on anal, pectoral, and dorsal fins without serrations. Dorsal fin origin posterior pelvic fin origin. Scales tiny, cycloid, resembling a trout. Lateral line complete, lateral scales 85–100, scale rows above lateral line 26–28. Smooth ventral keel extends from vent to pelvic fin base. Dorsal rays 8, pectoral fin 16–21, anal fin falcate, rays 13–14, pharyngeal teeth 4—4, moderately long and bluntly rounded. Gill rakers long, comb-like, length 40 times width and not fused into a porous, net-like plate. Intestine long and looped, 3–5 times TL. Dark gray above, dark mottlings on side, white below; clear fins. Exotic, widely introduced into Hudson Bay, Great Lakes, Mississippi River, Atlantic Slope, and Gulf Coastal basins from SD to ME, south to FL, west to CO and TX, and Pacific Slope of WA, CA, NV, and NM. Occasional. Large rivers in pools and runs associated with woody debris and soft substrates. Filter-feeding planktivore. Open substrate pelagophil (A.1.1). Maximum size 1,400 mm TL.

68   STRIPED SHINER—*Luxilus chrysocephalus chrysocephalus* Rafinesque. Deep, strongly compressed body, large scales twice higher than wide, dorsal fin origin over or slightly behind pelvic fin origin. Large oblique, terminal mouth. Lateral scales 36–46, scales around body at dorsal fin origin 24–29, predorsal scales 12–13, pharyngeal teeth 2,4—4,2. Olive above, dark stripes along middle of back converge posterior dorsal fin insertion to form large Vs, dark crescents on side, silver side, white below. Spawning adults with pink or red body and fins. Great Lakes, Mississippi River basins from NY to WI, south to LA, around Gulf from GA to LA. Abundant. Small headwater creeks to medium-sized rivers including pools below riffles. Benthic and drift insectivore. Brood-hiding lithophil (A.2.3). Maximum size 130 mm TL.

66 SILVER CARP—
Hypophthalmichthys molitrix

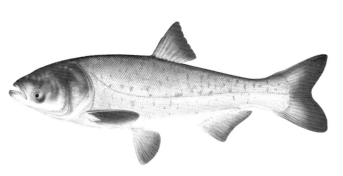

67 BIGHEAD CARP—
Hypophthalmichthys nobilis

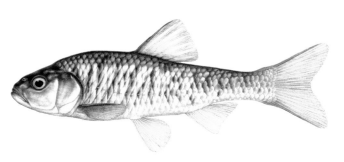

68 STRIPED SHINER—
Luxilus chrysocephalus

69 COMMON SHINER—*Luxilus cornutus frontalis* (Mitchill). Deep, strongly compressed body, large scales twice higher than wide, dorsal fin origin over or slightly behind pelvic fin origin. Large oblique, terminal mouth. Lateral scales 36–46, scales around body at dorsal fin origin 30–35, predorsal scales greater than 15, pharyngeal teeth 2,4—4,2. Olive above, dark stripes 1–2 along middle of back not converging to form large Vs, dark crescents on side, silver side, white below. Spawning adults with pink or red body and fins. Great Lakes, Atlantic Slope, Hudson Bay, and Mississippi River basins. Occasional. Small headwater creeks to medium-sized rivers including pools below riffles. Benthic and drift water column insectivore. Brood-hiding lithophil (A.2.3). Maximum size 130 mm TL.

70 SCARLETFIN SHINER—*Lythrurus fasciolaris* (Cope). Fairly deep, laterally compressed body, small scales on nape and anterior dorsal origin, large eye. Anal rays 9–(usually 10)–12, lateral scales 38–53, pharyngeal teeth 2,4—4,2. Olive to steel blue above, dusky stripe along back, black spots on back and upper side, dusky lips and chin; dark blotch at dorsal fin origin. Spawning male with red fins, orange lower side and head, with vertical stripes 9–12. Ohio River, south to AL and east to VA. Common. Rock pools and runs in headwater creeks, streams, and small rivers. Benthic and drift insectivore. Open substrate lithopelagophil (A.1.2). Maximum size 86 mm TL.

71 RIBBON SHINER—*Lythrurus fumeus* (Evermann). Fairly slender, laterally compressed body, large eye. Small scales on nape and anterior dorsal origin, scales edged in black. Lateral scales 35–45, anal rays 11–12, pharyngeal teeth 2,4—4,2. Olive above, dusky stripe along back, silvery-black stripe darkest posterior but usually weak, dusky lips and chin; dark blotch at dorsal fin origin mostly on body and less on fin. Spawning male with yellow fins. Mississippi River and Gulf Coast basins from IL south to AL, west to OK, and LA to TX. Rare. Turbid headwater creeks, streams, and small rivers in quiet pools over sand and muck substrates. Surface-feeding insectivore. Open substrate lithopelagophil (A.1.2). Maximum size 76 mm TL.

69 COMMON SHINER—
Luxilus cornutus frontalis

70 SCARLETFIN SHINER—
Lythrurus fasciolaris

71 RIBBON SHINER—
Lythrurus fumeus

72   REDFIN SHINER—*Lythrurus umbratilis cyano-cephalus* (Girard). Deep, laterally compressed body, large eye. Small scales on nape and anterior dorsal origin, without dark-edged scales. Lateral scales 37–56, anal rays 10–11, pharyngeal teeth 2,4—4,2. Olive above to steel blue, dusky stripe along back, black spots on back and upper side, herringbone lines on upper side, silver side, white below; red fins, dark prominent blotch on dorsal fin origin. Spawning male blue to purple head and body, with dark membranes on red fins. Great Lakes and Mississippi River basins from NY to MN, south to LA, and Gulf Coast from LA to TX. Common. Headwater creeks, streams, and small rivers in quiet and flowing pools over sand and gravel substrates. Benthic and drift insectivore. Open substrate lithophil (A.1.3). Maximum size 80 mm TL.

73   SILVER CREEK SHINER—*Lythrurus* cf. *umbratilis* nov. sp. Deep, laterally compressed body, large eye. Small scales on nape and anterior dorsal origin, without dark-edged scales. Lateral scales 37–56, anal rays 10, pharyngeal teeth 2,4—4,2. Olive above to steel blue, dusky stripe along back, black spots on back and upper side, without herringbone lines on upper side, silver side, white below; red fins, dark prominent blotch on dorsal fin origin. Spawning male with blue stripes on head and body, without dark membranes on red fins. Ohio River basin occurring in Silver Creek, IN. Locally common. Headwater creeks, streams, and small rivers in quiet and flowing pools over sand and gravel substrates. Benthic and drift insectivore. Open substrate lithophil (A.1.3). Maximum size 82 mm TL.

74   SHOAL CHUB—*Macrhybopsis hyostoma* (Girard). Slender, barely compressed body, deepest under nape, flattened below. Long, bulbous snout overhangs mouth. Long barbel in corner of subterminal mouth. Small, upward-directed eyes. Dorsal fin origin over or in front of pelvic fin origin. Complete lateral line, lateral line scales 34–41, anal rays 7–8, pharyngeal teeth 0,4—4,0 or 1,4—4,1. Translucent, light olive to straw-yellow above, with silver flecks and blue reflections, may have dusky stripe, with X and Y markings on body. Mississippi River south to Gulf Coast from OH and WV to MN south from AL. Occasional. Small and large rivers over sand and gravel runs. Benthic-hunting insectivore. Open substrate lithopelagophil (A.1.2). Maximum size 76 mm TL.

72   NORTHERN REDFIN SHINER—
Lythrurus umbratilis cyanocephalus

73   SILVER CREEK SHINER—
Lythrurus cf. *umbratilis*

74   SHOAL CHUB—
Macrhybopsis hyostoma

75 SILVER CHUB—*Macrhybopsis storeriana* (Kirtland). Slender, barely compressed body, flattened below. Short, rounded snout, overhangs mouth. Short, barbel in corner of subterminal mouth. Large, upward-directed eyes on upper half of head. Dorsal fin origin in front of pelvic fin origin. Complete lateral line, lateral line scales 35–48, anal rays 8, pharyngeal teeth 1,4—4,1. Light olive above, white to silver sides and ventral; paired and median fins clear, white edge on dusky lower lobe of caudal fin. Lake Erie basin west to Red River of the North, south in the Mississippi River from NE to NY, south to Gulf Coast from west AL to LA. Common. Large and great rivers over sand and gravel substrates. Planktivore/invertivore. Open substrate lithopelagophil (A.1.2). Maximum size 231 mm TL.

76 HORNYHEAD CHUB—*Nocomis biguttatus* (Kirtland). Large, stout, barely compressed body. Moderate rounded snout, not overhanging mouth. Barbel in corner of large, slightly subterminal mouth. Moderate eyes on upper half of head. Dorsal fin origin slightly in front or just behind pelvic fin origin. Complete lateral line, lateral line scales 38–45, anal rays 7, pharyngeal teeth 1,4—4,1. Dark olive to brown above, grading into iridescent green above dusky lateral line that extends from snout to caudal peduncle base. Yellow streak above lateral line, black caudal spot (darkest on juveniles), all fins clear. Breeding male pink below with pinkish to orange fins; tubercles present on top of head. Great Lake basin from NY west to Red River of the North, south to Ohio River, south in Ozarks. Common. Creeks to small rivers over gravel and cobble substrates in pools and runs. Invertivore. Brood-hiding lithophil (A.2.3). Maximum size 215 mm TL.

77 RIVER CHUB—*Nocomis micropogon* (Cope). Large, stout, barely compressed body. Long rounded snout, not overhanging mouth. Barbel in corner of large, slightly subterminal mouth. Small eyes on upper half of head. Dorsal fin origin slightly in front or just behind pelvic fin origin. Complete lateral line, lateral line scales 38–41, anal rays 7, pharyngeal teeth 0,4—4,0. Dark olive to brown above, grading into brassy iridescent green above, dark-edged scales on back and upper sides above lateral line, white to light yellow below; olive to light orange caudal fin, all other fins either yellow to pink. Breeding male pink to blue head, body, and fins; large tubercles on snout (anterior nostrils); large hump on head. Atlantic Slope from NY to VA, including the Great Lakes basin, south throughout Ohio River drainage to northern GA and AL. Common. Small to moderate-sized rivers over gravel and cobble substrates in pools and runs. Invertivore. Brood-hiding lithophil (A.2.3). Maximum size 245 mm TL.

75 SILVER CHUB—
Macrhybopsis storeriana

76 HORNYHEAD CHUB—
Nocomis biguttatus

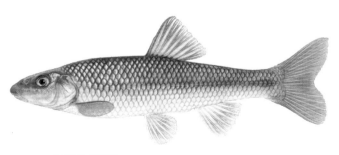

77 RIVER CHUB—
Nocomis micropogon

78 GOLDEN SHINER—*Notemigonus crysoleucas* (Mitchell). Strongly compressed body. Pointed snout, small upturned mouth. Keel scaleless from pelvic to anal fins. Dorsal fin origin behind pelvic fin origin. Lateral line strongly decurved, lateral line scales 44–54, dorsal rays 7–9, anal rays 11–14. Gill rakers on first arch 17–19, pharyngeal teeth 0,5—5,0. Silver to golden above and along sides with dusky stripe along side and herringbone lines on upper side, white below; dusky paired and median fins with caudal fin orange to golden. Atlantic and Gulf Slope from NS to TX, found in Great Lakes, Hudson Bay, and Mississippi River basins. Common. Small creeks to small and moderate-sized rivers in pools, vegetated ponds, swamps, lakes, and backwaters. Particulate-feeding, surface and water column insectivore. Open substrate phytophil (A.1.5). Maximum size 280 mm TL.

79 PUGNOSE SHINER—*Notropis anogenus* Forbes. Fairly compressed body. Pointed snout, small, sharply upturned mouth. Dorsal fin origin over pelvic fin origin. Lateral line complete, lateral line scales 34–38, anal rays 8 (often 7). Pharyngeal teeth 0,4—4,0. Olive above, thin dark line along back, scales darkly outlined except above dark lateral stripe, dark stripe along side and around snout including chin, lower lip, and side of upper lip, black peritoneum, silver to white below; dusky paired and median fins with black wedge on caudal fin base. Breeding male with yellow body and fins. Lake Ontario to southeastern North Dakota and central Illinois. Restricted to Great Lakes, Mississippi River, and Hudson Bay basins. Rare or possibly extirpate. Clear lakes with submerged aquatic plants and vegetated pools and runs of small creeks to small-sized rivers. Insectivore. Reproductive guild unknown. Maximum size 60 mm TL.

80 POPEYE SHINER—*Notropis ariommus* (Cope). Fairly deep, compressed body. Moderately pointed snout, huge eye (largest among genus). Dorsal fin origin over to slightly behind pelvic fin origin. Lateral line complete, lateral line scales 35–39, anal rays 9 (sometimes 10). Pharyngeal teeth 2,4—4,2. Light brown above, darkly outlined scales on back and upper side, grayish-black stripe along back, dusky stripe along silver side that is darkest at rear and expands into black caudal spot; median and paired fins dusky. Ohio River drainage from Pennsylvania west to IN, south to Tennessee River. A single record from the Maumee River, OH, population extirpated. Rare to occasional. Creeks and small rivers in flowing pools and runs over gravel substrates. Insectivore. Reproductive guild unknown. Maximum size 82 mm TL.

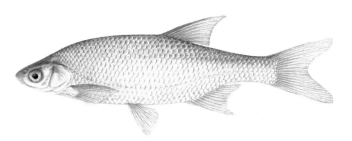

78 GOLDEN SHINER—
Notemigonus crysoleucas

79 PUGNOSE SHINER—
Notropis anogenus

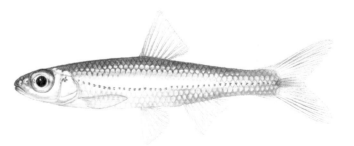

80 POPEYE SHINER—
Notropis ariommus

81   EMERALD SHINER—*Notropis atherinoides* Rafinesque. Slender, compressed body. Pointed snout (slightly rounded), large terminal mouth. Dorsal fin origin behind pelvic fin origin. Lateral line complete, lateral line scales 35–40, anal rays 10–12, pelvic rays 8, pharyngeal teeth 2,4—4,2. Light olive above, narrow dusky stripe along back, partly dusky, silver stripe with emerald reflections along side, silver or white below; fins clear or with dusky membranes. St. Lawrence to Hudson Bay south in Great Lakes and Mississippi River to Gulf of Mexico from AL to TX. Abundant. Large and great rivers, large inland lakes, and Great Lakes in pools and runs over sand and gravel substrates. Particulate-feeding, selective picker planktivore. Open substrate pelagophil (A.1.1). Maximum size 102 mm TL.

82   RIVER SHINER—*Notropis blennius* (Girard). Slender, compressed body. Moderately pointed snout, overhangs large, slightly subterminal mouth. Mouth extends to beneath eye. Dorsal fin origin over or slightly behind pelvic fin origin. Lateral line complete, lateral line scales 35–36 (34–41), anal rays 7. Pharyngeal teeth 2,4—4,2 (often 1,4—4,1). Breast mostly scaled. Light tan above, dark midline stripe extends around the dorsal fin, scales on upper side faintly outlined, side silver with faint dusky stripe along rear half of body; fins clear. Hudson Bay south to Mississippi River drainage from WV to eastern CO, south to Gulf Coastal Plain. Common. Large and great rivers in pools and main channel border habitats over sand and gravel substrates. Benthic and drift insectivore. Reproductive guild unknown. Maximum size 126 mm TL.

83   BIGEYE SHINER—*Notropis boops* Gilbert. Slender, fairly compressed body. Long, pointed snout, large terminal mouth (almost to anterior margin of eye), large eye, much larger than snout. Dorsal fin origin over pelvic fin origin. Lateral line complete, lateral line scales 34–40, anal rays 8. Pharyngeal teeth 1,4—4,1. Olive to yellowish above, thin dark stripe along back, scales darkly outlined on back and upper side above variably dusky lateral stripe. Clear stripe above black stripe along silver side and around snout including both lower and upper lip, black peritoneum, silver to white below; dusky paired and median fins with black pigmentation on anal fin membranes at anterior base. Lake Erie to Mississippi River basin from eastern KY to eastern OK, south to LA. Common. Small creeks to medium rivers in pools with emergent aquatic plants and clear pools. Drift insectivore. Reproductive guild unknown. Maximum size 66 mm TL.

81 EMERALD SHINER—
Notropis atherinoides

82 RIVER SHINER—
Notropis blennius

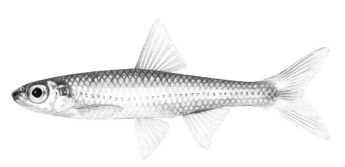

83 BIGEYE SHINER—
Notropis boops

84 GHOST SHINER—*Notropis buchanani* Meek. Body compressed, strong arch anterior of dorsal fin origin tapering to narrow caudal peduncle. Fairly large eye, rounded snout, small subterminal mouth. Dorsal fin origin over pelvic fin origin. Complete lateral line, lateral scales on anterior half of body deeper than wide, lateral line scales 30–35, anal rays 8, no infraorbital canal (rarely short segment present). Pharyngeal teeth 0,4—4,0. Fins large, pointed at tips, depressed pelvic fin touches anal fin origin. Body translucent to milky white, scales on back faintly outlined, sometimes black specks present on snout, along lateral line, and underside of caudal peduncle, transparent below; fins clear with dusky edge at tips. Mississippi River from MN south to northern AL, and from PA to central TX. Introduced into Maumee River, OH. Occasional. Small to large rivers in slow-flowing pools and backwaters over sand substrates. Benthic insectivore. Reproductive guild unknown. Maximum size 64 mm TL.

85 IRONCOLOR SHINER—*Notropis chalybaeus* (Cope). Compressed body, deepest at dorsal fin origin, usually arched. Pointed snout, small, oblique terminal mouth. Black pigment inside mouth. Large eye (longer than snout). Dorsal fin origin over pelvic fin origin. Incomplete lateral line, lateral line scales 31–37, anal rays 8. Pharyngeal teeth 2,4—4,2. Straw-colored above, dusky stripe along back widest and darkest anterior dorsal fin. Scales above lateral line darkly outlined except just above black stripe where golden-orange streak may be present. Black stripe from snout (covering both lips) to caudal fin base spot, silver-white below; fins clear. Breeding male orangish-golden body and fins. Atlantic, Gulf, and Mississippi River basins, from NY to FL west to LA, north in Mississippi River embayment to southeast MO, disjunct populations in northern IL and IN. Occasional. Creeks and small rivers in clear, vegetated sand substrate pools and slow runs. Insectivore. Open substrate lithopelagophil (A.1.2). Maximum size 55 mm TL.

86 BIGMOUTH SHINER—*Notropis dorsalis* (Agassiz). Slender, strongly arched body; head flattened below, long snout, large subterminal mouth. Dorsal fin origin over pelvic fin origin. Punctate lateral line (anterior half of body), nape with exposed scales, lateral line complete, lateral line scales 33–39, anal rays 8. Pharyngeal teeth 1,4—4,1. Straw-colored to olive above, dark stripe along back; faintly outlined scales on back and upper side, silver side, silver to white below; fins clear. Great Lakes, Hudson Bay, and Mississippi River basins from MI to WY, disjunct populations in NY, PA, WV, OH, and western MI. Rare, range margin in IN. Headwater creeks and small and medium-sized rivers in silty runs and pools of headwaters over sand substrates. Benthic insectivore. Reproductive guild unknown. Maximum size 69 mm TL.

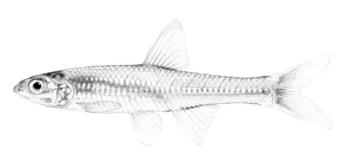

84 GHOST SHINER—
Notropis buchanani

85 IRONCOLOR SHINER—
Notropis chalybaeus

86 EASTERN BIGMOUTH SHINER—
Notropis dorsalis

87 BLACKCHIN SHINER—*Notropis heterodon* (Cope). Fairly compressed body, slender caudal peduncle. Pointed snout, small oblique mouth terminating below nostril. Large eye (longer than snout). Dorsal fin origin over to slightly in front of pelvic fin origin. Incomplete lateral line, lateral line scales 34–38, anal rays 8 (often 7). Pharyngeal teeth 1,4—4,1. Olive to straw above, scales darkly outlined except pale stripe above dark stripe along side, dusky stripe along back widest and darkest anterior dorsal fin. Scales above lateral line darkly outlined except just above black stripe where golden-orange streak may be present, concentrations of black pigment at lateral line pore appears as a zigzag on front half of body. Dusky or black stripe lips and chin, silver-white below; fins clear. Great Lakes and Mississippi River basins, from VT to IA, localized in Atlantic Slope, upper Ohio River, and Hudson Bay basins. Rare. Creeks and small rivers and lakes in clear, vegetated sand substrate pools and slow runs. Invertivore. Open substrate phytophil (A.1.5). Maximum size 61 mm TL.

88 BLACKNOSE SHINER—*Notropis heterolepis* Eigenmann and Eigenmann. Slender, slightly compressed body. Rounded, elongate snout, small, nearly horizontal subterminal mouth, round eye. Dorsal fin origin slightly behind pelvic fin origin. Incomplete lateral line, 37–39 lateral scales, 13 or more predorsal scales, anal rays 8. Pharyngeal teeth 0,4—4,0. Olive to straw-colored above, faint streak before dorsal fin; scales darkly outlined except above dark stripe along silver side. Black stripe along side and around snout but barely onto upper lip and absent on chin, black crescents within stripe, white below; fins clear. Atlantic, Great Lakes, Hudson Bay, and Mississippi River basins from NS west to SK, south to KS and northern TN. Rare. Creeks and small rivers and lakes in clear, vegetated sand substrate pools and slow runs. Invertivore. Open substrate phytophil (A.1.5). Maximum size 101 mm TL.

89 SPOTTAIL SHINER—*Notropis hudsonius* (Clinton). Body slender, laterally compressed. Short, rounded snout, large eye. Dorsal fin origin over or slightly in front of pelvic fin origin. Punctate (faint) lateral line anteriorly, lateral line scales 36–42, anal rays 8. Pharyngeal teeth usually 2,4—4,2. Olive to gray above, dusky dark stripe on back, dark-edged scales often forming wavy lines on back and upper side, dusky stripe along rear of silver side, large black caudal spot, white or silver below; fins clear. Atlantic and Gulf Coast drainages, Great Lakes, Hudson Bay, and Mississippi River basins from Arctic south to northern OH and southern IL. Abundant. Small to large rivers and nearshore of Great Lakes in littoral and pools and runs over sand and rock substrates. Invertivore. Open substrate lithopelagophil (A.1.2). Maximum size 122 mm TL.

87 BLACKCHIN SHINER—
Notropis heterodon

88 BLACKNOSE SHINER—
Notropis heterolepis

89 SPOTTAIL SHINER—
Notropis hudsonius

90 CARMINE SHINER—*Notropis percobromus* (Cope). Slender, elongate, laterally compressed body. Narrow, conical snout (equal to eye diameter), large eye. Dorsal fin origin behind pelvic fin origin. Lateral line complete, lateral line scales 36–45, anal rays 9–11. Pharyngeal teeth 0,4—4,0, gill rakers on lower limb short, 5–7. Olive above, silver side with punctate lateral line, cheek and operculum pink, silver below; fins clear. Breeding males with red snout, crimson on operculum and cheek, along pectoral girdle and fins, and along base of paired and median fins. Hudson Bay and Mississippi River basins from MB to West Fork White River IN. Disjunct populations in Ozarks of MO, OK, and KS. Common. Small to medium rivers in pools and runs over cobble and gravel substrates. Invertivore. Brood-hiding lithophil (A.2.3). Maximum size 90 mm TL.

91 SILVER SHINER—*Notropis photogenis* (Cope). Slender, elongate, laterally compressed body. Long snout, with two black crescents around nostrils, thickened tip of lower jaw projects beyond upper jaw, large eye. Dorsal fin origin behind pelvic fin origin. Lateral line complete, lateral line scales 36–40, anal rays 10–12, pelvic rays 9. Pharyngeal teeth 2,4—4,2. Light olive above, black stripe on back, dusky silver stripe with blue iridescence along side, front half of lips black, silver below; fins with dusky membranes or clear. Lake Erie and Ohio River basins from NY to MI, south to GA. Occasional. Small to large rivers in riffles and runs over rock substrates. Invertivore. Reproductive guild unknown. Maximum size 137 mm TL.

92 ROSYFACE SHINER—*Notropis rubellus* (Agassiz). Slender, elongate, laterally compressed body. Long, sharply pointed snout longer than eye diameter, eye moderate. Dorsal fin origin well behind pelvic fin origin (about middle of pelvic fin). Lateral line complete, lateral line scales 36–45, anal rays 9–11. Pharyngeal teeth 2,4—4,2 or 1,4—4,1. Olive above, often with a narrow dusky stripe along back, black streak just above silver stripe along side, iridescent blue along side, silver below; fins clear with faint red at base of dorsal fin. Breeding male blue above, with orange to bright rosy red head, front half of body, and fin bases. Atlantic Slope from St. Lawrence to VA including the Great Lakes, and Ohio River basin west to East Fork White River. Common. Small to large rivers and streams in flowing pools and runs over rock substrates. Invertivore. Brood-hiding lithophil (A.2.3). Maximum size 90 mm TL.

90   CARMINE SHINER—
     Notropis percobromus

91   SILVER SHINER—
     Notropis photogenis

92   ROSYFACE SHINER—
     Notropis rubellus

93   SILVERBAND SHINER—*Notropis shumardi* (Girard). Laterally compressed body, deep caudal peduncle. Short, pointed snout, terminal upturned mouth. Dorsal fin origin over to slightly behind pelvic fin origin, situated in middle of body. Dorsal fin tall, pointed fin, front rays extend well beyond rear rays when fin depressed. Lateral line complete, lateral line scales 33–39, anal rays 9 (often 8), pelvic fin rays 9. Pharyngeal teeth 2,4—4,2. Light olive above, dusky stripe along back, silver stripe along side becoming dusky at rear, white below; fins clear. Large rivers in the Mississippi River basin south to Gulf Coast drainages of TX. Common. Large rivers in flowing pools and runs over sand and gravel. Insectivore. Reproductive guild unknown. Maximum size 84 mm TL.

94   SAND SHINER—*Notropis stramineus* Cope. Slender, fairly compressed body. Rounded snout, small, slightly upturned subterminal mouth, eye large with nipple at anterior margin. Dorsal fin origin over to slightly behind pelvic fin origin. Lateral line complete, decurved, punctate in front half of body, lateral line scales 31–38, anal rays 7. Pharyngeal teeth 0,4—4,0. Straw-yellow above, faintly outlined scales on back and upper side, dark expanded wedge at dorsal fin origin, silver side with dusky stripe posteriorly, small black caudal spot or wedge, white below; fins clear. Great Lakes, Hudson Bay, and Mississippi River basin south to TN and TX, west MT and NM. Common. Creeks and small to large rivers and margins of lakes over sand substrates. Invertivore. Reproductive guild unknown. Maximum size 72 mm TL.

95   WEED SHINER—*Notropis texanus* (Girard). Fairly compressed body. Blunt snout, small terminal mouth (posterior margin terminates under nostril), eye large. Dorsal fin origin in front of pelvic fin origin. Lateral line complete or nearly complete, lateral line scales 32–39, anal rays 7. Pharyngeal teeth 2,4—4,2. Olive-yellow above, dark stripe along back much wider in front of dorsal fin, silver side, black stripe along side and around snout on both lips, some black-edged scales below lateral stripe, with clear stripe between black stripe and black-edged scales on upper side and back, black spot on caudal fin base connected to or barely separated from black stripe, streaked toward end of caudal fin, white below; fins clear with exception of 3–4 anal rays lined with black. Great Lakes lowlands, Hudson Bay, and Mississippi River basin north from MI, south to Gulf of Mexico from FL to TX. Rare. Creeks and small to medium rivers and margins of lakes over sand substrates. Particulate-feeding detritivore. Reproductive guild unknown. Maximum size 76 mm TL.

93 SILVERBAND SHINER—
Notropis shumardi

94 SAND SHINER—
Notropis stramineus

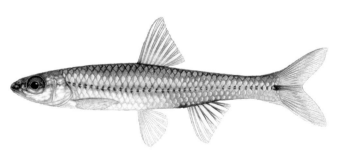

95 WEED SHINER—
Notropis texanus

96   MIMIC SHINER—*Notropis volucellus* (Cope). Slender, compressed body. Broad, rounded snout, small subterminal mouth, eye large. Dorsal fin origin over or to slightly behind pelvic fin origin. Lateral line complete, lateral line scales 32–38, scales along back in front of dorsal fin wider than those on upper side, scales on side anterior anus much deeper than wide, anal rays 8. Pharyngeal teeth 0,4—4,0. Body transparent gray to olive yellow above, dark stripe along back much wider in front of dorsal fin, often disconnected from anterior stripe, silver side, scales on back variably outlined on back and upper side, dusky stripe darkest at rear, stripe expanded just in front of caudal fin, white below with black pigment outlining anus; fins clear. Great Lakes, Hudson Bay, and Mississippi River from VT, east to Atlantic Slope and south to Gulf of Mexico from GA to TX. Occasional. Creeks, small to large rivers, and lake margins in pools and shallow sand littoral zones. Invertivore. Open substrate phytophil (A.1.5). Maximum size 76 mm TL.

97   CHANNEL SHINER—*Notropis wickliffi* Trautman. Broad, arched back, laterally compressed body with deeper caudal peduncle. Broad, rounded snout, small subterminal mouth, eye large. Dorsal fin origin over pelvic fin origin. Lateral line complete, lateral line scales 32–38, scales along back in front of dorsal fin wider than those on upper side, anal rays 8. Pharyngeal teeth 0,4—4,0. Body gray to olive-yellow above, dark stripe along back much wider in front of dorsal fin and often disconnected from anterior stripe, silver side, no or only a faint stripe along midline of nape, stripe not expanded in front of caudal fin, white below; fins clear. Great Lakes, Hudson Bay, and Mississippi River from QC to MT, Atlantic Slope from VA to NC, and south to Gulf of Mexico. Common. Small to large rivers in pools over shallow sand substrates. Insectivore. Open substrate psammophil (A.1.6). Maximum size 67 mm TL.

98   PUGNOSE MINNOW—*Opsopoeodus emiliae* Hay. Fairly slender body. Snout round, elongate, small, strongly upturned mouth. Small, crowded scales on front half of nape. Dorsal fin origin over to slightly behind pelvic fin origin. Lateral line usually complete, lateral line scales 36–40, dorsal rays 9, anal rays 8. Pharyngeal teeth 0,5—5,0. Dusky olive above, dark stripe along silver side including head and body, sometimes ending in small black spot on caudal fin base, white below; fins clear with exception of caudal fin, which has black streak emanating from caudal base. Great Lakes and Mississippi River basins to Gulf Coast from FL to TX. Rare. Vegetated lakes, swamps, oxbows, and basic gradient streams. Particulate-feeding, scooping detritivore. Nest-spawning speleophil (B.2.7). Maximum size 60 mm TL.

96   MIMIC SHINER—
Notropis volucellus

97   CHANNEL SHINER—
Notropis wickliffi

98   PUGNOSE MINNOW—
Opsopoeodus emiliae

99 SUCKERMOUTH MINNOW—*Phenacobius mirabilis* (Girard). Long, cylindrical body. Round snout, large fleshy lips on subterminal mouth, eye small. Dorsal fin origin in front of pelvic fin origin. Lateral line complete, lateral line scales 42–51, scale rows around caudal peduncle 15–17, anal rays 8. Pharyngeal teeth 0,4—4,0. Olive above, thin, dark stripe along back, darkly outlined scales on back and upper side, midlateral stripe from pectoral fin girdle to caudal fin base terminating in an intense, large black spot, white below; pectoral, dorsal and caudal fins with black pigment along membranes, others clear. Mississippi River basin, western Lake Erie basin, and isolated populations in Gulf Coast. Common. Moderate-sized creeks, small to large rivers in riffles and runs over gravel and cobble substrates. Benthic-grazing invertivore. Reproductive guild unknown. Maximum size 100 mm TL.

100 BLUNTNOSE MINNOW—*Pimephales notatus* (Rafinesque). Slender body nearly square in cross section. Blunt snout overhanging small, subterminal horizontal mouth, round eye. Dorsal fin origin slightly behind pelvic fin origin. Lateral line complete, lateral line scales 39–50, anal rays 7. Pharyngeal teeth 0,4—4,0. Scales crowded on nape, flattened. Light olive above, scales outlined (often with cross-hatched appearance), black streak on back, dusky or black stripe around snout and along silver side, black spot at base of caudal peduncle; fins clear except for dusky to black spot on midanterior dorsal fin. Breeding male black with silver bar behind opercle, about 16 large tubercles in 3 rows on snout, large gray fleshy nuptial pad on nape. Ubiquitously distributed in Mississippi River, Great Lakes, Hudson Bay, and Mobile Bay drainage in Gulf Coastal Plain. Abundant. Found in all types of aquatic habitats over all substrate types. Particulate-feeding, scooping detritivore. Intestine long with several loops; black peritoneum. Nest-spawning speleophil (B.2.7). Maximum size 110 mm TL.

101 FATHEAD MINNOW—*Pimephales promelas promelas* Rafinesque. Deep, compressed body. Blunt snout, terminal oblique mouth, head short, flat on top, round eye. Dorsal fin origin over pelvic fin origin. Lateral line incomplete, lateral line scales 40–54, anal rays 7. Pharyngeal teeth 0,4—4,0. Scales crowded on nape, flattened. Dark olive above and along side, dusky stripe along back and side mustard yellow to white below; fins clear, dusky black spot on midanterior dorsal fin. Breeding male black with two broad white to gold bars on side (behind head and beneath dorsal fin), large gray fleshy nuptial pad on nape, about 14–18 large tubercles arranged in 3 rows on snout. Colorado River to Atlantic Slope, from Hudson Bay to Ohio River, ubiquitous in Great Plains and Mobile Bay of Coastal Plain. Common. Headwater creeks, small rivers, and ponds in turbid pools over all substrate types. Particulate-feeding, scooping detritivore. Intestine long with several loops; black peritoneum. Nest-spawning speleophil (B.2.7). Maximum size 102 mm TL.

99 SUCKERMOUTH MINNOW—
Phenacobius mirabilis

100 BLUNTNOSE MINNOW—
Pimephales notatus

101 FATHEAD MINNOW—
Pimephales promelas promelas

102 BULLHEAD MINNOW—*Pimephales vigilax* (Baird and Girard). Slender body, nearly square in cross section. Rounded snout, small terminal mouth, eye large, directed upward, top of head and nape flattened. Dorsal fin origin over pelvic fin origin. Lateral line complete, lateral line scales 37–45, anal rays 7. Pharyngeal teeth 0,4—4,0. Scales crowded on nape, flattened. Dark olive above, scales darkly outlined, dusky to black stripe along silver side ending just before large caudal base spot, silver below, caudal peduncle with dark midline; fins clear, black spot on midanterior dorsal fin. Breeding male dark with black head, silver bar behind opercle, large gray fleshy nuptial pad on nape, about 5–9 large tubercles in 1–2 rows on snout. Mississippi River basin from PA to MN, south to Gulf of Mexico. Occasional to common. Large to great rivers with runs and flowing pools over sand, silt, or gravel substrates. Invertivore. Intestine short, silver peritoneum with black specks. Nest-spawning speleophil (B.2.7). Maximum size 89 mm TL.

103 LONGNOSE DACE—*Rhinichthys cataractae* (Valenciennes). Long, slender, streamlined body, deepest at nape, flattened below, with deep caudal peduncle. Long, fleshy snout overhanging lower jaw, without groove separating snout from upper lip, barbel in corner of mouth, eyes high on head. Straight-edged dorsal and anal fins, caudal fin moderately forked. Dorsal fin origin behind pelvic fin origin. Lateral line complete, lateral line 48–76 lateral line scales, dorsal rays 8, anal rays 7–9 (usually 8). Pharyngeal teeth 2,4—4,2. Olive brown above, brown-black spots and mottling on back and sides, dark stripe along side, dusky spot on caudal fin base, silver to yellow below; fins yellow. Breeding male with bright red lips, head, and fin bases. Arctic south to Appalachian Mountains, to Rocky Mountains of TX and Mexico, Atlantic Slope to VA. Occasional. Small to medium rivers and nearshore of Great Lakes in riffles and surf zone over gravel and cobble substrates. Invertivore. Open substrate lithopelagophil (A.1.2). Maximum size 75 mm TL.

104 WESTERN BLACKNOSE DACE—*Rhinichthys obtusus* (Hermann). Long, slender, streamlined body, deepest at nape, flattened below, with deep caudal peduncle. Snout pointed, snout slightly overhanging lower jaw, without groove separating snout from upper lip, barbel in corner of mouth, eyes high on head. Dorsal and anal fins rounded, caudal fin moderately forked. Dorsal fin origin behind pelvic fin origin. Lateral line complete, lateral line scales 53–70, anal rays 7. Pharyngeal teeth 2,4—4,2. Light brown above, black spots with silver spots on dorsal fin base, black spot along side through eye and onto snout, silver to white below; fins clear. Breeding male with nuptial pad on nape, with yellow-white pectoral and pelvic fins, white to red stripe below black lateral stripe. Atlantic, Great Lakes, Hudson Bay, Mississippi River, and upper Mobile Bay. Common. Coolwater springs, creeks, and small rivers in riffles over gravel and cobble substrates. Invertivore. Open substrate lithopelagophil (A.1.2). Maximum size 80 mm TL.

102 BULLHEAD MINNOW—
Pimephales vigilax

103 LONGNOSE DACE—
Rhinichthys cataractae cataractae

104 WESTERN BLACKNOSE DACE—
Rhinichthys obtusus

105   RUDD—*Scardinius erythrophthalmus* (Linnaeus). Deep, laterally compressed body. Small head, terminal oblique mouth. Dorsal fin origin behind pelvic fin origin. Lateral line incomplete, lateral line scales 36–45, scaled bony keel along belly from pelvic to anal fin, concave margin on dorsal and anal fin (tips from front rays reach beyond fin when depressed). Dorsal fin rays 9–11, anal fin rays 10–11. Pharyngeal teeth 3,5—5,3 with 10–13 rakers on first gill arch. Brown above, brassy yellow side, gold eye with red spot at top; fins golden-yellow with orangish-red caudal fin. Native to Europe and Asia, reproducing in Grand Calumet River (IN), Hudson River (NY), and ME. Lakes, basic gradient rivers of medium to large rivers in pools. Water column, drift-feeding insectivore. Open substrate phytolithophil (A.1.4). Maximum size 250 mm TL.

106   CREEK CHUB—*Semotilus atromaculatus* (Mitchill). Body barely compressed anteriorly, compressed at caudal peduncle. Pointed, short snout, short, broad head, small barbel in groove above corner of mouth, large terminal mouth. Dorsal fin origin behind pelvic fin origin. Lateral line complete, lateral line scales 47–65, anal rays 8. Pharyngeal teeth 2,5—4,2. Olive-brown above, dark black stripe along back, herringbone lines on upper side, dark black stripe along green side above midlateral through snout, upper lip, with black bar along back of gill cover, white below; fins clear. Breeding male with orange at dorsal fin base and on lower fins, pink on lower head and body, 6–12 large tubercles on head. Found in most of United States and Canada from Atlantic Slope, Great Lakes, Hudson Bay, Mississippi River, and Gulf Coastal Plain. Abundant. Small creeks, streams, and small rivers in riffle and run habitats over gravel and sand substrates. Insectivore, short intestine with silver peritoneum with black specks. Brood-hiding lithophil (A.2.3). Maximum size 305 mm TL.

LOACH FAMILY—COBITIDAE
(*SPECIES PLATE 107*)

The Cobitidae is a freshwater family with 26 genera and about 177 species distributed in Asia, Eurasia, and Morocco (Nelson 2006). The loaches have a fusiform body; subterminal mouth; 3–6 pairs of barbels present; erectile spine below eye; and a single row of pharyngeal teeth (Nelson 2006). The Cobitidae includes single pair of rostral barbels (rarely absent); conspicuous cephalic lateral line; and rounded or slightly emarginate caudal fin.

The Cobitidae is an introduced family that spread into Indiana from the Chicago waterways (Laird and Page 1996).

105 RUDD—
Scardinius erythrophthalmus

106 CREEK CHUB—
Semotilus atromaculatus

107 ORIENTAL WEATHERFISH—*Misgurnus anguillicaudatus* (Cantor). Worm-like, elongate, fusiform, nearly cylindrical body. Snout rounded, overhangs mouth, mouth thick and fleshy, subterminal, 6 barbels surround mouth, eye small. Spine on pelvic fin. Short dorsal fin positioned in middle of body. Dorsal fin origin over pelvic fin origin. Dorsal fin rays 9, pelvic fin rays 6–7, and anal fin rays 7–8. Tiny scales. Caudal fin rounded. Mottled olive above, black lateral stripe from head to caudal fin base, clay-brown to greenish-brown along side, creamy yellow to white below; paired fins clear and median fins with dark horizontal bands in dorsal, anal, and caudal fins. Introduced. Native to Southeast Asia. Great Lakes from MI to IL, isolated populations in FL, ID, CA, and HI. Common. Moderate to large rivers in mud substrates and in pools and runs of basic-gradient waters. Omnivore. Reproductive guild unknown. Maximum size 250 mm TL.

107 ORIENTAL WEATHERFISH—
Misgurnus anguillicaudatus

The Oriental weatherfish invaded into the Chicago waterways through ballast water. The species was established in the North Shore Canal prior to 1987 and in the Chicago Ship Canal by 1994. The Oriental weatherfish invaded into the Grand Calumet River by 2002 and was established in the Grand Calumet by 2005 (Simon et al. 2006). Its habitats range from muddy soft-bottomed rivers and are associated with woody debris or emergent wetland vegetation. Spawning periods occur during midsummer and females are known to have a mean fecundity of 2,000 eggs per female (Simon et al. 2006).

CATFISH FAMILY—ICTALURIDAE
(SPECIES PLATES 108–120)

The North American catfish family belongs in the order Siluriformes and includes 7 genera and 46 species (Nelson 2006), including 4 genera and 38 species in the United States and Canada. The *Ameiurus* have been raised from synonymy with the genus *Ictalurus* (Lundberg 1982) and includes 5 species. The revised *Ictalurus* includes 2 species, while *Noturus* includes 14 species in 3 subgenera. The genus *Pylodictis* is a monotypic genus and is considered the most divergent.

The North American catfish are diagnosed by 4 pair of barbels; skin naked; dorsal and pectoral fins with a spine; dorsal fin usually with 6 soft rays; palate toothless (Nelson 2006). The shape of the pectoral spine is a diagnostic character useful for specific identification (Figure 18).

Catfish are nocturnal and occupy various habitats in bodies of water ranging from small streams to large rivers, lakes, and reservoirs. Several genera are commercially desired, and aquaculture industries have developed to farm raise some species. The madtom are small, secretive species that are seldom seen. They possess venom associated with the pectoral and dorsal spines. The venom is not unique to madtoms but is present in varying degrees in other catfishes. Catfish are social animals and construct nests for spawning and for care of eggs and young. Spawning occurs in the spring to early summer. Larvae are large at hatching and develop rapidly with morphology

Bullheads	**Madtoms**	**Forktail Catfish**
Ameiurus catus	*Noturus eleutherus*	*Ictalurus furcatus*
Ameiurus melas	*Noturus flavus*	*Ictalurus punctatus*
Ameiurus natalis	*Noturus gyrinus*	**Flathead Catfish**
Ameiurus nebulosus	*Noturus miurus*	*Pylodictis olivaris*
	Noturus nocturnus	
	Noturus stigmosus	

Figure 18. Pectoral spine morphology of catfish genera and species.

similar to adults by the time yolk is absorbed (Simon and Wallus 2004). Most catfish are benthic species that feed on aquatic insects (Goldstein and Simon 1999). The bullheads are tolerant to a variety of anthropogenic stress, while the madtoms are among the most sensitive.

KEY TO THE CATFISHES OF INDIANA

1 a) Adipose fin with its posterior margin flap-like and free, not fused to back or to caudal fin posteriorly...............................2

   b) Adipose fin with its posterior margin fused to back and to caudal fin and separated from caudal fin by not more than an incomplete notch 8

2 a) Caudal fin deeply forked...3

   b) Caudal fin not deeply forked, its rear margin rounded, straight, or with a slight notch...5

3 a) Caudal fin moderately (less than 50% caudal fin length) forked; anal fin rays 22–24 (25); gill rakers 18–21 (23) .... **WHITE CATFISH**—*Ameiurus catus*

  b) Caudal fin deeply (greater than 50% caudal fin length) forked; anal fin rays greater than (23) 25–28 (30); gill rakers 13–15 (18) 4

4 a) Outer margin of anal fin rounded; anal fin rays 24–27 including rudimentary rays. Body with dark spots except in large adults. Swim bladder of paired lateral chambers, no posterior chamber ....**CHANNEL CATFISH**—*Ictalurus punctatus*

  b) Outer margin of anal fin straight, anal fin rays 30–36 including rudimentary rays. Body without dark spots. Swim bladder with paired lateral chambers and a posterior chamber .. .. **BLUE CATFISH**—*Ictalurus furcatus*

5 a) Lower jaw protruding beyond upper jaw. Tooth patch on upper jaw with elongate lateral backward extensions. Length of anal fin base (A) less than distance from back of eye to rear margin of operculum (B). Pectoral fin spine strongly toothed along both anterior (teeth pointing toward base) and posterior (teeth pointing toward tip) edges ....**FLATHEAD CATFISH**—*Pylodictis olivaris*

  b) Upper jaw extending beyond lower jaw. Tooth patch on upper jaw without lateral backward extensions. Length of anal fin base (A) greater than distance from back of eye to rear margin of operculum (B). Pectoral fin spine slightly rough to strongly toothed along posterior edge; along anterior edge weakly notched near tip 6

6 a) Anal fin rays 24–27 including rudimentary rays. Chin barbels white. Caudal fin rounded ....**YELLOW BULLHEAD**—*Ameiurus natalis*

  b) Anal fin rays 15–24 including rudimentary rays. Chin barbels gray to black. Caudal fin squarish and slightly notched 7

7 a) Pectoral fin spine toothless along posterior edge or with irregular or poorly developed teeth. Side not mottled. Interradial membranes of fins jet black. Adults with whitish bar at caudal fin base. Anal fin rays 15–21 including rudimentary rays.........................**BLACK BULLHEAD**—*Ameiurus melas*

  b) Pectoral fin spine with strong, saw-like teeth along posterior edge. Side mottled. Interradial membranes of fins dark but not jet-black. Adults without whitish bar at caudal fin base.

Anal fin rays 21–24 including rudimentary rays......................
.......................**BROWN BULLHEAD**—*Ameiurus nebulosus*

8 a) Dorsal surface uniformly gray, lacking pale saddles, or with only 2 pale saddles (posterior to head and under posterior edge of dorsal fin); posterior pectoral fin serrae not nearly as long as diameter of spine; pectoral spine with posterior margin straight and with posterior serrae, if present, not recurved toward body 9

b) Dorsal surface marked with 3–4 pale saddles (located behind head, under dorsal fin, anterior to adipose fin, and posterior to adipose fin); posterior serrae on pectoral fin spine as long as diameter of the spine; pectoral spine with posterior margin concave and the posterior serrae recurved toward the body...12

9 a) Pale dorsal area behind head and at posterior end of dorsal fin; premaxillary tooth patch with posterior extensions; posterior pectoral fin serrae less developed than anterior serrae. Tip of upper jaw projecting well beyond lower jaw ....
.... **STONECAT**—*Noturus flavus*

b) Dorsum uniformly gray; premaxillary tooth patch lacking posterior extensions; anterior pectoral fin serrae never longer than posterior serrae; tips of jaws about equal 10

10 a) Pectoral fin spine with prominent posterior serrae; dorsal, caudal, and anal fins with dark submarginal bands (Note: species has not been collected from Indiana)..........................
....................................**SLENDER MADTOM**—*Noturus exilis*

b) Pectoral fin spine without prominent posterior serrae...... 11

11 a) Mouth terminal; upper and lower jaws equal. Usually 3 dark longitudinal streaks on each side and dark lines outlining the muscle segments. No transverse light bands behind head and dorsal fin. Anal, caudal, and dorsal fins not dark edged; preoperculomandibular pores normally 10 (9–12); anal fin rays 13–16 ....**TADPOLE MADTOM**—*Noturus gyrinus*

b) Mouth inferior, lower jaw included (upper jaw overhangs lower). Dark, longitudinal streaks on sides absent; muscle segments not outlined with dark lines. Anal, caudal, and dorsal fins usually dark edged. Preoperculomandibular pores either 10–11; anal rays 16–18 (15–20)................................
.... **FRECKLED MADTOM**—*Noturus nocturnus*

12 a) Adipose fin nearly separated from caudal fin and forming a free posterior flap; dark pigment on adipose fin not extending to edge of margin (generally less than 50% of adipose fin); anal fin rays 13–14 (12–16); dark bar present at base of caudal peduncle.... **MOUNTAIN MADTOM**—*Noturus eleutherus*

b) Adipose fin not separated from caudal fin; dark pigment on adipose fin extending past middle of adipose fin sometimes to margin; anal fin rays 14–15 (13–16); dark bar not present at base of caudal peduncle 13

108 WHITE CATFISH—*Ameiurus catus* (Linnaeus). Deep bodied, with large, rounded head. Snout short, rounded, eye small. Upper jaw projecting beyond lower jaw, extends before anterior eye. Short anal fin, rounded in outline. Short adipose fin base, free from back and caudal fin. Moderately forked caudal fin. Anal fin rays 22–25, pectoral fin spines with 11–15 saw-like teeth on rear margin of pectoral fin. Gray to bluish-black above, dusky blue or black on back to adipose fin, white or yellow chin barbels, lips dusky blue above, no dark blotch at dorsal fin base, white or yellow below; dusky gray fins. Atlantic and Gulf Coast from NY to MS. Introduced into IN. Occasional. Backwaters and deep pools of large rivers, lakes, and reservoirs. Benthic whole body invertivore-carnivore. Guarding, nest-spawning speleophil (B.2.7). Maximum size 592 mm TL.

109 BLACK BULLHEAD—*Ameiurus melas* (Rafinesque). Deep bodied, with large, rounded head. Snout short, rounded, eye small. Upper jaw projecting beyond lower jaw, extends before anterior eye. Short anal fin, rounded in outline. Short adipose fin base, free from back and caudal fin. Slightly notched caudal fin. Anal fin rays 19–23—rays at front of anal fin distinctly longer than rear rays, pectoral fin spines without any saw-like teeth on rear margin. Dark olive to black above, side yellowish-green, brown or slate-gray above, dusky or black chin barbels, no mottling or black blotch on dorsal fin base, white or yellow below; dusky gray or black fins, pale rays with black anal and caudal fin membranes. Great Lakes, Hudson Bay, and Mississippi River basins, south to Gulf of Mexico. Introduced into Atlantic Slope. Abundant. Creeks, streams, small and large rivers, backwaters of lakes, wetlands, and reservoirs over soft substrates. Benthic, whole body invertivore-carnivore. Guarding, nest-spawning speleophil (B.2.7). Maximum size 380 mm TL.

13 a) Black bar beneath middle of adipose fin extends posteriorly and connects with basicaudal dark blotch; caudal fin typically with 2 black bands; total caudal fin rays 54 or fewer .... **NORTHERN MADTOM**—*Noturus stigmosus*

b) Black bar beneath middle of adipose fin separate from basicaudal dark blotch; caudal fin typically with a single submarginal band; caudal fin rays 56 or more ....**BRINDLED MADTOM**—*Noturus miurus*

108 WHITE CATFISH—
Ameiurus catus

109 BLACK BULLHEAD—
Ameiurus melas

110 YELLOW BULLHEAD—*Ameiurus natalis* (Lesueur). Deep bodied, with large, rounded head. Snout short, rounded, eye small. Upper jaw projecting beyond lower jaw, extends before anterior eye. Moderately long anal fin, nearly straight in outline. Short adipose fin base, free from back and caudal fin. Rounded or nearly straight caudal fin. Anal fin rays 24–27—rays at front only slightly longer than rear rays, pectoral fin spines with 5–8 saw-like teeth on rear margin. Yellowish-olive above and lighter side, white or yellow chin barbels, lips dusky above and yellow below, no dark blotch at dorsal fin base, bright yellow to white below; dusky gray fins, anal fin often with stripe in middle of fin. Atlantic and Gulf Coastal Plain from NY to Mexico, Great Lakes and Mississippi River basins. Introduced outside native range. Abundant. Creeks, streams, small and large rivers, backwaters of lakes, wetlands, and reservoirs over soft substrates. Benthic, whole body invertivore-carnivore. Guarding, nest-spawning speleophil (B.2.7). Maximum size 380 mm TL.

111 BROWN BULLHEAD—*Ameiurus nebulosus* (Lesueur). Deep bodied, with large, rounded head. Snout short, rounded, eye small. Upper jaw projecting beyond lower jaw, extends before anterior eye. Short anal fin, rounded in outline. Short adipose fin base, free from back and caudal fin. Square or slightly emarginate caudal fin. Anal fin rays 18–24, pectoral fin spines with 5–8 saw-like teeth on rear margin. Brown to black above, mottled or spotted along side with black, brown, and white, dusky or brown chin barbels, no dark blotch at dorsal fin base, white or yellow below; no dark membranes contrasting with pale rays on anal and caudal fins. Atlantic and Gulf Coastal Plain from NS to Mobile Bay, AL, Great Lakes, Hudson Bay, and Mississippi River. Widely introduced. Abundant. Backwaters and deep pools of large rivers, lakes, and reservoirs. Benthic, whole body invertivore-carnivore. Guarding, nest-spawning speleophil (B.2.7). Maximum size 532 mm TL.

112 BLUE CATFISH—*Ictalurus furcatus* (Lesueur). Deep bodied, steeply sloping head, and straight predorsal profile. Elongate snout, small eye. Long straight-edged anal fin, tapering posteriorly. Anal fin rays 30–35. Pale blue to olive above and side, white chin barbels, silver-blue on side, white below; fins clear or white, except black or borders on dorsal and caudal fins. Mississippi River basin from PA west to SD, south to Gulf Coast from AL to TX, including Atlantic Slope of Mexico. Occasional. Deep, turbid, pools of large and great rivers over mud, sand, and gravel. Benthic, whole body carnivore. Guarding, nest-spawning speleophil (B.2.7). Maximum size 1,194 mm TL.

110 YELLOW BULLHEAD—
Ameiurus natalis

111 BROWN BULLHEAD—
Ameiurus nebulosus

112 BLUE CATFISH—
Ictalurus furcatus

113   CHANNEL CATFISH—*Ictalurus punctatus* (Rafinesque). Slender bodied, steeply sloping head, and straight predorsal profile. Elongate pointed snout, small eye. Long rounded anal fin along edge. Anal fin rays 24–29. Pale blue to olive above and side, white to dusky chin barbels, silver-blue on side with scattered dark spots on light back and side (juveniles) absent in large adults, white below; fins similar color as adjacent body. Great Lakes, Hudson Bay, and Mississippi River basin, south to Gulf. Introduced into most of United States. Common. Deep pools and runs of large and great rivers and lakes over mud, sand, and gravel. Benthic, whole body carnivore. Guarding, nest-spawning speleophil (B.2.7). Maximum size 1,270 mm TL.

114   MOUNTAIN MADTOM—*Noturus eleutherus* Jordan. Thick, stout body with deep caudal peduncle. Long and low adipose with posterior margin high and nearly free from caudal fin. Elongate snout overhanging lower jaw, eye moderate. Long pectoral spine with 6–10 prominent saw-like teeth on rear edge with large teeth on front edge. Rear edge of caudal fin straight. Anal rays 12–16. Dark brown above, usually dark mottling with 4 faint saddles, dark brown bar on caudal fin base, light below, usually no dark specks on belly; dark bands or mottling on other fins, dark band near clear edge of caudal fin. Ohio River basin from PA to IL, south to TN and GA, also MO and AR. Occasional. Small to large rivers in fast current of riffles over gravel, cobble, or boulder substrates. Benthic, lie-in-wait invertivore. Guarding, nest-spawning speleophil (B.2.7). Maximum size 89 mm TL.

115   STONECAT—*Noturus flavus* Rafinesque. Elongate, slender body with deep caudal peduncle. Long and low adipose fin joined to or slightly separated from caudal fin. Elongate snout overhanging lower jaw, eye small. No or few weak saw-like teeth on rear edge of pectoral fin. Rear edge of caudal fin straight or with slightly rounded corners. Anal rays 15–18. Brown or tan above; light blotch on nape; yellow, slate, or olive side; pale or white below. Pelvic and anal fins dusky; pectoral, dorsal, and adipose fins dark at base. St. Lawrence, Great Lakes, Hudson Bay, Atlantic Slope in Hudson River, and Mississippi River basins from QC to AB, south to AL and west to OK. Common. Creeks, small to large rivers in riffles and runs over gravel, cobble, boulder, or bedrock substrates. Benthic, lie-in-wait invertivore. Guarding, nest-spawning speleophil (B.2.7). Maximum size 312 mm TL.

113 CHANNEL CATFISH—
Ictalurus punctatus

114 MOUNTAIN MADTOM—
Noturus eleutherus

115 STONECAT—
Noturus flavus

116 TADPOLE MADTOM—*Noturus gyrinus* (Mitchill). Thick, stout body with deep caudal peduncle. Long and low adipose fin joined to or slightly separated from caudal fin. Rounded snout, terminal mouth with equal jaws, eye small. Moderate pectoral spine without any prominent saw-like teeth on rear or front edge. Anal rays 13–18. Light tan or chocolate brown above, uniformly colored along side, yellow below; fins gray or brown. Great Lakes, Hudson Bay, and Mississippi River basins from QC to AB south to northern AL, west to OK. Common. Creeks, streams, small rivers, and lakes over detritus, sand, and gravel substrates. Benthic, particulate-feeding invertivore. Guarding, nest-spawning speleophil (B.2.7). Maximum size 110 mm TL.

117 BRINDLED MADTOM—*Noturus miurus* Jordan. Thick, stout body with deep caudal peduncle. Adipose and caudal fin broadly joined. Elongate snout overhanging lower jaw, head rounded above, eye moderate. Long pectoral spine with 5–9 prominent saw-like teeth on rear edge. Caudal fin rounded. Anal rays 13–17. Light yellow or brown above, dark mottling on sides with 4 faint saddles, black blotch on outer third of dorsal fin extends across first 3–5 rays, dark saddle under adipose fin extends to fin edge, white or yellow below; brown or black border on caudal fin. Lower Great Lakes, Ohio River, and lower Mississippi River basin west to KS, south to Gulf Coast LA and MS. Occasional. Creeks, small rivers, and lakes in riffles and flowing pools over gravel and sand substrates. Benthic invertivore. Guarding, nest-spawning speleophil (B.2.7). Maximum size 89 mm TL.

118 FRECKLED MADTOM—*Noturus nocturnus* Jordan and Gilbert. Slender, elongate body with deep caudal peduncle. Long and low adipose fin joined to or slightly separated from caudal fin. Elongate pointed snout, overhanging lower jaw, eye small. Long pectoral spine with 2–3 weak saw-like teeth on rear edge. Anal fin short, usually 16–18 rays. Light to dark brown or gray above, yellow or white below, dark fin bases, lighter toward margins, belly mostly without dark specks; anal fin with dusky black edge. Mississippi River basin from KY west to IA, south to Gulf Coast from AL to TX. Occasional. Creeks to large rivers in riffles and runs over sand and gravel near debris and tree roots and undercut banks. Benthic, lie-in-wait invertivore. Guarding, nest-spawning speleophil (B.2.7). Maximum size 67 mm TL.

116 TADPOLE MADTOM—
Noturus gyrinus

117 BRINDLED MADTOM—
Noturus miurus

118 FRECKLED MADTOM—
Noturus nocturnus

119 NORTHERN MADTOM—*Noturus stigmosus* Taylor. Thick, stout body with deep caudal peduncle. Long adipose fin, rear edge high, nearly free from caudal fin. Elongate pointed snout, overhanging lower jaw, eye moderate. Long pectoral spine with 5–10 prominent saw-like teeth on rear edge with large teeth on front edge. Straight or slightly rounded caudal fin. Anal fin rays 13–16. Yellow or medium tan above, brown or black mottling along sides, brown or black saddle extends into upper half of adipose fin but not to edge. Front edge of first saddle irregular, usually enclosing 2 large light spots to front of dorsal fin. Dark crescent-shaped band in middle of caudal fin usually extends forward across upper and lower caudal rays to caudal peduncle, another clear band adjacent to clear edge, white or yellow below; blotched or banded fins, dark band near clear edge of dorsal fin. Lake Erie and Ohio River basin from PA to KY, western TN, south to MS. Rare. Small to large rivers in fast current or in deep, fast riffles or runs over sand, gravel, cobble, or boulder substrates. Benthic, lie-in-wait invertivore. Guarding, nest-spawning speleophil (B.2.7). Maximum size 120 mm TL.

120 FLATHEAD CATFISH—*Pylodictis olivaris* (Rafinesque). Slender, compressed body with deep caudal peduncle. Short, high adipose fin with rear edge free from back and far from caudal fin. Elongate snout overhanging lower jaw, eye small on top of head, wide, flat head, lower jaw projecting beyond upper jaw (except in small young). Backward projections on each side of premaxillary tooth patch. Short pectoral spine with 6–10 prominent saw-like teeth on rear edge with large teeth on front edge. Anal fin short, rounded outline, fin rays 14–17. Rear edge of caudal fin rounded or slightly notched. Yellow to dark purple above, with black or brown mottling on back and side, chin barbels white to yellow, white to yellow below; fins mottled. Lower Great Lakes and Mississippi River basin from PA to MO, south to LA from AL to Mexico. Introduced elsewhere. Common. Large rivers, lakes, and reservoirs in pools with logs and woody debris in low to moderate gradients in fast current over sand or cobble substrates. Benthic, whole body, passive carnivore. Guarding, nest-spawning speleophil (B.2.7). Maximum size 1,410 mm TL.

SMELT FAMILY—OSMERIDAE
(*Species plate 121*)

The smelt family is circumpolar in distribution and includes 7 genera and about 11 species, all restricted to the Arctic and north temperate regions. Most members of the family are marine and anadromous. The genus *Osmerus* is sister lineage with *Allosmerus, Thaleichthys,* and *Spirinchus* and is considered derived to the more primitive members *Mallotus* and *Hypomesus* (Nelson 2006).

119   NORTHERN MADTOM—
      Noturus stigmosus

120   FLATHEAD CATFISH—
      Pylodictis olivaris

Smelts are small fishes with elongate, compressed bodies and large mouths; teeth are well or weakly developed on the mesopterygoid, glossohyal, vomer, palatine, premaxilla, maxilla, and dentary bones; spines and pelvic axillary scales are lacking; an adipose fin is present; and scales are thin and cycloid (Nelson 2006). *Osmerus mordax* has been introduced into the Great Lakes and has invaded the Ohio River through the Chicago Sanitary and Ship Canal (Mayden et al. 1987; Burr and Mayden 1980).

SALMON, TROUT, CHARR, AND WHITEFISH FAMILY—SALMONIDAE
(*SPECIES PLATES 122–139*)

The Salmonidae comprise 3 subfamilies, 11 genera, and 66 species, including the Coregoninae, Thymallinae, or Salmoninae. The family is diagnosed by a deep posterior myodome with eye musculature passing through and attaching to trunk muscles; adipose fins present; mesocoracoid present; gill membranes extending far forward; free from isthmus; pelvic axillary process present; last 3 vertebrae upturned; 11–210 pyloric caeca; 7–20 branchiostegal rays; vertebrae 50–75; parr marks on young on most species (Nelson 2006).

The subfamily Coregoninae includes the whitefishes, which contain 3 genera and 32 species. The subfamily is diagnosed by possessing fewer than 16 dorsal fin rays; scales large, fewer than 110 along lateral line; no teeth on maxilla; vomer usually small and without teeth; orbitosphenoid present; suprapreopercular absent. The Salmoninae includes the trout, salmon, and charr, which contain 7 genera and about 30 species. The subfamily is diagnosed by possessing fewer than 16 dorsal fin rays; scales small, more than 110 along lateral line; teeth on maxilla; orbitosphenoid present; suprapreopercular present. The third subfamily is the Thymallinae, which includes the grayling, containing a single genus and either 4 or 5 species. The subfamily includes 17 dorsal fin rays; teeth on maxilla; orbitosphenoid absent; suprapreopercular absent.

The whitefish are pelagic invertivores that are broadcast-spawning species in the Great Lakes. The complex flocks are difficult to understand because many of the species exhibit overlapping variation. Significant extirpation has occurred within the Great Lakes as a result of anthropogenic stressors; thus, complete understanding of species relationships may never be attained. The salmon are nest-constructing spawners that are Holarctic in distribution. They are obligate coldwater species that require well-oxygenated water. Only 2 native charr occur in Indiana; however, both are limited to Lake Michigan.

The remaining salmon species are Pacific drainage natives that were introduced intentionally. The exotic Brown trout has been extensively stocked in northern headwater streams, as were Atlantic salmon and Rainbow trout, which have been stocked in public lands for pay fishing. The Salmonidae are extremely sensitive to pollutants and habitat impacts.

KEY TO THE SALMON, TROUT, CHARR, AND WHITEFISHES OF INDIANA

1 a) Mouth large; maxillary extends behind center of eye. Teeth on lateral parts of upper and on lower jaws. Scales in lateral series more than 100. Eyelids normal...................................... 2

    b) Mouth small; maxillary does not extend beyond center of eye. Absence of teeth on lateral parts of upper and lower jaws. Scales in lateral line fewer than 100................................ ....**WHITEFISH AND CISCOES**

2 a) Anal rays 9–12, rarely 13..3

    b) Anal rays 13–20... 8

3 a) Back of body and dorsal fin with few to many small, dark, defined black and brown spots. No distinct vermiculations (like worm tracks) on back. The flattened vomer with 1 or 2 rows of teeth extending along the shaft. Posterior end of maxillary in mature specimens extending only to posterior edge of eye or slightly beyond. Scales along lateral line fewer than 140.. 4

    b) Dorsal half of body including the dorsal fin with distinct vermiculations and without distinct, small, black or brown spots. The vomer has a toothless shaft, posterior edge of maxillary in mature specimens extending past eye. Scales more than 190 along lateral line... 6

4 a) Anal fin rays 9; vomerine teeth little developed, those on the shaft of the bone few; adults with X-shaped spots on side ....**ATLANTIC SALMON**—*Salmo salar*

    b) Anal fin rays usually 10–13. Vomerine teeth well developed, those on the shaft of the bone numerous, arranged in a single zigzag and 2 alternating rows. Side usually with round spots..5

5 a) Black or brown spots large and diffuse, scarce on the caudal fin; reddish spots developed laterally, surrounded by a light border. Adipose fin orange or red-orange, without dark margins or spots. No pink or rose stripe along side of body........ ....**BROWN TROUT**—*Salmo trutta*

b) Black (or brown) spots small and distinct, well developed on caudal fin; red spots totally absent. Adipose fin olive, with black margin or spots. Broad pink to rose stripe present along side of body..............................**RAINBOW TROUT**— .... *Oncorhynchus mykiss*

6 a) Lower fins each with black stripe near leading edge. Body red spotted in live specimens. Caudal fin little forked. Mandibular pores 7–8 on each side.. ....**BROOK TROUT**—*Salvelinus fontinalis*

b) Lower fins without black stripes on leading edge. Body not red spotted in live specimens. Caudal fin strongly forked. Mandibular pores usually 9–10 on each side........................ 7

7 a) Body depth (A) into total length (b) 3.8–5.5 times, narrow. Top of head and nape visually a straight line from back of head to tip of snout ....**LAKE TROUT**—*Salvelinus namaycush namaycush*

b) Body depth (A) into total length (B), 3.1–3.8 times, robust. Laterally, top of head is a bent line from above eye and has a shortened snout...**SISCOWET**— .... *Salvelinus namaycush siscowet*

8 a) Large black spots on back and both lobes of caudal fin, largest the size of eye. Breeding males with distinct humpback. Scales in lateral series 147–205 ....**PINK SALMON**—*Oncorhynchus gorbuscha*

b) Spots on back and caudal fin small, largest size of pupil of eye. Breeding males without humpback. Scales in lateral line 112–165.. 9

9 a) Small black spots on both lobes of caudal fin. Anal fin rays 14–19. Entire mouth, including gums, black............................. .... **CHINOOK SALMON**—*Oncorhynchus tshawytscha*

b) Small black spots, when present on caudal fin, on upper lobe only. Anal fin rays 11–15. Gums white...................................... ....**COHO SALMON**—*Oncorhynchus kisutch*

KEY TO THE WHITEFISH AND CISCOES OF INDIANA

1 a) Single flap between nostrils. Gill rakers fewer than 22..........
........**ROUND WHITEFISH**—*Prosopium cylindraceum*

  b) Two flaps between nostrils. Gill rakers usually more than 22... 2

2 a) Premaxillaries point backward, giving front of snout a rounded profile. Upper jaw length usually contained 3 or more times in head. Mouth subterminal. Gill rakers 19–33 ....**LAKE WHITEFISH**—*Coregonus clupeaformis*

  b) Premaxillaries point forward, giving front of snout a pointed profile. Upper jaw seldom contained more than 3 times in head length. Mouth terminal. Gill rakers usually more than 31 3

3 a) Tip of lower jaw extending beyond upper jaw..................... 4

  b) Lower jaw equal to or shorter than upper jaw..................... 6

4 a) Lower jaw stout (ramus thick), no pigment; symphyseal knob usually absent. Gill rakers, medium in length, 36–43 (33–46) ....**LONGJAW CISCO**—*Coregonus alpenae*[*]

  b) Lower jaw frail (ramus thin), medium pigment; symphyseal knob present..5

5 a) Gill rakers, medium length, 36–41 (34–45); gill rakers about same length as gill filaments. Paired fins long, pelvics usually reaching to anus or beyond. Body deeper anterior than medially. Eye very large, equal or nearly equal to snout length ....
....**KIYI**—*Coregonus kiyi*

  b) Gill rakers long, longer than longest gill filament, and usually 41–44 (40–47). Paired fins long, but pelvic fins seldom reach anus. Body deepest medially. Eye large but less than length of snout.......................... **BLOATER**—*Coregonus hoyi*

6 a) Lower jaw oblique and equal to upper jaw; posterior end of upper jaw usually reaching anterior edge of pupil 7

  b) Lower jaw underslung (ventral) and usually shorter than upper jaw; posterior end of upper jaw often reaching middle of pupil.. 9

7 a) Gill rakers usually fewer than 33...
.....................**DEEPWATER CISCO**—*Coregonus johannae*[*]

  b) Gill rakers usually 46–50... 8

8 a) Body deepest medially. Lower jaw weak; symphyseal knob present. Body elongate and almost round in cross section ... .**CISCO** or **LAKE HERRING**—*Coregonus artedii*

  b) Body deepest anterior. Lower jaw stout; symphyseal knob absent. Body broad and very deep.. ....**BLACKFIN CISCO**—*Coregonus nigripinnis**

9 a) Snout long, snout into head length usually 3.3–3.6. Premaxillaries at angle of 60–70° with horizontal. Gill rakers usually 38–42 and approximately equal to length of gill filaments.

121 RAINBOW SMELT—*Osmerus mordax* (Mitchill). Slender, elongate, laterally compressed body. Snout pointed, large mouth, upper jaw reaches middle of eye or beyond, eye small. Two large canine teeth in roof of mouth, large teeth on tongue. Dorsal fin origin above or in front of pelvic fin origin. Gill rakers on first arch 28–32. Incomplete lateral line, lateral line scales 62–72. Anal fin rays 11–16. Caudal fin forked. Olive above, blue or pink iridescence on silver side, usually a silver stripe along side, dark specks on upper sides, silver or white below; fins dusky. Introduced. Holarctic. Atlantic drainages from NF to DE, Great Lakes, and Pacific drainages. Common. Cool lakes, medium to large rivers and nearshore coastal waters, midwater pelagic schooling species. Anadromous. Benthic and drift, whole body, carnivore. Non-guarding, open substrate phytolithophil (A.1.4). Maximum size 250 mm TL.

WHITEFISH SUBFAMILY, COREGONINAE

122 LONGJAW CISCO—*Coregonus alpenae* (Koelz). Slender, elongate, laterally compressed body. Greatest depth in the middle of the body, greatest body depth 3.8–4.3 times into TL. Gill rakers medium long, longest equal to longest gill filaments 36–43. Dorsal fin origin over or slightly in front of pelvic fin origin. Dorsal fin rays 10–11, anal fin rays 11–12 (9–13). Lateral line scales 78–85. Silver above, pink or blue iridescence on sides strongest above lateral line, silver or white below. Great Lakes endemic species including Lakes Huron, Michigan, and Erie. Extinct. Extinction of Longjaw cisco was a result of overfishing, pollution, and food chain disruption. The Longjaw cisco may not be a separate species but a distinctive population of large-bodied individuals of Shortjaw cisco (*Coregonus zenithicus*). Deep water usually at depths of 100 m or more. Pelagic schooling species. Particulate-feeding planktivore. Non-guarding, open substrate pelagophil (A.1.1). Maximum size 380 mm TL.

Paired fin medium in length ....
.... **SHORTJAW CISCO**—*Coregonus zenithicus**

b) Snout short, snout into head length usually 3.4–4.0. Premax-
illaries at large angle, often vertical (90°) with horizontal.
Gill rakers usually 34–38 and shorter than gill filaments.
Paired fins short ....
.... **SHORTNOSE CISCO**—*Coregonus reighardi**

*This species is either extremely rare or considered extirpated from
Indiana's Lake Michigan coastal waters.

121 RAINBOW SMELT—
Osmerus mordax

122 LONGJAW CISCO—
Coregonus alpenae

123   CISCO or LAKE HERRING—*Coregonus artedii* Lesueur. Slender, elongate, laterally compressed body. Body almost round in cross section, deepest in middle. Lower jaw equal to or slightly projecting beyond upper jaw, upper jaw extends to front of pupil. Symphyseal knob at tip of lower jaw. Pelvic fins far back on body, distance from snout to pelvic fin origin equal to distance from pelvic fin origin to caudal fin. Gill rakers long, slender, usually 46–50 on first arch. Lateral line scales 63–94. Dark blue to green above, silver side; fins clear with dusky black-tipped pelvic fins. Canada and Great Lakes, Hudson Bay, Arctic, and upper Mississippi River basins. Rare. Open waters of lakes and large rivers and coastal pelagic waters. Pelagic schooling species. Particulate-feeding planktivore. Non-guarding, open substrate pelagophil (A.1.1). Maximum size 500 mm TL.

124   LAKE WHITEFISH—*Coregonus clupeaformis* (Mitchill). Slender, elongate, laterally compressed body. Greatest body depth half the distance from head to dorsal fin origin. Snout rounded, upper jaw overhangs lower jaw, just barely projecting to front of eye. Dorsal fin origin over or slightly in front of pelvic fin origin. Gill rakers on first arch 26–33. Lateral line scales 70–97. Dark brown to navy blue above, silver side, silver or white below; dorsal, anal, and caudal fins with black stripes. Great Lakes, Arctic, and Hudson Bay. Common. Open waters of lakes and large rivers. Pelagic schooling species. Particulate-feeding planktivore. Non-guarding, open substrate lithopelagophils (A.1.2). Maximum size 798 mm TL.

125   BLOATER—*Coregonus hoyi* (Gill). Slender, elongate, compressed body. Pointed snout, lower jaw projecting slightly beyond upper jaw. Upper jaw less dusky, small eye (usually less than snout length). Body deepest at middle, pelvic fin seldom reaching anus. Gill rakers longer than longest gill filament, usually 40–47 on first arch. Dark brown above, silver side silver or white below; caudal fin dusky. Great Lakes (except Erie) endemic and Lake Nipigon (probably extirpated). Rare. Large lakes generally at depths greater than 100 m. Pelagic schooling species. Particulate-feeding planktivore. Non-guarding, open substrate lithopelagophils (A.1.2). Maximum size 360 mm TL.

126   DEEPWATER CISCO—*Coregonus johannae* (Wagner). Slender, elongate, compressed body. Pointed snout, lower jaw moderately stout, about equal to upper jaw. Gill rakers short, longest generally shorter than the longest gill filaments 27–32. Lateral line scales 80–90. Pale green above, sides pink to purple iridescent above lateral line with silver side, white below. Former Great Lakes endemic occurring in Lakes Michigan and Huron. Extinct. Open waters of large lakes at depths 55–165 m. Pelagic schooling species. Particulate-feeding planktivore. Non-guarding, open substrate lithopelagophils (A.1.2). Maximum size 360 mm TL.

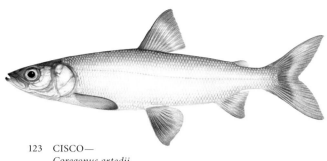

123 CISCO—
Coregonus artedii

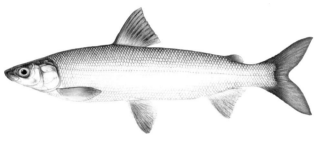

124 LAKE WHITEFISH—
Coregonus clupeaformis

125 BLOATER—
Coregonus hoyi

126 DEEPWATER CISCO—
Coregonus johannae

127 KIYI—*Coregonus kiyi* (Koelz). Slender, elongate, compressed body. Pointed snout, lower jaw projecting slightly beyond upper jaw, symphyseal knob at tip of lower jaw. Large eye nearly equal to snout length. Long paired fins, pelvic fin usually reaches to anus or beyond. Body deepest beneath nape. Silver with faint pink to purple iridescence, silver below; dorsal and caudal fins with black edges. Great Lakes endemic. Open water at depths greater than 100–180 m. Pelagic schooling species. Particulate-feeding planktivore. Non-guarding, open substrate lithopelagophils (A.1.2). Maximum size 300 mm TL.

128 BLACKFIN CISCO—*Coregonus nigripinnis* (Gill). Slender, elongate, compressed body. Dusky upper jaw. Stout lower jaw equal to upper jaw, reaches to front of pupil, lacks symphyseal knob. Greatest body depth under nape. Gill rakers long, usually longer than gill filaments with 46–50 on first arch. Blue-green to blue-black above, silver side, silver below; usually dusky blue-black fins. Great Lakes and Lake Nipigon endemic. Rare. Extirpated from Lakes Michigan and Huron. Open water at depths 90–160 m. Pelagic schooling species. Particulate-feeding planktivore. Non-guarding, open substrate lithopelagophils (A.1.2). Maximum size 420 mm TL.

129 SHORTNOSE CISCO—*Coregonus reighardi* (Koelz). Slender, elongate, only slightly compressed body. Greatest body depth anterior to dorsal fin going 3.9–4.5 times into TL. Snout short, jaw extending to about middle of pupil. Lower jaw stout, usually shorter and included within upper jaw. Lateral line scales 72–81. Gill rakers short, longest shorter than longest gill filament, 34–38. Pale green to blue-green above, pink iridescence on silver side, silver or white below. Great Lakes endemic. Extirpated. Open water at depths between 37 and 110 m. Pelagic schooling species. Particulate-feeding planktivore. Non-guarding, open substrate lithopelagophils (A.1.2). Maximum size 300 mm TL.

130 SHORTJAW CISCO—*Coregonus zenithicus* (Jordan and Evermann). Slender, elongate, laterally compressed body. Greatest body depth at front of dorsal fin origin going 4.2–4.8 times into TL. Lower jaw stout with no symphyseal knob, usually shorter than upper jaw. Gill rakers moderately long with the longest equal in length to gill filaments 38–42. Lateral line scales 74–84. Dark blue-green to pale green above, sides silver, silver or white below; dorsal fin margin and distal half of pectoral and caudal fins smoky to black, sometimes black on pelvic and anal fins. Great Lakes, Great Slave Lake, and Hudson Bay. Extirpated. Open water at depths between 20 and 180 m. Pelagic schooling species. Particulate-feeding planktivore. Non-guarding, open substrate lithopelagophils (A.1.2). Maximum size 450 mm TL.

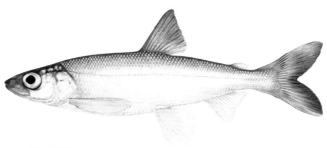

127 KIYI—
Coregonus kiyi kiyi

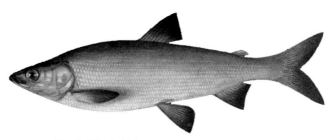

128 BLACKFIN CISCO—
Coregonus nigripinnis

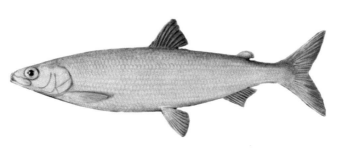

129 SHORTNOSE CISCO—
Coregonus reighardi

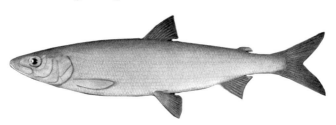

130 SHORTJAW CISCO—
Coregonus zenithicus

131 ROUND WHITEFISH—*Prosopium cylindraceum* (Pennant). Elongate, cylindrical body, not laterally compressed. Greatest body depth halfway between head and dorsal fin origin. Pointed snout, single flap between nostrils, eye moderate less than snout length, head short 4.9–5.6 times into TL. Gill rakers 16–18. Lateral line scales 83–96. Dark brown to bronze above, sides brown, young with 2 or more longitudinal rows of dark spots on sides with row of 10 or more spots along midlateral; paired and anal fins orange. Arctic, Hudson Bay, and Great Lakes. Rare. Open shallow water at depths 7–22 m. Pelagic schooling species. Invertivore. Non-guarding, open substrate lithopelagophils (A.1.2). Maximum size 305 mm TL.

SALMON, TROUT, CHARR
SUBFAMILY, SALMONINAE

132 PINK SALMON—*Oncorhynchus gorbuscha* (Walbaum). Body streamlined, laterally compressed. Eye small, snout greatly elongate, mouth terminal, maxillary extending beyond eye. Lateral line scales 147–205. Gill rakers 24–35. Dorsal fin rays 10–15, anal fin rays 13–19. Pharyngeal teeth 95–224. Metallic blue or blue-green above. Large, mostly oval black spots on back and both lobes of caudal fin. Male with hooked jaw. Young without parr marks. Arctic and Pacific drainages. Introduced into Great Lakes. Occasional. Anadromous, ocean and coastal streams of Great Lakes. Invertivore/carnivore. Non-guarding, brood-hiding lithophil (A.2.3). Maximum size 610 mm TL.

133 COHO SALMON—*Oncorhynchus kisutch* (Walbaum). Body streamlined, laterally compressed. Eye small, snout greatly elongate, mouth large terminal, maxillary extending beyond eye. Lateral line scales 112–148. Gill rakers 18–25. Dorsal fin rays 9–12, anal fin rays 12–17. Steel blue or green above, back and upper sides with black spots, side silver, white below; base of dorsal fin and upper lobe of caudal fin with small dark spots. Breeding males with dark blue-green head, lower gum usually pale or gray. Young blue-green on back, silver side with 8–12 narrow parr marks, caudal fin and most of anal fin orange. Arctic and Pacific drainages from AK to CA. Introduced into Great Lakes. Common. Anadromous, ocean and coastal streams of Great Lakes. Invertivore/carnivore. Non-guarding, brood-hiding lithophil (A.2.3). Maximum size 650 mm TL.

131 ROUND WHITEFISH—
Prosopium cylindraceum

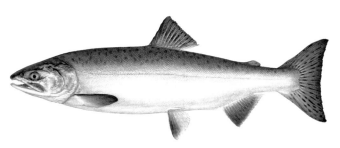

132 PINK SALMON—
Oncorhynchus gorbuscha

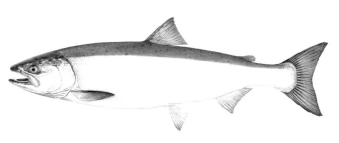

133 COHO SALMON—
Oncorhynchus kisutch

134 RAINBOW TROUT (STEELHEAD)—*Oncorhynchus mykiss* (Walbaum). Body streamlined, laterally compressed. Eye small, snout elongate, mouth large terminal, maxillary extending beyond eye. Lateral line scales 100–150. Gill rakers 16–22. Dorsal fin rays 10–12, anal fin rays 8–12. Blue, blue-green, brown above and top of head, silver sides, pink or rose stripe, many small dark black spots above lateral line, white below; dorsal and caudal fins with rows of dark spots, adipose fin with black border and a few spots. Breeding males with hook jaws, blue and silver sides, only faintly spotted. Young blue to silver, white on sides and below, 5–10 dark marks on back between head and dorsal fin and 5–10 dark oval parr marks, spaces between parr marks wider than the parr marks, some dark spots above but not below lateral line, black border of adipose fin with either single or no breaks, dorsal fin with a white to orange edge and a dark leading edge. Arctic and Pacific drainages. Introduced into Great Lakes. Common. Anadromous, ocean and coastal streams of Great Lakes. Invertivore/carnivore. Non-guarding, brood-hiding lithophil (A.2.3). Maximum size 1,000 mm TL.

135 CHINOOK SALMON—*Oncorhynchus tshawytscha* (Walbaum). Body streamlined, laterally compressed. Eye small, snout elongate, mouth large terminal, maxillary extending beyond eye. Lateral line scales 100–150. Gill rakers 16–22. Dorsal fin rays 10–12, anal fin rays 8–12. Blue, blue-green, brown above and top of head, silver sides, pink or rose stripe, many small dark black spots above lateral line, white below; dorsal and caudal fins with rows of dark spots, adipose fin with black border and a few spots. Breeding males with hook jaws, blue and silver sides, only faintly spotted. Young blue to silver, white on sides and below, 5–10 dark marks on back between head and dorsal fin and 5–10 dark oval parr marks, spaces between parr marks wider than the parr marks, some dark spots above but not below lateral line, black border of adipose fin with either single or no breaks, dorsal fin with a white to orange edge and a dark leading edge. Arctic and Pacific drainages. Introduced into Great Lakes. Common. Anadromous, ocean and coastal streams of Great Lakes. Invertivore/carnivore. Non-guarding, brood-hiding lithophil (A.2.3). Maximum size 1,000 mm TL.

136 ATLANTIC SALMON—*Salmo salar* Linnaeus. Elongate, slender, laterally compressed body. Upper jaw reaches below middle of eye. Hooked lower jaw. Lateral line scales 109–121. Slightly forked caudal fin. Branchiostegal rays 12, dorsal fin rays 11. Brown, green, or bronze above, black spots on head and body, 2–3 large spots on gill cover, sides darker bronze or yellow, 8–11 narrow parr marks along side of young, red spots between each pair; no white edge on pelvic and anal fins, caudal fin unspotted. Atlantic coast drainage. Introduced in Indiana. Occasional. Anadromous, small rivers and headwater streams. Invertivore/carnivore. Non-guarding, brood-hiding lithophil (A.2.3). Maximum size 900 mm TL.

134 RAINBOW TROUT—
Oncorhynchus mykiss

135 CHINOOK SALMON—
Oncorhynchus tshawytscha

136 ATLANTIC SALMON—
Salmo salar

137   BROWN TROUT—*Salmo trutta* Linnaeus. Slender, laterally compressed body. Upper jaw extends to center of eye. Breeding male with hooked lower jaw. Lateral line scales 120–130. Branchiostegal rays 10, dorsal fin rays 9. Caudal fin edge straight. Olive to dark brown above, silver sheen on yellow-brown side often with X marks, red and black spots on head and body, many spots on gill cover, bold black spots on head, back, dorsal, and adipose fin extending below lateral line on side (spots usually surrounded by pale halos), few red spots along lateral line, rust red spots on side, white to yellow below; adipose fin usually orange or red, caudal fin unspotted or faintly spotted, no white edge on pelvic or anal fins. Young with 9–14 short, narrow parr marks along side. Alien. Introduced from Europe, northern Africa, and Western Asia. Common. Coolwater headwater streams, cold lakes, and Lake Michigan and coastal streams. Invertivore/carnivore. Non-guarding, brood-hiding lithophil (A.2.3). Maximum size 826 mm TL.

138   BROOK TROUT—*Salvelinus fontinalis* (Mitchill). Slender, elongate, laterally compressed body. Caudal fin slightly forked to straight. Gill rakers 14–22 with marginal teeth on first gill arch. Olive to black above, light wavy lines or blotches on back and dorsal fin, blue halos around pink or red spots on side; black lines on caudal fin, black line behind white edge on red lower fins. Breeding male is brilliant orange or red below, black below. Young with 8–10 regularly arranged parr marks on side. Hudson Bay, Atlantic Slope, Great Lakes, and Mississippi River basins from Appalachian Mountains to MN. Rare. Coldwater headwater streams and nearshore Great Lakes and coastal streams. Invertivore/carnivore. Non-guarding, brood-hiding lithophil (A.2.3). Maximum size 450 mm TL

139   LAKE TROUT—*Salvelinus namaycush* (Walbaum). Body elongate, rounded. Mouth extends past eye when closed. Gill rakers 12–24. Lateral line scales 185–210. Deeply forked caudal fin. Two forms exist, including the native lean form from Lake Michigan and a fat form from deep waters of Lake Superior called the siscowet. A hybrid form between Lake trout and Brook trout called a splake has also been widely introduced. Olive to black above, many small cream or yellow-colored bean-shaped spots on dark green to gray head, body, dorsal, and caudal fins. Narrow white edge on orange-red lower fins. Breeding male with lateral stripe. Young with 7–12 narrow often interrupted parr marks. Arctic, Hudson Bay, and Great Lakes basin. Occasional. Deep waters of large lakes over rubble and cobble substrates. Invertivore/carnivore. Non-guarding, brood-hiding lithophil (A.2.3). Maximum size 1,260 mm TL.

137   BROWN TROUT—
       Salmo trutta

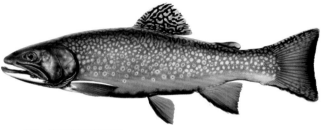

138   BROOK TROUT—
       Salvelinus fontinalis

139   LAKE TROUT—
       Salvelinus namaycush namaycush

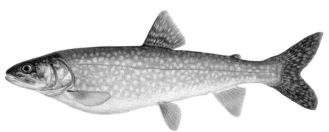

       SISCOWET—
       Salvelinus namaycush siscowet

PIKE FAMILY—ESOCIDAE
(SPECIES PLATES 140–142)

The pike are Holarctic and circumpolar in distribution. Five species belong to the family, with single species being circumpolar, another endemic to Siberia, and 3 others endemic to eastern North America (Scott and Crossman 1973). Esocidae are elongate, laterally compressed fishes that possess a forked tail; dorsal and anal fins set far back on the body, equal to subequal in size, and placed opposite each other. Head large; snout elongate, flat, and shaped like a duck's bill. Jaw articulated behind the posterior edge of orbit. Teeth on jaws, large and prominent. Large patches of cardiform teeth on vomer, palatines, and tongue. Inframandibular present, in contrast to mudminnows. Gill rakers reduced to patches of sharp denticles. Pectoral fins low on body; pelvic fins abdominal. Mesocoracoid absent from pectoral girdle. The pikes are phystostomous, but there is no known ability to breathe atmospheric oxygen.

The genus contains 5 freshwater species, including *Esox reicherti* Dybowski from Siberia, *E. lucius,* which is circumpolar in distribution, and *E. masquinongy, E. niger,* and *E. americanus,* which are found in eastern North America. Crossman (1978) summarized the taxonomy of the genus, and Nelson (2006) provided a phylogenetic analysis. Nelson (2006) recognized 2 subgenera, including *Esox* s.s., which includes *E. lucius, E. reicherti,* and *E. masquinongy,* and *Kenzoa* Jordan and Evermann, which contains the pickerels *Esox americanus* and *E. niger.* Three species inhabit Indiana; however, 2 subspecies of *Esox masquinongy* are known from the Great Lakes and Ohio River basin.

KEY TO THE PIKES OF INDIANA

1 a) Sensory pores on undersurface of jaw, 4 on each side (rarely 3–5). Cheek and opercle fully scaled. Prominent dark teardrop present .... **GRASS PICKEREL**—*Esox americanus*

  b) Sensory pores on undersurface of jaw usually 5 or more on each side. Cheek and opercle not fully scaled. Teardrop either absent or faint 2

2 a) Sensory pores on undersurface of jaw, 5 on each side (rarely 4–6). Cheek fully scaled; only upper portion of opercle scaled. Branchiostegal rays 14–16 on each side. Body color a dark background color with horizontal rows of light-colored, slanted ovals in adults ....
  ....**NORTHERN PIKE**—*Esox lucius*

  b) Sensory pores on undersurface of jaw, 6–9 on each side. Only upper portions of cheek and opercle scaled. Body a light background color with dark spots or narrow vertical bars...
  ....**MUSKELLUNGE**—*Esox masquinongy*

MUDMINNOW FAMILY—UMBRIDAE
(SPECIES PLATE 143)

The mudminnows are a group of primitive Salmoniform fishes that occur in both North America and Europe. In North America, 3 genera and 4 species are recognized. The mudminnows are most closely related to the pikes (Nelson 2006).

The mudminnows are small fish, characterized by unpored lateral line scales; dorsal and anal fins situated far back on the body; and a rounded caudal fin preceded by a vertical bar of dark pigment. They bear a slight resemblance to topminnows but lack the protractile jaws characteristic of that family. They have been variously classified and are now considered close relatives of the esocids. Mudminnows have a functional duct from the pharynx to the swim bladder and are capable of breathing atmospheric oxygen.

140 GRASS PICKEREL—*Esox americanus vermiculatus* Gmelin. Elongate, fusiform, nearly cylindrical body. Snout elongate, duck-like, fully scaled cheek and opercle, terminal mouth, eye small. Short dorsal and anal fins positioned far back on body. Dorsal fin origin slightly in front of pelvic fin origin. Caudal fin forked. Lateral line scales 92–118, branchiostegal rays 11–13, submandibular pores 4 (rarely 3–5). Dark olive to brown above, head with black suborbital bar obliquely descending from eye, 15–36 dark green to brown wavy bars along side, white to golden below; fins clear, yellow, or dusky. Atlantic Slope, Great Lakes, and Mississippi River basins, west from NE to FL. Common. Lakes, marshes, backwaters of pools in creeks, streams, and small rivers in basic-gradient waters. Whole body, ambush carnivore. Non-guarding, open substrate phytophil (A.1.5). Maximum size 381 mm TL.

141 NORTHERN PIKE—*Esox lucius* Linnaeus. Elongate, fusiform, slightly compressed cylindrical body. Snout elongate, duck-like, cheek scaled and partly scaled opercle (upper part only), terminal mouth, eye small. Short dorsal and anal fins positioned far back on body. Dorsal fin origin slightly in front of pelvic fin origin. Caudal fin forked. Lateral line scales 105–148, branchiostegal rays 13–16, submandibular pores 5–6. Olive, gray, to black back, no suborbital bar, rows of yellow or white bean-shaped spots, yellow or white wavy bars on young appearing to be dark bars on a light-colored body; white below; usually with black spots on all fins except pectoral fins, median fins either red, yellow, or dusky green. Holarctic. Atlantic, Arctic, Great Lakes, and Mississippi River basins, also occurring in Europe. Occasional. Clear vegetated lakes, pools and backwaters of creeks, and small to large rivers. Whole body, ambush carnivore. Non-guarding, open substrate phytophil (A.1.5). Maximum size 1,333 mm TL.

142 MUSKELLUNGE—*Esox masquinongy* Mitchill. Elongate, fusiform, slightly compressed cylindrical body. Snout elongate, duck-like, cheek and opercle partly scaled (upper parts only not extending onto cheek or lower opercle), terminal mouth, eye small. Short dorsal and anal fins positioned far back on body. Dorsal fin origin slightly in front of pelvic fin origin. Caudal fin forked. Lateral line scales 130–167, branchiostegal rays 16–19, submandibular pores 6–10. Dark spots, blotches, or bars on light yellow-green back, no suborbital bar, light yellow-green side, cream to white below with small brown to gray blotches; silver below. Great Lakes–St. Lawrence River, Hudson Bay, and Mississippi River basins, west to IA, south to GA. Two subspecies are recognized in IN. *E. m. masquinongy* Mitchill, Great Lakes muskellunge, formerly occurred in Lake Michigan and is considered extinct, while *E. m. ohioensis* Mitchill, Ohio River muskellunge, formerly occurred throughout the Ohio River drainage and is only seen in the Little Blue River. The species is rare. Clear vegetated lakes, pools and backwaters of creeks, and small to large rivers. Whole body, ambush carnivore. Non-guarding, open substrate phytophil (A.1.5). Maximum size 1,638 mm TL.

140 GRASS PICKEREL—
Esox americanus vermiculatus

141 NORTHERN PIKE—
Esox lucius

142 MUSKELLUNGE—GREAT LAKES MUSKELLUNGE—
Esox masquinongy masquinongy

OHIO RIVER MUSKELLUNGE—
Esox masquinongy ohioensis

TROUT-PERCH FAMILY—PERCOPSIDAE
(SPECIES PLATE 144)

The family includes 2 living species and 3 extinct species that are endemic to North America. The Percopsiformes include the trout-perch, pirate perch, and cavefishes. This relationship is a paraphyletic grouping that does not resolve the relationship of the trout-perch. The Percopsidae are among the most primitive of the Percopsiformes (Patterson 1982; Nelson 2006) and are evolutionarily intermediate among bony fish.

Members of the genus possess an adipose fin and the head is scaleless, pleisiomorphic characters typical of several less-

143 CENTRAL MUDMINNOW—*Umbra limi* Linnaeus. Elongate, cylindrical body. Short dorsal fin set far back on body in front of anal fin origin. Dorsal fin rays 13–17. Pectoral fin small with 11–16 rays. Anal fin base about half length of dorsal fin base with 7–10 rays. Small pelvic fin with 6–7 rays. Round caudal fins. No lateral line, lateral scales large 30–37. Green to brown above, black above and on side, black bar on caudal fin base, as many as 14 dark brown bars occasionally on side, white or yellow below; fins brown without any spots. Breeding male with iridescent blue-green anal and pelvic fins. Great Lakes, Hudson Bay, and Mississippi River basin from OH to TN, west to AR. Abundant. Marshes, lakes, and quiet pools of streams associated with vegetation and mud substrates. Benthic and drift invertivore. Guarding, substrate-choosing phytophil (B.1.4). Maximum size 117 mm TL.

144 TROUT-PERCH—*Percopsis omiscomaycus* (Walbaum). Fairly deep body, slender caudal peduncle. Long, pointed snout. Large eye high on head. Large head flattened below, pearl organs on lower jaw and edge of cheek, no preopercle spines. Dorsal fin origin over pelvic fin origin. Complete lateral line, caudal fin forked. Transparent body, yellow to tan above with silver flecks, 7–12 dusky spots on back, upper side, and side, transparent or white below; fins clear. Atlantic, Arctic, Great Lakes, and Mississippi River basins, west to MO, and south to VA. Rare. Lakes, deep flowing pools of creeks, and small rivers usually over sand. Benthic invertivore. Nonguarding, open substrate lithophil (A.1.3). Maximum size 152 mm TL.

advanced families. Fin spines and ctenoid scales, which are present in other percoid fishes, occur in percopsids. Fin spines are weak in extant percopsids, and the position of the paired fins is intermediate between those of lower and more advanced fish species.

Trout-perch are a group of small fish that have little economic or management significance. In the Great Lakes, the species is an important diet item for walleye, Northern pike, burbot, Lake trout, Brook trout, sauger, Yellow perch, and Freshwater drum. It provides an important link in the transfer of energy from lower to upper trophic levels.

143   CENTRAL MUDMINNOW—
Umbra limi

144   TROUT-PERCH—
Percopsis omiscomaycus

PIRATE PERCH FAMILY—APHREDODERIDAE
(SPECIES PLATE 145)

The pirate perch is a monotypic family that is endemic to eastern North America. The family is a sister group to the cavefishes. The 3 Percopsiform families, including the Aphredoderidae, Amblyopsidae, and Percopsidae, are positioned intermediately between the lower and higher bony fishes and are collectively placed in the superorder Paracanthopterygii (Nelson 2006). Two subspecies are recognized, including an Atlantic Coast form and a Great Lakes–Mississippi River basin form.

CAVEFISH FAMILY—AMBLYOPSIDAE
(SPECIES PLATES 146–147)

The cavefishes are 1 of 3 families that live a subterranean life. It is a small family of 5 genera, 4 of which are monotypic, and 6 highly specialized fishes (Nelson 2006). The Amblyopsidae are diagnosed by a reduction in pigment, jugular position of the anus and urogenital openings, absence or reduction of eyes, lack of pelvic fins, minute scales, and an elaborate sensory system with many papillose sensory structures over the head and body, and without a lateral line. All species have flat, naked heads, relatively large mouths, and moderately elongate bodies (Nelson 2006).

The family is confined to caves, springs, and swamps of unglaciated south-central and southeastern United States. The distribution of cavefishes is closely correlated with limestone formations and dispersal is independent of surface waters.

145 PIRATE PERCH—*Aphredoderus sayanus* (Gilliams). Short, deep body. Large mouth, lower jaw protruding, large head. Ctenoid scales on head and body. Single dorsal containing both spines and rays. Pelvic fins thoracic. No or incomplete lateral line. The anus and urogenital opening positioned normally as juvenile but migrates forward beneath throat of adult. Square, slightly notched caudal fin. Grayish-purple to black above, black teardrop, black bar on caudal fin base, often speckled with black, yellow-white below; fins dusky to black. Atlantic, Gulf Slope, Great Lakes, to Mississippi River. Common. Swamps, vegetated backwaters, ponds, lakes, creeks, and small to large rivers. Invertivore. Bearing, external gill chamber brooder (C.1.4). Maximum size 144 mm TL.

KEY TO THE CAVEFISHES OF INDIANA

1 a) Sensory papillae on tail fin in 4–6 rows; dorsal fin rays usually 7, often 8............................ **NORTHERN CAVEFISH**—...*Amblyopsis spelaea*

   b) Sensory papillae on tail in 2 rows; dorsal fin rays 8 or 9................ **SOUTHERN CAVEFISH**—*Typhlichthys subterraneus*

BURBOT FAMILY—LOTIDAE
(*Species plate 148*)

Formerly the Lotidae was included as a part of the Gadidae in the subfamily Lotinae (Nelson 2006). The revised family is comprised of 6 genera with 23 species. The burbot is the only freshwater representative of this group. The family distribution is Holarctic, found in the northern parts of Eurasia and North America.

The group includes 1 or 2 dorsal fins and 1 anal fin, chin barbel always present but no barbels on snout, caudal fin rounded, egg with oil globule. The burbot of North America was described as more than a single species, but by the late nineteenth century all forms, including the Eurasian burbot, were considered *Lota lota*. Three subspecies were designated, including *L. l. lota* from Eurasia, *L. l. leptura* from eastern Siberia and northwestern North America, and *L. l. lacustris* (= *maculosa*) from central and northeastern North America (Hubbs and Schultz 1941). The division was based on characters that appeared to be clinal with broad areas of intergradation. Further systematic study of this group is warranted.

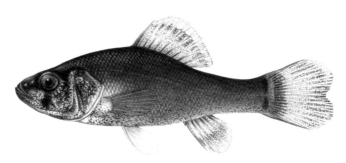

145   PIRATE PERCH—
      Aphredoderus sayanus

146 NORTHERN CAVEFISH—*Amblyopsis spelaea* DeKay. Club-shaped body, slightly lateral compressed. Short, rounded snout. Large, broad head, no eyes (vestigial eye tissues under skin). Extremely small pelvic fins (rarely absent). Caudal fin with 4–6 rows of papillae. Dorsal fin rays 9–11, anal fin rays 9–10, caudal fin rays 11–13. Pink-white over entire body. Karst regions of south-central IN south to northern KY and Mammoth Cave. Rare. Subterranean waters, karst streams, and cave springs. Insectivore. Bearing, external gill chamber brooder (C.1.4). Maximum size 105 mm TL.

147 SOUTHERN CAVEFISH—*Typhlichthys subterraneus* Girard. Club-shaped body, moderately compressed laterally. Long, pointed snout. Large, broad head, no eyes (vestigial eye tissues under skin). No pelvic fins. Caudal fin with 0–2 rows of papillae. Dorsal fin rays 8–9 (7–10), anal fin rays 9–11, caudal fin rays 10–15. Pink-white coloration over entire body. East of Mississippi River from southern IN to northern AL, Ozark Plateau in southern MO to northeast AR. Rare. Subterranean waters. Insectivore. Bearing, external gill chamber brooder (C.1.4). Maximum size 78 mm TL.

148 BURBOT—*Lota lota* (Linnaeus). Long, slender body, strongly compressed posteriorly. Long, pointed snout, long thin barbel at tip of chin. Large, wide head, eye small. Two dorsal fins, first short with 8–16 rays and second long with 60–80 rays. Long anal fin, small pelvic fin located in front of pectoral fin. Scales very small and embedded. Light brown to yellow above, brown to black mottling on back and side, tan to light brown below; second dorsal and anal fins with dark edge. Holarctic including Arctic, Hudson Bay, Great Lakes, Atlantic, Pacific, and Atlantic Slope basins. Occasional. Deep, cold waters to depths of 90 m of large lakes and rivers. Whole body, stalking carnivore. Non-guarding, open substrate lithopelagophil (A.1.2). Maximum size 1,043 mm TL.

146   NORTHERN CAVEFISH—
       Amblyopsis spelaea

147   SOUTHERN CAVEFISH—
       Typhlichthys subterraneus

148   BURBOT—
       Lota lota

TOPMINNOW FAMILY—FUNDULIDAE
(*Species plates 149–153*)

The Fundulidae is a New World family of killifish comprised of 4 genera. The family is distributed from the lowlands of North and Middle America from southeast Canada to the Yucatan, including Bermuda and Cuba (Nelson 2006). The killifishes and topminnows are represented by about 40 species, 29 occurring in freshwaters of North America (Mayden et al. 1992).

The genus *Fundulus* is characterized by an elongate body with conical jaw teeth, usually in more than a single series. Gill openings are unrestricted, so that the upper part is not adnate to the shoulder girdle. The dorsal fin origin is vertically aligned so that it may be anterior, over, or posterior to the origin of the anal fin (Wiley 1986).

The topminnows are surface-dwelling species that occupy the margins of streams, ponds, lakes, and wetlands (Foster 1967). With their flattened dorsums and upturned mouths, they are well adapted to the lifestyle of feeding at the surface. They are often seen lying motionless near the surface with only their pectoral fins rotating for stability and their caudal fins bent. The species are sexually dimorphic and males of some species are extremely colorful.

KEY TO THE TOPMINNOWS OF INDIANA

1. a) Dorsal fin rays 13–16; anal fin rays 14–18 .... **NORTHERN STUDFISH**—*Fundulus catenatus*

   b) Dorsal fin rays 7–13; anal fin rays 10–13 2

2. a) Dorsal fin origin distinctly in advance of anal fin origin. Lateral series of scales 39–43. No broad dark lateral stripe or dark blotch under eye .... **BANDED KILLIFISH**—*Fundulus diaphanus*

   b) Dorsal fin origin distinctly behind anal fin origin. Lateral series of scales fewer than 38. Either broad, dark lateral stripe or dark blotch under eye present 3

3 a) Broad, dark lateral stripe present; no thin, dotted horizontal stripes. No dark blotch ("teardrop") under eye. Body depth into SL generally greater than 4.. 4

   b) Broad, dark lateral stripe absent; instead, 7–8 thin, dotted horizontal stripes. Dark blotch ("teardrop") under eye. Body depth into SL usually 4 or less..
   ....**NORTHERNSTARHEAD**
   ....**TOPMINNOW**—*Fundulus dispar*

4 a) Upper side without black spots or with spots that are irregular or with spots that are irregular in outline and not as dark as midlateral stripe ....**BLACKSTRIPE TOPMINNOW**—
   .... *Fundulus notatus*

   b) Upper side with few to many black spots that are regular in outline and as dark as the midlateral stripe ....
   ...**BLACKSPOTTED TOPMINNOW**—*Fundulus olivaceus*

LIVEBEARER FAMILY—POECILIIDAE
(SPECIES PLATE 154)

The Poeciliidae are a large family of 30 genera and about 293 species of fresh- and brackish-water fishes that occur in North and South America, Africa, and Madagascar (Nelson 2006). Poeciliids are ovoviviparous or viviparous fishes; that is, eggs are fertilized internally and develop within the ovary or oviduct. Internal fertilization is accomplished by means of a male intromittent organ, the gonopodium, which consists of modified anterior anal fin rays and is the family's most conspicuous feature. The young are born free-swimming.

Diagnostic family characters include usually small fins; caudal fin well developed, usually rounded or truncate, never forked; mouth small, directed upward (an adaptation for feeding at the surface and that allows the fish access to the thin, oxygen-rich layer at the water-air interface); teeth usually in 2 rows on both premaxillary and dentary bones.

The common name "livebearers" is partially a misnomer, since only the New World members of the family, subfamily Poeciliinae (about 190 species), would be accurately described.

149 NORTHERN STUDFISH—*Fundulus catenatus* (Storer). Body round, laterally compressed posteriorly. Snout long, head large, eye moderate. Dorsal fin origin over or slightly in front of anal fin origin. Dorsal fin rays 12–17, anal fin rays 13–18. Lateral line scales 41–50, usually 19 scales around caudal peduncle. Caudal fin emarginate. Light yellow or brown above, short gold stripe in front of dorsal fin origin, silver-blue side, rows of small brown or red-brown spots on side; fins with rows of small brown spots on dorsal and caudal fins. Breeding male bright blue side, red spots on head and fins, usually yellow paired fins, orange edged, often a submarginal black band on caudal fin. Male possesses tubercles on side of head, body, and caudal peduncle, and on dorsal, anal, and paired fins. Upper East Fork White River from IN to VA, KY, TN, and AL, west to MO, and south to MS. Common. Introduced into Bean Blossom Creek. Moderate rivers and creeks along backwaters, pools, and stream margins over sand and gravel substrates. Insectivore. Non-guarding, open substrate phytolithophil (A.1.4). Maximum size 178 mm TL.

150 BANDED KILLIFISH—*Fundulus diaphanus menoa* (Lesueur). Long, slender body. Dorsal fin in front of anal fin origin, Lateral line scales 40–44. Dorsal fin rays 13–15, pectoral fin rays 14–15, anal fin rays 10–12. Caudal fin emarginate with rounded edges. Dark olive to tan above, brown stripe along back, white to yellow below, 10–20 green-brown bars along silver side, back and upper side with many brown spots, bars on caudal peduncle fused at middle into dark stripe; clear to dusky olive-yellow fins. Breeding male with wide green bars along side, yellow throat and fins. St. Lawrence–Great Lakes and Mississippi River basins from QC to MN, south to IL. Common. Lakes, ponds, and basic gradient streams over sand substrates often associated with aquatic vegetation. Insectivore. Non-guarding, open substrate phytophil (A.1.5). Maximum size 75 mm TL.

151 NORTHERN STARHEAD TOPMINNOW—*Fundulus dispar* (Agassiz). Long, slender body. Dorsal fin origin behind anal fin origin. Lateral line scales 30–36. Dorsal rays 6–8, anal fin rays 8–11. Olive-green above, large blue-black suborbital bar, large iridescent gold spot on top of head, small iridescent gold spot at dorsal fin origin, 6–8 thin brown to red-brown stripes or rows of dots along the side. Green, red, and blue flecks on silver-yellow side, white below; fins yellow. Lake Michigan and Mississippi River basin from MI to LA. Common. Lakes, ponds, and basic gradient streams in pools and backwaters over sand and mud substrates often associated with aquatic vegetation. Insectivore. Non-guarding, open substrate phytolithophil (A.1.4). Maximum size 72 mm TL.

149   NORTHERN STUDFISH—
Fundulus catenatus

150   EASTERN BANDED KILLIFISH—
Fundulus diaphanus menoa

151   NORTHERN STARHEAD TOPMINNOW—
Fundulus dispar

152   BLACKSTRIPE TOPMINNOW—*Fundulus notatus* (Rafinesque). Long, slender body. Snout elongate, head moderate, eye moderate. Dorsal fin origin behind anal fin origin. Lateral line scales 31–36. Dorsal fin rays 8–10, anal fin rays 12–13. Olive-tan above, wide blue-black stripe along side, around snout, and onto caudal fin; silver-white spot on top of head, usually few to many dusky or dark spots on upper side, light blue along upper edge of stripe; yellow fins. Lakes Erie and Michigan, Mississippi River basins, from ON, west to IA, south to Gulf. Abundant. Margins of creeks, streams, small rivers, ponds, and lakes usually associated with aquatic vegetation and overhanging grasses. Particulate-feeding, drift herbivore/insectivore. Non-guarding, open substrate phytophil (A.1.5). Maximum size 74 mm TL.

153   BLACKSPOTTED TOPMINNOW—*Fundulus olivaceus* (Storer). Long, slender body. Snout more elongate than *F. notatus,* head moderate, eye moderate. Dorsal fin origin behind anal fin origin. Lateral line scales 33–37. Dorsal fin rays 9–10, anal fin rays 11–12. Olive-tan above, wide blue-black stripe along side, around snout, and onto caudal fin; silver-white spot on top of head, usually few to many dark spots on upper side, light blue along upper edge of stripe; yellow fins. Mississippi River basin from Interior River Lowlands south to Gulf from GA to TX. Rare. Margins of creeks, ditches, streams, and small rivers usually associated with aquatic vegetation and overhanging grasses. Insectivore. Non-guarding, open substrate phytophil (A.1.5). Maximum size 97 mm TL.

154   WESTERN MOSQUITOFISH—*Gambusia affinis* (Baird and Girard). Deep bodied with deep caudal peduncle. Moderate pointed snout, broad head, large eye. Small dorsal fin, origin behind anal fin origin. Dorsal fin rays 6. Lacking prominent teeth on gonopodial ray 3 of males. Caudal fin rounded. Light olive-gray to yellowish-brown above, dark stripe along back to dorsal fin, large black suborbital bar, no dark spots or stripes on side, yellow and blue iridescence on transparent silver-gray side; fins with 1–3 rows of black spots on dorsal and caudal fins. Atlantic and Gulf Slopes, Mississippi River from central IN to Mexico, north to NJ. Occasional. Lentic waters, ponds, lakes, and stream pools associated with aquatic vegetation over sand, gravel, or mud substrates. Drift, surface-feeding insectivore. Bearing, internal-bearing viviparous (C.2.1). Maximum size 36 mm TL (males) and 59 mm TL (females).

152 BLACKSTRIPE TOPMINNOW—
Fundulus notatus

153 BLACKSPOTTED TOPMINNOW—
Fundulus olivaceus

154 WESTERN MOSQUITOFISH—
Gambusia affinis

SILVERSIDE FAMILY—ATHERINOPSIDAE
(SPECIES PLATES 155–156)

The Atherinopsidae is a relatively large family of fishes found in marine and euryhaline habitats worldwide with about 29 genera and 160 species currently recognized (Nelson 2006). The species are primarily marine, but the family includes many either freshwater or coastal river inhabitants, especially in parts of North and South America and Australia. Nelson et al. (2004) place Atherinopsidae (New World silversides) in the order Atheriniformes. Under current classifications, Atheriniformes, along with Beloniformes, the needlefishes and flying fishes and their close relatives, and Cyprinodontiformes, the killifishes, are placed in the series Atherinomorpha, superorder Acanthoptergii. Atherinopsids were formerly included in the family Atherinidae (Nelson 2006). Six genera and 11 species occur in the coastal and freshwaters of the United States, with 2 genera present in the east, the strictly freshwater monotypic genus *Labidesthes* and the euryhaline *Menidia*.

The Atherinopsidae possess a bright metallic, silvery streak along the sides; thin, elongate bodies with flattened dorsums; beak-like snouts with small, terminal mouths; 2 widely separated dorsal fins, the first with 3–8 weak, flexible spines and the second with 1 spine followed by soft rays; anal fin much longer than the soft dorsal fin, usually preceded by a single spine; pectoral fins inserted high on the sides near top of gill openings; lateral line greatly reduced or absent; and relatively large cycloid scales, usually 31–50 in lateral series, more in *Labidesthes.*

Brook silverside occur in the Mississippi River and adjacent areas with Inland silverside. Scale counts and snout shape differ markedly between the 2 species. In *Labidesthes,* the dorsolateral scales are nearly microscopic in all but the largest specimens; in *Menidia,* these scales are easily visible. Position of anal fin origin relative to soft dorsal fin origin and numbers of anal fin rays are also useful characters for distinguishing adults of these 2 species.

KEY TO THE SILVERSIDES OF INDIANA

1   a) Scales small, predorsal scales (counted on the dorsal mid-line) about 40; anal fin rays 21 or more; snout and jaws produced into a beak .... **BROOK SILVERSIDE**—
.... *Labidesthes sicculus*

   b) Scales larger, predorsal scales about 20; anal fin rays 20 or fewer; snout not greatly produced ....
.... **INLAND SILVERSIDE**—*Menidia beryllina*

MULLET FAMILY—MUGILIDAE
(*Species plate 157*)

The Mugilidae occur worldwide in all tropical and temperate marine waters. The family is comprised of about 17 genera and 66 or more species (Nelson 2006). Most mullets occur strictly in marine environments, but some species, including the Striped mullet, *Mugil cephalus,* frequently travel into inland freshwaters (Etnier and Starnes 1993; Nelson 1994; Ross 2001).

   The mullets closely resemble the silversides in the family Atherinopsidae (Nelson 2006). The Mugilidae has 2 widely separated dorsal fins, the first usually consisting of only 4 spines and the second with 1 spine followed by soft rays; pelvic fins with a single spine and 5 soft rays; pelvic fins are subabdominal in position and the pelvic girdle does not articulate with the cliethra; scales large and cycloid; lateral line absent or poorly developed; gill rakers long; branchiostegal rays 5 or 6, membranes free from the isthmus. All mullets are similar in appearance, with *Mugil* characterized by prominent adipose eyelids and cycloid or very weakly ctenoid scales.

155 BROOK SILVERSIDE—*Labidesthes sicculus sicculus* (Cope). Elongate, strongly compressed, silver-sided body. Long, beak-like snout about 1.5 times eye diameter, terminal mouth, large eye. Two widely separated dorsal fins with the first small and with spines. First dorsal fin origin above anal fin origin. Scales on the head. Pectoral fins long, pointed, and upturned, anal fin sickle shaped, caudal fin forked. Lateral line scales 74–87, anal rays 22–25. Pale green above, translucent sides with silver to greenish iridescence, scales faintly outlined, silver translucent below; fins clear. Great Lakes with exception of Lake Superior, Mississippi River basins from MN south to Gulf of Mexico, and Atlantic and Gulf Coastal Plain. Common. Surface of marshes, lakes, ponds, and backwater habitats of creeks and small to large rivers. Insectivore. Non-guarding, open substrate phytolithophil (A.1.4). Maximum size 168 mm TL.

156 INLAND SILVERSIDE—*Menidia beryllina* (Cope). Elongate, strongly compressed, silver-sided body. Long beak-like snout about equal to eye diameter, superior mouth, large eye. Two widely separated dorsal fins with the first small and with spines. First dorsal fin origin in front of anal fin origin. Scales on head absent. Pectoral fins large, pointed, and upturned, anal fin sickle shaped, caudal fin forked. Lateral line scales 36–44, anal rays 16–18. Pale yellow-green above, translucent sides with silver to greenish iridescence, scales faintly outlined, silver translucent below; fins clear. Marine species that ascends great rivers. Found in Mississippi and Ohio rivers to southern IL, reported from Ohio River near Madison. Rare. Surface of clear waters in main channel of large rivers, lakes, and reservoirs. Insectivore. Non-guarding, open substrate phytolithophil (A.1.4). Maximum size 150 mm TL.

157 STRIPED MULLET—*Mugil cephalus* Linnaeus. Subtriangular to terete, laterally compressed posteriorly, silver-sided body. Short, rounded snout, head small and dorsally flattened, eye small. First dorsal fin origin in front of anal fin origin. Dorsal rays 11–12, anal rays 26–29, lateral scales 52–57. Silver above and below; iris silver. Marine species that ascends great rivers. Temperate and tropical oceans along coastal waters from Atlantic Slope near Cape Code to northern Mexico. Ascends the Mississippi River to Ohio River and lower TN rivers from Gulf of Mexico. Rare. Deep pools and main channel of large rivers and reservoirs. Herbivore. Marine spawning. Maximum size 420 mm TL.

155 BROOK SILVERSIDE—
Labidesthes sicculus

156 INLAND SILVERSIDE—
Menidia beryllina

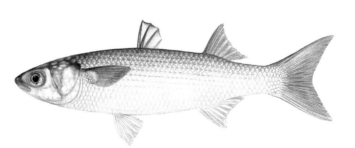

157 STRIPED MULLET—
Mugil cephalus

TEMPERATE BASS FAMILY—MORONIDAE
(*Species plates 158–161*)

The Moronidae are freshwater or euryhaline fishes, with 2 genera—*Morone,* including 4 species from North America, and the closely related *Dicentrarchus*, with 2 species from Europe and North Africa (Nelson 2006). The 4 North American species are White perch, *Morone americana,* White bass, *M. chrysops,* Yellow bass, *M. mississippiensis,* and Striped bass, *M. saxatilis* (Nelson et al. 2004).

The family is diagnosed by a laterally compressed, deep body; a skull somewhat elevated and strongly ossified, with lateral canals at least partially enclosed in bone; well-developed jaws, armed with numerous teeth; maxillary expanded posteriorly; opercle usually with 2 flat spines; branchiostegal rays 7; dorsal fin separated 2 two distinct sections that may be slightly connected at base, the first section with 8–10 spines, the second with 1 spine and 10–13 soft rays; anal fin with 3 spines and 9–12 soft rays; thoracic pelvic fins with 1 spine and 5 rays and no auxiliary process; ctenoid scales; lateral line well developed and complete, extends well onto caudal fin; 24 or more vertebrae (Scott and Crossman 1973).

The Moronidae are predaceous fishes highly desired by anglers. White and Yellow bass are important freshwater game fishes, and the anadromous Striped bass, a highly prized species, is now present in introduced landlocked populations in the United States. The White perch, a mostly brackish-water species of the Atlantic seaboard, is a popular food fish. Moronids have been widely transplanted outside their native ranges, and the production and stocking of artificial hybrids of these species has become an important management tool in controlling forage populations in reservoirs and production of sport food fish (White 2000).

KEY TO THE TEMPERATE BASSES OF INDIANA

1. a) First and second dorsal fins definitely connected with membranes between all spines... 2

   b) First and second dorsal fins separate 3

2. a) Spinous and soft dorsal fins well connected with membranes. No teeth on tongue. Body without dark longitudinal lines although light spots on the scales may appear as many pale longitudinal lines .... **WHITE PERCH**—*Morone americana*

   b) Spinous and soft dorsal fins slightly connected by membrane. Anal spines of differential weight, second spine much heavier than third. Soft anal rays 8–10. Lower lateral stripes broader and usually sharply broken and offset above origin of anal fin. Color largely yellowish or olive ....**YELLOW BASS**—*Morone mississippiensis*

3. a) Body elongate, greatest depth distinctly less than head length. Longitudinal streaks uniform and continuous on the scale row above or below in some individuals. Base of tongue with 2 patches of teeth, clearly separate and about equal in size..................**STRIPED BASS**—*Morone saxatilis*

   b) Body short and deep, greatest depth about equal to head length. Longitudinal stripes weaker and frequently interrupted. No vertical bars, even in young. Base of the tongue with 2 patches of teeth that are usually unequal in size and so close together that they appear as a single patch .... **WHITE BASS**—*Morone chrysops*

158 WHITE PERCH—*Morone americana* (Gmelin). Compressed, deep bodied. Large mouth without teeth on tongue, large spine on gill cover with sawtoothed-like preopercle. Body deepest between dorsal fins. Two dorsal fins, first with 9 spines and the second with 1 spine and 11–14 rays. Anal fin with 3 spines and 9–10 rays. Second anal spine about as long as third spine. Caudal fin truncate. Olive-brown to dark green-brown above, silver-green with brassy side, no dark stripe along side, white to greenish-yellow below; fins with dusky membranes and stripe on second dorsal fin. Native range is Atlantic Slope invading Great Lakes. Rare. Mostly estuarine but found in pools and quiet waters of lakes, moderate-sized rivers, and Lake Michigan. Insectivore. Non-guarding, open substrate phytolithophil (A.1.4). Maximum size 488 mm TL.

159 WHITE BASS—*Morone chrysops* (Rafinesque). Compressed, deep bodied. Large mouth with 1–2 tooth patches on rear of tongue, large spine on gill cover with sawtoothed-like preopercle. Body strongly arched behind head, deepest between dorsal fins. Two dorsal fins, first with 9 spines and the second with 1 spine and 11–13 rays. Anal fin with 3 spines and 9–10 rays. Second anal spine distinctly smaller than third spine. Caudal fin truncate. Olive-brown to bluish-gray above, yellow eye, 4–7 dark gray-brown stripes on silver-white sides, white below; fins gray with dusky membranes. Great Lakes, Hudson Bay, and Mississippi River to Gulf Coast. Common. Lakes and pools of lakes, moderate to large rivers, and Lake Michigan. Insectivore. Non-guarding, open substrate phytolithophil (A.1.4). Maximum size 420 mm TL.

160 YELLOW BASS—*Morone mississippiensis* Jordan and Eigenmann. Compressed, deep bodied. Large mouth without teeth on tongue, large spine on gill cover with sawtoothed-like preopercle. Body deepest between dorsal fins. Two dorsal fins, first with 9 spines and the second with 1 spine and 11–14 rays. Anal fin with 3 spines and 9 rays. Second anal spine about as long as third spine. Caudal fin truncate. Olive to gray above, silver-yellow to brassy side, 5–7 dark stripes along side—usually broken and offset on lower side, white to greenish-yellow below; fins clear to blue-gray. Lake Michigan and Mississippi River to Gulf Coast. Occasional. Large rivers and inland lakes in pools and quiet waters of lakes, moderate-sized rivers. Insectivore. Non-guarding, open substrate phytolithophil (A.1.4). Maximum size 275 mm TL.

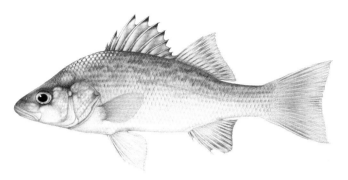

158 WHITE PERCH—
Morone americana

159 WHITE BASS—
Morone chrysops

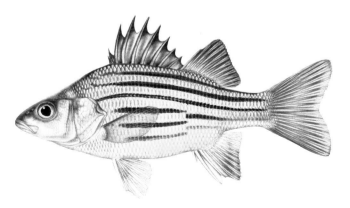

160 YELLOW BASS—
Morone mississippiensis

161 STRIPED BASS—*Morone saxatilis* (Walbaum). Compressed, deep bodied. Large mouth with 1–2 tooth patches on rear of tongue, large spine on gill cover with sawtoothed-like preopercle. Smoothly arched dorsal profile, body deepest between dorsal fins. Two dorsal fins, first with 9 spines and the second with 1 spine and 11–14 rays. Anal fin with 3 spines and 11 (9–13) rays. Second anal spine about as long as third spine. Caudal fin truncate. Olive-brown to blue-gray above, silver-white side, 6–9 dark gray stripes along side, white below; fins with clear to greenish-gray. Native range is Atlantic Slope and Gulf Coast and widely introduced elsewhere into Great Lakes, inland lakes, and Ohio River. Occasional. Mostly marine but found in pelagic zones of deep waters and pools of lakes, moderate-sized rivers, and Lake Michigan. Whole body carnivore. Non-guarding, open substrate phytolithophil (A.1.4). Maximum size 2,000 mm TL.

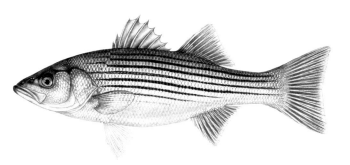

161   STRIPED BASS—
Morone saxatilis

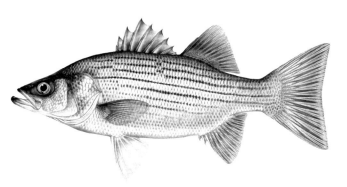

Morone HYBRID

PERCH FAMILY—PERCIDAE
(Species plates 162–199)

The Percidae is a North American family with 10 genera and about 201 species worldwide (Nelson 2006; Table 4). Three subfamilies are recognized, including the Percinae, Luciopercinae, and Etheostomatinae. The Blue pike, a form previously occurring in Lake Erie, is considered extinct (Nelson et al. 2004).

The perch are diagnosed by 2 dorsal fins, separate or narrowly joined; usually 1 or 2 anal spines; premaxilla protractile or non-protractile; branchiostegal rays 5–8; branchiostegal membranes not joined to isthmus (may be united to each other or not); psuedobranchiae well developed to rudimentary; no subocular shelf; supramaxilla absent; single or no predorsal bones (rarely 2); vertebrae 32–50 (Nelson 2006).

The Percinae includes the genera *Perca, Gymnocephalus,* and *Percarina.* This subfamily includes an anteriormost interhaemal bone greatly enlarged; anal spines usually well developed; preopercle strongly serrate; usually 7–8 branchiostegal rays; body compressed; anal spines prominent; and swim bladder well developed. The Luciopercinae includes the genera *Sander, Zingel,* and *Romanichthys.* The subfamily possesses anteriormost interhaemal no larger than posterior one; anal spines weak; and lateral line extends onto caudal fin. The Etheostomatinae or darters of North America is comprised of 4 genera, the *Ammocrypta, Crystallaria, Percina,* and *Etheostoma.* The Etheostomatinae has an anteriormost interhaemal bone greatly enlarged; anal spines usually well developed; preopercle margin smooth or partly serrated; usually 5–6 branchiostegal rays; body slightly compressed or fusiform; anal spines moderately prominent; and swim bladder reduced or absent.

Perch range in size from the smallest being about the size of a penny to largest reaching about 780 mm TL. The darters have exhibited explosive radiation, with numerous species recognized and further species yet to be described. Habitats range from small headwater streams to large rivers and reservoirs. Spawning runs of the more primitive species occur in the spring when adults ascend streams and rivers and concentrate in riffles and below dams (Simon 1999). Spawning generally occurs over gravel substrates (Simon 1999; Simon and Wallus

TABLE 4. BASIN DISTRIBUTION OF
FAMILY PERCIDAE IN INDIANA

Species/Basin	Lake Michigan	Lake Erie	Ohio River	Mississippi River
Ammocrypta clara			X	
Ammocrypta pellucida		X	X	X
Crystallaria asprella			X	X
Etheostoma asprigene			X	
Etheostoma cf. *asprigene*			X	
Etheostoma blennioides			X	
Etheostoma caeruleum			X	X
Etheostoma camurum			X	X
Etheostoma chlorosoma			X	X
Etheostoma exile	X			
Etheostoma flabellare flabellare			X	X
Etheostoma flabellare lineolatum			X	
Etheostoma gracile			X	
Etheostoma histrio			X	
Etheostoma maculatum			X	
Etheostoma microperca	X	X	X	X
Etheostoma nigrum nigrum	X	X	X	X
Etheostoma cf. *nigrum*	X		X	X
Etheostoma pholidotum			X	
Etheostoma proeliare			X	
Etheostoma spectabile spectabile	X	X	X	X
Etheostoma squamiceps			X	
Etheostoma tippecanoe			X	
Etheostoma variatum			X	
Etheostoma cf. *zonale*				X
Etheostoma zonale			X	
Perca flavescens	X	X	X	X
Percina caprodes caprodes	X	X	X	X
Percina copelandi		X	X	
Percina evides			X	
Percina maculata	X	X	X	X
Percina phoxocephala			X	
Percina sciera sciera		X	X	X
Percina shumardi			X	
Percina uranidea			X	
Percina vigil			X	
Percina zebra	X		X	
Sander canadense			X	X
Sander vitreus	X		X	X

2006); however, numerous reproductive behaviors and strategies have been adapted for new habitats. Most darters are benthic species that feed on aquatic insects (Goldstein and Simon 1999). The genus *Etheostoma* has a variety of mouth shapes, with some species adapted for selecting invertebrate from the substrates, while others are more pointed for digging into substrates or for flipping stones. The perch are among the most sensitive species to anthropogenic stress and are reduced in number with increasing impacts.

KEY TO THE PERCH OF INDIANA

1 a) Caudal fin deeply forked; preopercle strongly serrate; mouth large, the maxilla extending backward to at least to middle of eye; genital papillae absent or reduced............................. 2

   b) Caudal fin usually not forked, with exception of *Crystallaria asprella;* preopercle smooth or weakly serrate; mouth small, the maxilla not extending backward to middle of eye; genital papillae prominent in females... 4

2 a) Canine teeth present; pelvic fins widely separated; body terete; anal rays greater than 11; body pattern variable........3

   b) Canine teeth lacking; pelvic fins slightly separated; body deep and slab-sided; anal rays less than 8; coloration includes 6–8 black or olive-green vertical bars......................................
      ....**YELLOW PERCH**—*Perca flavescens*

3 a) First dorsal fin with round, discrete black spots forming a series of rows; first dorsal fin without a prominent black basal spot posteriorly; cheeks usually partly scaled; rays of soft dorsal fin 17–21; back with 3–4 dusky saddles; pyloric caeca 5–8...................................**SAUGER**—*Sander canadense*

   b) First dorsal fin with mottling but without rows of discrete black spots; prominent black basal spot in posterior rays of spinous dorsal fin; rays of soft dorsal 19–23; back and sides with 4–14 dark saddles or single color; pyloric caeca 3..........
      .... **WALLEYE**—*Sander vitreus*

4 a) Body usually incompletely scaled, translucent in life, white in preservation; snout long and pointed; body elongate and cylindrical; dorsal fin well separated......................................5

   b) Body fully or mostly scaled, opaque; snout variable; body shape variable; dorsal fin usually closely placed.................. 7

5 a) Caudal fin deeply forked; premaxillary frenum present; dorsal fin rays 12–15, usually 3–14; dorsum with 4 large dark saddles; body completely scaled ....
      .... **CRYSTAL DARTER**—*Crystallaria asprella*

   b) Caudal fin truncate or only shallowly forked; no premaxillary frenum present; dorsal rays 8–13, usually 10 or 11; dorsum without dorsal saddles; body incompletely scaled...... 6

6 a) Opercle with a needle-like backward-projecting spine; blotches along lateral line, if present, irregular in outline and connected by a weak row of melanophores; generally, dorsum above lateral line scales above the lateral line and outlined with pigment... ....**WESTERN SAND DARTER**—*Ammocrypta clara*

   b) Opercle without a needle-like backward-projecting spine; 12–19 sharply defined blotches along lateral line, usually not connected by melanophores; several rows of scales above lateral line sharply outlined with pigment............................... ....**EASTERN SAND DARTER**—*Ammocrypta pellucida*

7 a) Male with an enlarged tooth scale between pelvic fin bases; belly of male and breast of female usually with a midventral row of enlarged scales; lateral line complete; anal fin usually of similar size as soft dorsal fin; anal spines 2 8

   b) Male without an enlarged tooth scale between pelvic fin bases; belly midline usually with normal scales but sometimes naked; lateral line highly variable in number of pored scales; anal fin usually smaller than second dorsal fin 2 (sometimes 1) anal fin spine 2 (sometimes single)....................................16

8 a) Conical snout projecting well beyond upper jaw; mouth subterminal; black spot at base of caudal peduncle; dorsal spines and rays usually 14 or more; scales in lateral line more than 80; sides of body with more than 16 narrow, dark vertical bars 9

   b) Snout not projecting beyond upper jaw; mouth terminal; dorsal spines and rays usually fewer than 14; scales in lateral line fewer than 80; sides of body without dark vertical bars 10

9 a) Bars without terminal blotch, some extending past midline ....**LOGPERCH**—*Percina caprodes*

   b) Bars terminating at midline with a blotch............................... .... **MANITOU DARTER**—*Percina zebra*

10 a) Upper lip separated from snout by a groove, or if present, a weakly developed frenum; anal fin of male, when depressed, extending far behind end of depressed second dorsal fin 11

   b) Upper lip bound to snout by a well-developed frenum; anal fin of male, when depressed, extending slightly behind tip of depressed second dorsal fin 14

11 a) Dorsal saddles moderate to distinct, usually less than 5; caudal peduncle scales 19 or more (rarely 18); anal fin rays 10–13,

usually 10–12; anal fin of adult male elongated, sometimes extending to caudal fin...12

b) Dorsal saddles usually 8 poorly defined; caudal peduncle scales 18 or fewer; anal rays 7–10, usually 8 or 9; anal fin of adult not elongate .... **CHANNEL DARTER**— .... *Percina copelandi*

12 a) Spinous dorsal fin with an anterior and posterior black blotch; dark distinct teardrop; mid-dorsum mottled or with 5 or more weakly defined saddles; anterior lateral blotches deeper than long; teardrop slightly forward............................ .... **RIVER DARTER**—*Percina shumardi*

b) Spinous dorsal fin without an anterior or posterior black blotch; mid-dorsum with either less than 5 or more than 6 dorsal saddles; teardrop either vertical or directed slightly posterior...13

13 a) Dorsum with 5 dark saddles that do not extend ventrally and do not connect to midlateral row of dark blotches; body slender, head small.. ....**SADDLEBACK DARTER**—*Percina vigil*

b) Dorsum with 4 dark saddles that extend ventrally and connect to lateral dark blotches; anal rays usually 11; first dorsal fin with a small dark basal spot anteriorly................................ .... **STARGAZING DARTER**—*Percina uranidea*

14 a) Snout pointed sharply, snout distance from front of eye to tip of snout greater than distance from back of eye to posterior edge of opercle; body slender; spinous dorsal fin with a submarginal row of orange spots; mid-dorsum with 11–13 obscure greenish or brownish blotches; sides with 10–16 round dark blotches..............**SLENDERHEAD DARTER**— ....*Percina phoxocephala*

b) Snout not pointed, snout distance from front of eye to tip of snout less than distance from back of eye to posterior edge of opercle; body robust; spinous dorsal fin without a submarginal row of orange dots; mid-dorsum with 7–10 squared black blotches; sides with 6–10 black blotches......15

15 a) Dorsal saddles directly over lateral blotches and usually connected with them; body and fins with red, orange, yellow, blue, and green....................**GILT DARTER**—*Percina evides*

b) Dorsal saddles and lateral blotches alternating and separate from each other; body and fins without bright colors 16

16 a) A single median caudal spot at base of caudal peduncle; teardrop strongly developed; gill covers not connected at isthmus; spinous dorsal fin with a black basal spot ....**BLACKSIDE DARTER**—*Percina maculata*

   b) Three distinct spots at base of caudal peduncle; teardrop weakly developed or absent; gill covers moderately joined at isthmus; spinous dorsal fin without a black basal spot ....**DUSKY DARTER**—*Percina sciera*

17 a) Upper lip separated from snout by groove; anal spines either 1 or 2; mouth terminal...18

   b) Upper lip joined to snout medially by frenum; anal spines 2; mouth position variable but usually subterminal 22

18 a) Gill covers broadly joined by membrane across isthmus; sides of body with prominent V- or U-shaped markings or large irregular blotches 19

   b) Gill membranes not broadly joined across isthmus; sides of body with many small flecks or X-, W- or Y-shaped markings 20

19 a) Snout extremely blunt; overhanging mouth; anterior half of maxillary fused with preorbital region; pelvic fins without discrete markings; distinct U-shaped markings on lower sides ....**EASTERN GREENSIDE DARTER**— ....*Etheostoma blennioides*

   b) Snout snubnosed, overhanging mouth; maxillary separated from preorbital region by a groove; pelvic fins with discrete brown markings ....**PRAIRIE DARTER**— ....*Etheostoma pholidotum*

20 a) Lateral line incomplete; cheeks scaled; dorsal fins widely separated; dark bridle continuing around front of snout, due to absence of frenum; snout profile forming a continuous U-shape..**BLUNTNOSE DARTER**— ....*Etheostoma chlorosoma*

   b) Lateral line complete; cheeks usually naked; dorsal fins narrowly separated; dark bridle interrupted medially on snout; snout rather pointed in lateral profile....................................21

21 a) Head, cheek, and nape fully scaled ....**SCALY DARTER**—*Etheostoma* cf. *nigrum* nov. sp.

   b) Head, cheek, and nape not scaled or only weakly scaled .... **JOHNNY DARTER**—*Etheostoma nigrum*

22 a) Lateral line absent or extremely short (fewer than 8 anterior pored scales); dorsal spines, usually fewer than 8; pelvic fin

of male angular, extending to or beyond anus; maximum size less than 50 mm TL.. 23

b) Lateral line complete or incomplete but consisting of more than 10 pored scales; dorsal spines greater than 8; pelvic fin rounded and not extending to anus; maximum size greater than 50 mm TL... 24

23 a) Cheeks naked; lateral line usually with 0 or 2 pores; dorsal spines 6–7; mouth small, upper jaw reaching behind front of eye; breast with evenly spaced melanophores.....................
.... **LEAST DARTER**—*Etheostoma microperca*

b) Cheeks with embedded scales; lateral line usually with 3–7 anterior pores; dorsal spines 7–8; mouth large, upper jaw reaching behind front of eye; breast stippled with fin melanophores ....**CYPRESS DARTER**—*Etheostoma proeliare*

24 a) Lateral line highly flexed upward to within 3 scale rows of dorsal fin base; body coloration consisting of bright green bars in life; spinous dorsal fin with distal edge of red spots .
...............................**SLOUGH DARTER**—*Etheostoma gracile*

b) Lateral line not flexed upward to within 3 scale rows of dorsal fin base; color variable but not consisting of green body bars and red spots on distal edge of spinous dorsal fin............. 25

25 a) Spinous dorsal fin shorter (in height) than soft dorsal fin; caudal fin boldly marbled with 4 or more black bands; dorsal spines of male usually with fleshy knobs at tips; conspicuous dark humeral spot above pectoral fin base 26

b) Spinous dorsal fin not shorter than soft dorsal fin; caudal fin without marbling or indistinct and usually with fewer than 6 dusky bands; dorsal spines of male without knobs at tips; dark humeral spot present or absent.................................... 27

26 a) Nape scaled; opercles and breast with some scales; gill cover narrowly connected at isthmus so that juncture is V-shaped; caudal peduncle with 3 intense caudal spots; lateral line extending to rear or soft dorsal fin...
...................**SPOTTAIL DARTER**—*Etheostoma squamiceps*

b) Nape, opercles, and breast scaleless; gill covers moderately to broadly joined at isthmus; caudal peduncle without 3 conspicuous caudal spots; lateral line extending only to front of dorsal fin ...**FANTAIL DARTER**—*Etheostoma flabellare*

27 a) Gill covers broadly joined at isthmus; mouth terminal; sides of body without bright green bars (*E. histrio* green in winter, brown in summer) 28

b) Gill covers not broadly joined at isthmus; mouth subterminal; sides of body without bright green bars........................ 30

28 a) Nape, breast, opercles, and cheeks unscaled; underside of head, breast, and fins with widely spaced coarse black spots; pectoral fins enlarged, extending well beyond tips of pelvic fins; spinous dorsal fin with anterior and posterior dark blotch........... **HARLEQUIN DARTER**—*Etheostoma histrio*

b) Nape, breast, opercles, and cheeks scaled; underside of head, breast, and fins without coarse black spots; pectoral and pelvic fins extending backward an equal distance; spinous dorsal fin without anterior and posterior dark blotch 29

29 a) Greatest body depth equal anterior and posterior dorsal fin origin................... **BANDED DARTER**—*Etheostoma zonale*

b) Greatest body depth anterior dorsal fin origin ....**JADE DARTER**—*Etheostoma* cf. *zonale* nov. sp.

30 a) Lateral line complete; dark horizontal line present on side; red spots present on side of male; adult size greater than 50 mm TL 32

b) Lateral line incomplete; dark horizontal line absent on side; red spots absent on side of male ....**TIPPECANOE DARTER**—*Etheostoma tippecanoe*

31 a) Snout pointed; cheek scaled; lateral line scale 51–68.............. ....**SPOTTED DARTER**—*Etheostoma maculatum*

b) Snout blunt; cheek unscaled; lateral line scales 47–70 .... **BLUEBREAST DARTER**—*Etheostoma camurum*

32 a) Lateral line short, not extending to soft dorsal fin, highly arched; dorsal spines 8–9; body terete; sides with a series of quadrate dark blotches separated by red or orange patches; eye diameter greater than snout length.................................... .... **IOWA DARTER**—*Etheostoma exile*

b) Lateral line extending to middle of soft dorsal fin, nearly straight; dorsal spines 10–11; body somewhat compressed; sides with dark vertical bars; eye diameter less than snout length 33

33 a) Cheek scaled; bands at caudal base well developed and more prominent than other lateral line bands 34

b) Cheek unscaled; band at caudal base no more prominent than other lateral bands 35

34 a) Vertical bands 5–7 .... **MUD DARTER**—
....*Etheostoma asprigene*

 b) Vertical bands usually 9 ....**TANGLE DARTER**—
....*Etheostoma* cf. *asprigene* nov. sp.

162 WESTERN SAND DARTER—*Ammocrypta clara* Jordan and Meek. Slender, laterally compressed, translucent body. Snout pointed, premaxillary frenum narrowly formed, mouth terminal, eye moderate, located high on head. Spine on opercle. Dorsal fin spines 9–13, dorsal rays 9–13, pectoral fin rays 12–15, anal fin rays 8–11. Scale rows above lateral line 0–2, below lateral line 1–5. Lateral scales 63–81. Caudal fin truncate. Dark green blotches along back and side, 12 dorsal blotches, 12–14 lateral brown to greenish-brown stripes from head to caudal fin base, translucent below; paired and median fins clear. Mississippi River from WI south to TX and Lake Michigan from WI. Occasional. Moderate to large rivers over clean sand substrates in runs. Benthic insectivore. Non-guarding, open substrate psammophil (A.1.6). Maximum size 72 mm TL.

163 EASTERN SAND DARTER—*Ammocrypta pellucida* (Agassiz). Slender, laterally compressed, translucent body. Snout pointed, premaxillary frenum narrowly formed, mouth terminal, eye moderate, located high on head. No spine on opercle. Dorsal fin spines 7–12, dorsal rays 8–12, pectoral fin rays 12–16, anal fin spines 1, anal rays 7–11. Scale rows above lateral line complete, below lateral line 4–7. Lateral scales 65–84. Caudal fin truncate. Dark green blotches along back and side, 12–16 small olive dorsal blotches, 9–14 oblong dusky olive spots along lateral from head to caudal fin base, translucent to silver below; paired and median fins clear. Eastern Great Lakes and Ohio River from NY to KY. Occasional. Moderate to large rivers over clean sand substrates in runs. Benthic insectivore. Non-guarding, open substrate psammophil (A.1.6). Maximum size 70 mm TL.

164 CRYSTAL DARTER—*Crystallaria asprella* Jordan. Slender, laterally compressed body. Snout pointed, mouth terminal, eye moderate, located high on head. Dorsal fin spines 7–12, dorsal rays 8–12, pectoral fin rays 15–17, anal fin spines 1, anal rays 12–15. Body completely scaled, lateral scales 81–93. Caudal fin forked. Back with 4 dark brown saddles, dark brown mottling along side, snout with dark brown on lip from eye to eye, sides tan to yellow, translucent to silver below. Paired and median fins clear but pectoral and soft dorsal fins with concentric rows of light pigment. Mississippi River from WI to LA, former range in Ohio River from TN to IN, north to OH, Gulf Coast from FL to AL. Extirpated in IN. Moderate to large rivers over clean sand and fine gravel substrates. Benthic insectivore. Non-guarding, open substrate psammophil (A.1.6). Maximum size 156 mm TL.

35 a) Vertical bands on sides rather uniform and about equal to interspaces in width; male with red or orange spot in blue-green anal fins; sides of body without checkerboard (longitudinal rows) of dark spots; pectoral rays 13–15; gill covers slightly connected at isthmus........ **RAINBOW DARTER**—
....*Etheostoma caeruleum*

b) Vertical bands on sides less uniform, narrower than interspaces and widened along lateral line; male without red or orange spot in blue-green anal fin, typically black without any bright coloration; sides of body with some short checkerboard (longitudinal rows) of dark spots that usually terminate at anus; pectoral fin rays 11–12; gill covers not connected at isthmus .... **ORANGETHROAT DARTER**—
....*Etheostoma spectabile*

162   WESTERN SAND DARTER—
Ammocrypta clara

163   EASTERN SAND DARTER—
Ammocrypta pellucida

164   CRYSTAL DARTER—
Crystallaria asprella

165   MUD DARTER—*Etheostoma asprigene* (Forbes). Deep, laterally compressed body, deepest beneath middle of spinous dorsal fin. Snout pointed, mouth terminal, eye moderate. Head with fully scaled cheek, opercle, and nape. Lateral line incomplete, lateral line scales 45–51. Dorsal fin spines 9–12, dorsal rays 10–14, pectoral fin rays 11–15, anal fin spines 2, anal rays 6–8. Caudal fin truncate. Olive-brown back with 6–10 dark saddles, 9–11 dark blue bars on side, large black blotch at rear, orange or white below; fins usually clear. Spinous dorsal fin with middle red band, blue edge and base, middle red band on soft dorsal fin. Mississippi River basin from WI to LA and west from Gulf Slope to TX. Common. Small creeks to moderate-sized rivers, backwaters, and sloughs, usually associated with submerged vegetation and fine substrates. Benthic insectivore. Guarding, substrate-choosing phytophil (B.1.4). Maximum size 65 mm TL.

166   TANGLE DARTER—*Etheostoma* cf. *asprigene* nov. sp. Deep, laterally compressed body, deepest beneath middle of spinous dorsal fin. Snout pointed, mouth terminal, eye moderate. Head with fully scaled cheek, opercle, and nape. Lateral line incomplete, lateral line scales 44–54. Dorsal fin spines 9–12, dorsal rays 10–14, pectoral fin rays 11–15, anal fin spines 2, anal rays 6–8. Caudal fin truncate. Olive-brown back with 6–10 dark saddles, 5–8 faint red bars on side, large black blotch at rear, orange or white below. Fins usually clear, spinous dorsal fin with middle red band, black edge and base, middle red band with black edge and base on soft dorsal fin. Ohio River basin within White and Wabash rivers. Common. Moderate- to large-sized rivers, stream nearshore margins associated with root wads, or associated with submerged vegetation. Benthic insectivore. Guarding, substrate-choosing phytophil (B.1.4). Maximum size 68 mm TL.

167   EASTERN GREENSIDE DARTER—*Etheostoma blennioides* Rafinesque. Slender, terete body. Snout blunt, mouth subterminal, head shape narrow, eye moderate. Lip tip short, belly and opercles with small, naked area or completely scaled. Broadly joined branchiostegal membranes. Lateral line complete, lateral line scales 58–72. Dorsal fin spines 9–11, dorsal rays 13–15, pectoral fin rays 13–17, anal fin spines 2, anal rays 6–10. Caudal fin truncate. Olive-green to brown back, 4–7 dark green dorsal saddles from nape to caudal peduncle. Side with 4–10 dark green U- or W-shaped bars, white below. Spinous dorsal fin 2 stripes, soft dorsal 2–3 stripes, pectoral fins 3–4 concentric stripes, caudal fin 3–4 stripes, pelvic and anal fins unpigmented. Ohio River restricted, north and south tributaries from Green River confluence, KY, east to Potomac and north to Genesee River basins, NY, headwater tributaries of Allegheny and Monongahela basins; introduced into Potomac River. Common. Rocky riffles of creeks, small to medium rivers, and shores of large lakes. Benthic insectivore. Guarding, substrate-choosing phytophil (B.1.4). Maximum size 138 mm TL.

165 MUD DARTER—
Etheostoma asprigene

166 TANGLE DARTER—
Etheostoma cf. *asprigene*

167 EASTERN GREENSIDE DARTER—
Etheostoma blennioides

168 RAINBOW DARTER—*Etheostoma caeruleum* Storer. Deep, laterally compressed body. Snout pointed, mouth terminal. Infraorbital canal complete. Greatest body depth beneath middle of spinous dorsal fin. Cheek and breast unscaled. Branchiostegal membrane orange. Lateral line incomplete, lateral line scales 41–50. Pectoral fin rays 13. Caudal fin truncate. Brown back, dorsal saddles 6–10. Dark bars 10–13 along side from pectoral girdle to caudal peduncle. Blue cheek, white below. Pelvic fin blue; dorsal, anal, and caudal fins red with blue edges; red pectoral fins. Great Lakes, Mississippi and Ohio rivers from western NY to Red River of the North, MN, south to LA, and west Arkansas River, MO to northern VA. Common. Creeks, small to medium rivers in fast current over gravel and cobble substrates. Benthic insectivore. Non-guarding, brood-hiding lithophil (A.2.3). Maximum size 68 mm TL.

169 BLUEBREAST DARTER—*Etheostoma camurum* (Cope). Deep, laterally compressed body. Snout rounded, mouth terminal. Nape unscaled. Branchiostegal membrane broad. Lateral line scales 47–70. Back gray to black, dusky teardrop, male with bright red or female with brown spots, without black halo outline, blue breast, light green to white below. Soft dorsal, caudal, and anal fins with black edge. Ohio River basin from western NY to eastern IL, south to Tennessee River, TN, and NC. Rare. Small to medium rivers in fast, rocky riffles with cobble substrates. Benthic insectivore. Guarding, substrate-choosing lithophil (B.1.3). Maximum size 66 mm TL.

170 BLUNTNOSE DARTER—*Etheostoma chlorosoma* (Hay). Slender, terete body. Extremely blunt snout, no premaxillary frenum. Lateral line incomplete, lateral scales 49–60. Anal spine 1. Olive above, dusky saddles 6, black bridle connecting around snout, black teardrop, sides and back with brown Xs and Ws, horizontal dusky to black blotches along side, white below. Spinous dorsal fin with black edge. Mississippi River basin from MN to LA, Gulf Slope from Mobile Bay, AL, to TX. Extirpated from Lake Michigan, IL. Rare. Backwaters of creeks, small to medium rivers, lakes, ponds, and swamps with aquatic vegetation over fine substrates. Benthic insectivore. Guarding, substrate-choosing phytophil (B.1.4). Maximum size 55 mm TL.

168 RAINBOW DARTER—
Etheostoma caeruleum

169 BLUEBREAST DARTER—
Etheostoma camurum

170 BLUNTNOSE DARTER—
Etheostoma chlorosoma

171   IOWA DARTER—*Etheostoma exile* (Girard). Slender, terete body with long, slender caudal peduncle. Snout pointed, eye moderate. Lateral line incomplete, lateral scales 45–69 arched in front, with 19–34 pored scales. Infraorbital canal incomplete with 8 pores. Tan above, black teardrop, dark brown or black mottling along side, breeding male with alternating blue and brick red bars on side, belly orange or white below. Spinous dorsal fin with blue edge and base and red middle stripe, soft dorsal and caudal fins with scattered pigment. Arctic, Great Lakes, Mississippi and Ohio river basins from QC west to Yukon Territory, south to central OH to CO. Occasional. Lakes, ponds, lagoons, and slow-flowing rivers with abundant aquatic vegetation and substrates of peat, sand, and organic debris. Benthic invertivore. Guarding, substrate-choosing phytophil (B.1.4). Maximum size 58 mm TL.

172   BARRED FANTAIL DARTER—*Etheostoma flabellare flabellare* Rafinesque. Slender, laterally compressed body. Snout pointed, protruding lower jaw, upturned mouth, eye moderate. Nape unscaled. Branchiostegal membranes broadly connected. Infraorbital canal interrupted 4 anterior pores and 3 posterior pores. Lateral line incomplete, lateral line scales 45–55. Dorsal spines 8–11, dorsal fin rays 10–13. Olive to dark brown above, teardrop narrow or absent, black bars, mottling, or rows of black spots on side, yellow to white below. Black stripes on soft dorsal and caudal fins. Nuptial male with golden knobs on tips of spinous dorsal fin and with black head and large swollen nape. Great Lakes and Mississippi River basins from western NY to southwestern MN, south to Cumberland River basin, TN, and KY. Common. Small creeks, streams, and small rivers in riffles with gravel and cobble substrates. Benthic invertivore. Guarding, nest-spawning speleophil (B.2.7). Maximum size 76 mm TL.

STRIPED FANTAIL DARTER—*Etheostoma flabellare lineolatum*. Lateral line scales 42–55. Dorsal spines 8–9, dorsal fin rays 12–14. Olive to dark brown above, teardrop narrow or absent, black bars, mottling, or rows of black spots on side, yellow to white below. Black stripes on soft dorsal and caudal fins. Nuptial male with golden knobs on tips of spinous dorsal fin and with black head and large swollen nape. Ohio and Mississippi river basins from Ohio, Wabash, and White rivers, IN, west to MO. Common. Small creeks, streams, and small rivers in riffles with gravel and cobble substrates. Benthic invertivore. Guarding, nest-spawning speleophil (B.2.7). Maximum size 76 mm TL.

171 IOWA DARTER—
Etheostoma exile

172 FANTAIL DARTER—BARRED FANTAIL DARTER—
Etheostoma flabellare flabellare

STRIPED FANTAIL DARTER—
Etheostoma flabellare lineolatum

173   SLOUGH DARTER—*Etheostoma gracile* (Girard). Slender, laterally compressed body. Snout pointed, mouth terminal, eye moderate. Branchiostegal membrane narrowly connected. Lateral line incomplete, lateral line scales 40–55 with 13–27 pored scales. Breast unscaled. Infraorbital canal complete 8 pores. Dorsal spines 7–8, dorsal rays 9–14, pectoral rays 12–14, anal spines 2, anal rays 5–8. Yellow above, green saddles and vermiculated lines along back, 10–11 green bars on side, yellow or white below. Dorsal fin with middle red stripe, blue-gray anal fin along base, soft dorsal and caudal fin with 2–5 vertical bands, pectoral and pelvic fins clear. Mississippi River and Gulf Slope basins from southern IN to northeast MO, southwest to KS and OK, east to MS and TX. Occasional. Swamps, sloughs, basic gradient streams, and creeks with submerged aquatic vegetation over fine substrates. Benthic invertivore. Guarding, substrate-choosing phytophil (B.1.4). Maximum size 50 mm TL.

174   HARLEQUIN DARTER—*Etheostoma histrio* (Jordan and Gilbert). Deep, laterally compressed body. Snout overhanging terminal mouth, eye moderate. Branchiostegal membrane broadly connected. Lateral line complete, lateral line scales 45–58. Dorsal spines 10–11, dorsal rays 12–14, pectoral rays 13–15, anal spines 2, anal rays 7–8. Caudal fin truncate. Green to yellow above, green dorsal saddles 6–7, black teardrop, dark brown blotches along side 7–11, 2 dark brown caudal spots, with brown or black specks beneath head and extending onto yellow belly. Spinous dorsal clear with red margin. Spawning male emerald green with brown and black mottling. Mississippi Embayment and Coastal Plain from western KY to MO south to LA, and from FL to TX. Rare to occasional. Small, medium, and large rivers in deep runs associated with submerged trees over sand, gravel, and bedrock substrates. Benthic invertivore. Guarding, substrate-choosing phytophil (B.1.4). Maximum size 69 mm TL.

175   SPOTTED DARTER—*Etheostoma maculatum* Kirtland. Deep, laterally compressed body. Snout pointed, mouth terminal, eye moderate. Branchiostegal membrane broadly connected. Lateral line complete, lateral line scales 53–68. Caudal fin round. Black to gray above, teardrop thin or absent, sides black to gray, male with red spots with black halos, females with black mottling, blue breast. Fins gray or blue. Ohio River basin from NY to PA, northern IN south to WV and KY. Rare, considered special concern; however, stable in Blue and East Fork White rivers but possibly extirpated from Tippecanoe River. Small, medium, and large rivers in riffles with cobble and boulder substrates. Benthic invertivore. Guarding, substrate-choosing lithophil (B.1.3). Maximum size 95 mm TL.

173 SLOUGH DARTER—
Etheostoma gracile

174 HARLEQUIN DARTER—
Etheostoma histrio

175 SPOTTED DARTER—
Etheostoma maculatum

176   LEAST DARTER—*Etheostoma microperca* Jordan and Gilbert. Deep, laterally compressed body. Snout rounded, mouth terminal, eye large. Breast unscaled. Infraorbital canal interrupted 2–3 pores. Lateral line scales 30–36, lateral line pores 0–3. Anal spines 2. Olive above, large teardrop, dark green saddles, green blotches along side, rows of dark green spots on sides, white to yellow below. First dorsal fin with black edge and red middle band. Spawning male with red or orange pelvic and anal fins. Caudal fin truncate. Great Lakes and Mississippi River basins from ON to MN, south to central OH, IL, and IN, west to MO, KS, AR, and OK. Common. Springs, headwater streams, and creeks, lakes, and ditches associated with aquatic macrophytes over mud and sand substrates. Benthic invertivore. Guarding, substrate-choosing phytophil (B.1.4). Maximum size 45 mm TL.

177   JOHNNY DARTER—*Etheostoma nigrum* Rafinesque. Slender, elongate, terete body with slender caudal peduncle. Snout protruding, blunt. No premaxillary frenum, mouth terminal, eye moderate, closely set. Infraorbital and supratemporal canals interrupted. Squamation reduced or absent on nape, cheek, and breast. Branchiostegal membranes narrowly joined. Lateral line complete, lateral line scales 50–65. Dorsal spines 6–10, dorsal rays 9–12, anal spines 1–2, anal rays 8–9. Straw above and sides, 6 dark brown saddles, black teardrop, many dark brown specks and Xs, Ws, and Ys on sides, translucent below. Black spot at front of spinous dorsal fin, pelvic, anal, and caudal fins with black margins. Breeding male with black head, body, pelvic and anal fins. Hudson Bay, Great Lakes, Mississippi River, and Gulf of Mexico from VA to WY and CO. Abundant. Lakes, headwater streams, creeks, and small, moderate, and large rivers over sand substrates. Benthic insectivore. Guarding, nest-spawning speleophil (B.2.7). Maximum size 70 mm TL.

178   SCALY DARTER—*Etheostoma* cf. *nigrum* nov. sp.. Slender, elongate, terete body with slender caudal peduncle. Snout blunt, premaxillary frenum absent, mouth terminal, eye moderate. Branchiostegal membrane narrowly joined. Extensive squamation of nape, cheek, and breast. Infraorbital and supratemporal canals interrupted. Lateral line complete, lateral line scales 40–51. Dorsal spines 6–9, dorsal rays 9–12, anal spines 2, anal rays 8–9. Straw above and sides, 6 dark brown saddles, black teardrop, many dark brown specks and Xs, Ws, and Ys on sides, translucent below. Melanophores marking on the cheek, black spot at front of spinous dorsal fin, pelvic, anal, and caudal fins with black margins. Breeding male with black head, body, pelvic, and anal fins. Lakes Michigan and Erie, Mississippi River, Hudson Bay from western MN and IA, east to northwest IN to ON, northern OH and PA; isolated in Neosho River, MO. Common. Lakes, headwater streams, creeks and small, moderate, and large rivers over sand substrates. Benthic insectivore. Guarding, nest-spawning speleophil (B.2.7). Maximum size 100 mm TL.

176 LEAST DARTER—
Etheostoma microperca

177 JOHNNY DARTER—
Etheostoma nigrum nigrum

178 SCALY DARTER—
Etheostoma cf. *nigrum*

179   PRAIRIE DARTER—*Etheostoma pholidotum* (Miller). Elongate, terete body. Snout blunt, rarely overhanging subterminal mouth, eye small, head narrow. Belly and opercle completely scaled. Dorsal spines 11–14, dorsal rays 12–14, anal spines 2, anal rays 9. Lateral line complete, lateral scales 58–62. Dark green above, teardrop present, 7–8 midlateral blotches form Us or Ws, white below. Spinous dorsal fin with middle or marginal stripe, soft dorsal with 2–3 concentric stripes, pectoral fins with scattered pigment, caudal fin with 4 vertical stripes, and pelvic and anal fins unpigmented. Wabash basin eastern IL and IN, across Maumee drainage OH and MI, north into ON, and east along Lakes Erie and Ontario, NY. Common. Streams, small and medium rivers in riffles over gravel substrates. Benthic invertivore. Guarding, substrate-choosing phytophil (B.1.4). Maximum size 138 mm TL.

180   CYPRESS DARTER—*Etheostoma proeliare* (Hay). Deep, laterally compressed body. Snout rounded, mouth terminal, eye large. Breast unscaled. Infraorbital canal interrupted 4 pores. Lateral line scales 34–38, lateral line pores 0–9. Anal spines 2. Olive above, thin teardrop, 6–9 dark brown saddles, black blotches along side, spots on sides, white to yellow below. First dorsal fin with anterior spot, black edge, and red middle band. Spawning male with black pelvic and anal fin. Caudal fin truncate. Mississippi River basins from IL to Gulf of Mexico. Rare. Basic gradient streams associated with aquatic macrophytes over mud and sand substrates. Benthic invertivore. Guarding, substrate-choosing phytophil (B.1.4). Maximum size 45 mm TL.

181   ORANGETHROAT DARTER—*Etheostoma spectabile* (Agassiz). Deep, laterally compressed body. Snout rounded, mouth terminal, eye moderate. Infraorbital canal interrupted. Supratemporal canal complete. Body deepest at nape. Lateral line incomplete, lateral line scales 40–53. Pectoral rays 11–12. Olive above, 7–10 dark saddles, teardrop, orange branchiostegal membranes, lateral bars from anus to caudal peduncle, checkerboard pattern from shoulder to anus, white to orange below. Blue margin with red median band on dorsal fin, male with blue anal fin, black pelvic fins, 2 orange spots on caudal fin base. Mississippi River, Lake Erie, Gulf Coast basins from MI to WY south to TX and TN. Abundant. Headwater streams, ditches, springs in gravel runs, riffles, and vegetated pools. Benthic invertivore. Non-guarding, brood-hiding lithophil (A.2.3). Maximum size 76 mm TL.

179 PRAIRIE DARTER—
Etheostoma pholidotum

180 CYPRESS DARTER—
Etheostoma proeliare

181 NORTHERN ORANGETHROAT DARTER—
Etheostoma spectabile spectabile

182 SPOTTAIL DARTER—*Etheostoma squamiceps* Jordan. Elongate, terete body. Snout rounded, mouth terminal, eye moderate. Infraorbital canal interrupted. Dorsal spines 9, dorsal rays 13 with small white knobs and 3 branches per ray, second and third branches equal in length, adnate and tipped with small white knob. Olive to brown above, 7–8 saddles, with 11–13 vertical bars along midlateral, 3 vertical spots at base of caudal peduncle, tan or yellow below. Soft dorsal and caudal fins with black and white horizontal stripes, spinous dorsal, pelvic, and anal fins black. Breeding male with black head. Lower Ohio River basin from KY and TN to IL and IN. Rare to occasional. Headwater streams and creeks with slab rock pools and sand riffles. Benthic invertivore. Guarding, nest-spawning speleophil (B.2.7). Maximum size 104 mm TL.

183 TIPPECANOE DARTER—*Etheostoma tippecanoe* Jordan and Evermann. Short, deep, laterally compressed body. Snout pointed, mouth terminal, eye moderate. Incomplete lateral line, lateral line scales 40–65. Brown or yellow above, blue-black bars on side, darkest at rear, last bar surrounding caudal peduncle, female with 2 yellow or male with 2 orange spots, yellow or blue below, fins orange or unpigmented. Breeding male is orange with electric blue breast, black specks on fins. Ohio River basin from PA to IN, south to VA and TN. Rare to occasional. Moderate to large rivers in riffles with cobble or large gravel substrates with clean interstitial spaces. Benthic invertivore. Guarding, substrate-choosing lithophil (B.1.3). Maximum size 52 mm TL.

184 VARIEGATE DARTER—*Etheostoma variatum* Kirtland. Large, terete body. Snout rounded, eye diameter equal to snout length, mouth terminal. Posterior margin of breast scaled. Branchiostegal membrane broadly joined. Lateral line complete, lateral scales 48–60. Brown above, 4 large brown saddles angled forward toward lateral line, green and orange bars on side, orange spots on side and fins, white or red below. Spinous dorsal fin with red margin and median blue band. Breeding male with deep blue and orange or red belly. Ohio River basin from NY to VA, KY to IN, below Kanawha Falls, WV. Occasional to common. Moderate-sized to large rivers in riffles with cobble or large gravel substrates. Benthic invertivore. Guarding, substrate-choosing lithophil (B.1.3). Maximum size 89 mm TL.

182   SPOTTAIL DARTER—
        Etheostoma squamiceps

183   TIPPECANOE DARTER—
        Etheostoma tippecanoev

184   VARIEGATE DARTER—
        Etheostoma variatum

185 JADE DARTER—*Etheostoma* cf. *zonale* nov. sp. Deep, laterally compressed body. Cheek, opercle, nape, and breast completely scaled. Body deepest at dorsal origin. Lateral line complete, lateral line scales 46. Dorsal spines 11, dorsal rays 10, anal spines 2, anal rays 6. Branchiostegal rays 6–6. Infraorbital canal pores 7, preoperculomandibular pores 10. Brown or olive above, lips yellow, green teardrop, 10 green dorsal bands connecting to 10 lateral bands, white or with turquoise breast below. Spinous and soft dorsal fin with orange or red stripe along base and jade edge, turquoise or jade-green pelvic and anal fins, caudal fin with vertical stripes. Upper Mississippi River from Meramec and Missouri rivers, MO, northward to Zumbro and Minnesota rivers, MN, east to Kankakee River, IN. Common. Moderate to large rivers in riffles with cobble or large gravel substrates. Benthic invertivore. Guarding, substrate-choosing phytophil (B.1.4). Maximum size 75 mm TL.

186 BANDED DARTER—*Etheostoma zonale* (Cope). Slender, laterally compressed body. Breast without or nearly without scales. Body deepest posterior dorsal fin origin. Lateral line complete, lateral line scales 39–57. Dorsal spines 8–11, dorsal rays 11–12, anal spines 2, anal rays 7–9. Branchiostegal rays 6–6. Infraorbital canal pores 7, preoperculomandibular pores 10. Brown or olive above, 6–10 green dorsal bands connected to 6–10 lateral bands, white or with green breast below. Spinous and soft dorsal fin with brick red basal band and green edge, pelvic and anal fin spines kelly green, caudal fins with vertical stripes. Ohio River above fall line including tributaries above Kentucky River in IN, OH, WV, western PA, and southwest NY. Common. Streams, moderate and large rivers in riffles with cobble or large gravel substrates. Benthic invertivore. Guarding, substrate-choosing phytophil (B.1.4). Maximum size 72 mm TL.

187 YELLOW PERCH—*Perca flavescens* (Mitchill). Deep, laterally compressed body. Pointed snout, large mouth extending to middle of eye, no canine teeth. Lateral line scales 52–61. Dorsal rays 12–14, anal rays 6–8. Forked caudal fin. Green to olive above, 6–9 green-brown saddles terminating in triangular tips, yellow sides, white below. Black blotch at front and back margins, yellow to red paired and caudal fins. Atlantic, Arctic, Great Lakes, and Mississippi River basins from NS to NT south to SC, west to NE. Lakes, ponds, and pools of creeks, streams, and small to large rivers usually associated with submerged aquatic vegetation. Common. Benthic invertivore. Non-guarding, open substrate phytolithophil (A.1.4). Maximum size 305 mm TL.

185 JADE DARTER—
Etheostoma cf. *zonale*

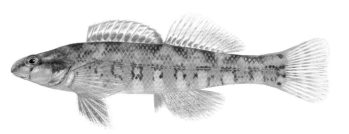

186 BANDED DARTER—
Etheostoma zonale

187 YELLOW PERCH—
Perca flavescens

188   LOGPERCH—*Percina caprodes* (Rafinesque). Slender, elongate, terete body. Snout conical with bulbous tip, mouth terminal, eye moderate. No scales on top of head, nape scaled. Dorsal spines 12–16, dorsal rays 12–18, anal spines 2, anal rays 8–11. Lateral line complete, lateral line scales 67–100. Olive back, dusky teardrop, numerous long alternating or equal-length bars terminating at or below the lateral line, white or translucent below. Spinous dorsal fin without orange edge. Great Lakes, Hudson Bay, and Mississippi River basins from NY to Gulf Coast from FL and AL to Mississippi River, LA. Medium, large, and great rivers over sand and gravel substrates in runs and littoral lake shorelines. Common to abundant. Benthic invertivore. Non-guarding, brood-hiding lithophil (A.2.3). Maximum size 200 mm TL.

189   CHANNEL DARTER—*Percina copelandi* (Jordan). Elongate, slender, terete body. Blunt snout, no premaxillary frenum, eye moderate. Cheek and opercle scaled, breast and preopercle unscaled. Lateral line complete, lateral scales 43–61. Dorsal spines 9–12, dorsal rays 10–14, anal spines 2, anal rays 7–10. Caudal fin emarginate to slightly notched. Olive above, dusky teardrop, 9–10 horizontal, oblong black blotches along side, black Xs and Ws on back and upper side, medial black caudal spot, translucent below. Spinous dorsal fin with black margin and base, second dorsal fin black at base, and caudal fin with several black vertical bands. Great Lakes and Mississippi River basins from QC south to LA along Gulf Slope. Rare. Medium, large, and great rivers in pools and margins of riffles on sand and gravel substrates. Benthic invertivore. Non-guarding, brood-hiding lithophil (A.2.3). Maximum size 61 mm TL.

190   GILT DARTER—*Percina evides* (Jordan and Copeland). Deep, laterally compressed body. Snout rounded, mouth terminal, eye moderate. Supratemporal pore canals present. Cheeks, breast, and belly unscaled, opercle and nape scaled. Lateral line scales 51–77. Dorsal spines 11–14, dorsal rays 10–13, anal spines 2, anal rays 6–9. Caudal fin slightly emarginated. Olive above, 6–8 black saddles connected to lateral bands, white or yellow areas at caudal fin base, yellow to bright orange underside of head, breast, and belly below. Spinous dorsal fin orange or yellow at base, orange band at base of all median fins with white margins along edge. Mississippi River from NY to MN south to AL west to AR; extirpated from Maumee River drainage and from OH, IA, and IL. Occasional. Medium and large rivers in riffle and run habitat over cobble and gravel substrates. Benthic invertivore. Non-guarding, brood-hiding lithophil (A.2.3). Maximum size 71 mm TL.

188 LOGPERCH—
Percina caprodes caprodes

189 CHANNEL DARTER—
Percina copelandi

190 GILT DARTER—
Percina evides

191 BLACKSIDE DARTER—*Percina maculata* (Girard). Elongate, laterally compressed body. Snout rounded, mouth terminal, eye moderate. Cheek scaled posterior eye, breast and preopercle unscaled. Nape, opercle, and belly variable, either completely scaled or unscaled. Branchiostegal membrane narrowly connected. Dorsal spines 12–17, dorsal rays 10–15, anal spines 2, anal rays 7–13. Caudal fin slightly emarginate. Olive above, prominent teardrop, wavy black lines connected horizontally above lateral line, 8–9 dark saddles, 6–9 large oval black blotches at midlateral, discrete medial black caudal spot, white below. Both dorsal fins dusky, first with black spot at front and along base. Great Lakes, Hudson Bay, and Mississippi River basins from NY to SK and south to LA, along Gulf Coast to AL. Common. Creeks, small to medium rivers, usually in pools over gravel or sand substrates. Benthic invertivore. Non-guarding, brood-hiding lithophil (A.2.3). Maximum size 101 mm TL.

192 SLENDERHEAD DARTER—*Percina phoxocephala* (Nelson). Elongate, laterally compressed body. Snout pointed and elongate, mouth terminal, eye moderate. Supratemporal canal pores present. Nape scaled, breast partially scaled. Cheek, opercle, preopercle, and belly unscaled. Branchiostegal membrane moderately connected. Dorsal spines 10–14, dorsal rays 10–14, anal spines 2, anal rays 7–10. Caudal fin emarginate. Olive to straw above, wavy brown horizontal stripes above lateral line, black teardrop, 10–16 round brown-black midlateral blotches, white to yellow below. Spinous dorsal fin with red edge, soft dorsal with red median band, caudal fin with vertical bands, all other fins unpigmented. Mississippi River basin from OH to SD to OK and east to northern AL. Common. Moderate to large rivers in riffles over large gravel and cobble substrates. Benthic invertivore. Non-guarding, brood-hiding lithophil (A.2.3). Maximum size 95 mm TL.

193 DUSKY DARTER—*Percina sciera* (Swain). Deep, laterally compressed body. Snout elongate and round, mouth terminal, eye moderate, serrate preopercle. Lateral line complete, lateral line scales 56–78. Dorsal spines 10–14, dorsal rays 10–14, anal spines 2, anal rays 7–10. Caudal fin truncate to slightly emarginate. Olive above, 7–9 saddles, discrete wavy lines separated between blotches and saddles, no teardrop, 8–9 horizontal blotches, 3 spots at caudal base, white below. Median fins with scattered pigment forming vertical stripes including caudal fin, fins mostly clear. Mississippi River basin from WV to IL and south to LA, along Gulf Coast from AL to TX. Common. Creeks, small to medium rivers in riffles and run habitats often associated with woody debris. Benthic invertivore. Non-guarding, brood-hiding lithophil (A.2.3). Maximum size 132 mm TL.

191 BLACKSIDE DARTER—
Percina maculata

192 SLENDERHEAD DARTER—
Percina phoxocephala

193 DUSKY DARTER—
Percina sciera sciera

194 RIVER DARTER—*Percina shumardi* (Girard). Elongate, terete body. Snout elongate and round, mouth terminal, eye large. Lateral line complete, lateral line scales 46–57. Dorsal spines 8–11, dorsal rays 12–14, anal spines 2, anal rays 8–12. Caudal fin slightly emarginate. Olive above, 8–15 black bars along side, black teardrop, small black caudal spot, white below. Small black spots at front and rear of spinous dorsal fin, membranes of all median fins dusky, pectoral and pelvic fins unpigmented. Great Lakes, Hudson Bay, Mississippi River basins, and Gulf Coastal Plain from AL to TX. Occasional. Moderate to large rivers in shoals and riffles associated with cobble and large gravel substrates. Benthic invertivore. Non-guarding, brood-hiding lithophil (A.2.3). Maximum size 73 mm TL.

195 STARGAZING DARTER—*Percina uranidea* (Jordan and Gilbert). Robust and terete body. Blunt snout, eye high on head, mouth terminal. Frenum absent, gill membranes narrowly joined. Cheeks scaled. Lateral line complete, lateral line scales 48–55. Dorsal spines 10–11, anal spines 2, elongate anal fin with 9 rays. Rusty above, 4 narrow dorsal saddles round at tips bifurcating into 2 blotches at terminus near lateral line, teardrop present, numerous brown specks on body, white below. Spinous and soft dorsal, anal, and caudal fins with black bands, pectoral and pelvic fins without pigmentation. Missouri River basin from MO, AR, and LA, extirpated from IN and IL. Rare and probably extirpated. Large and medium rivers from high-flow gravel runs. Benthic invertivore. Non-guarding, brood-hiding lithophil (A.2.3). Maximum size 78 mm TL.

196 SADDLEBACK DARTER—*Percina vigil* (Hoy). Robust and terete body. Snout blunt, eyes set on top of the head, mouth terminal. Branchiostegal membranes separate to slightly connected, narrow frenum, and an elongate anal fin on breeding male. Lateral line complete, lateral line scales 46–58. Dorsal spines 9–12, dorsal rays 12–15, anal spines 2, anal rays 10–11. Caudal fin emarginate. Yellow to olive above, back with 4 saddles and a small, less-defined saddle near caudal fin, side has 8–10 square blotches separate from saddles, distinct teardrop present in front and below eye, white or pale yellow below. Spinous dorsal fin black at base and margin, other fins are faintly banded or clear, a small but distinct spot present at base of the caudal fin. Mississippi River basin from IN and MO to LA from Gulf Coast from FL to AL. Rare. Small to medium rivers over sand and gravel runs in shoal areas. Benthic invertivore. Non-guarding, brood-hiding lithophil (A.2.3). Maximum size 72 mm TL.

194 RIVER DARTER—
Percina shumardi

195 STARGAZING DARTER—
Percina uranidea

196 SADDLEBACK DARTER—
Percina vigil

197 MANITOU DARTER—*Percina zebra* (Jordan). Body elongate, laterally compressed. Snout short, blunt, and less sloping that *P. caprodes,* head slender, eye large 3.5–4 times into head length, mouth small, subterminal, maxillary not reaching to eye. Cheeks and opercles with small scales, nape and breast unscaled. Dorsal spines 15, dorsal rays 14, anal spines 2, anal rays 10. Lateral line complete, lateral scales 90. Olive above, marbled pigment on back extending into about 20 short vertical bands that do not reach to lateral line, separate spiral blotches on midline, white to translucent below. Spinous dorsal with red edge, soft dorsal and caudal fins mottled. Great Lakes including the lakes of northern IN, MI, WI, and northward to Lake Superior. Common. Lakes and river flowages occurring in runs and littoral habitats over sand and gravel. Benthic invertivore. Non-guarding, brood-hiding lithophil (A.2.3). Maximum size 132 mm TL.

198 SAUGER—*Sander canadense* (Smith). Elongate, deep bodied. Long, pointed snout, large mouth extending beyond middle of eye, large canine teeth, eye gray and opaque. Lateral line complete, lateral scales 77–104. Dorsal spines 19–22, dorsal rays 17–19, anal rays 11–12. Pyloric caeca 5–8, forked caudal fin. Brown to olive-yellow above, dark green wavy marks, 3–4 dusky saddles extend onto side as broad bars, side brassy to brown, white below. Spinous dorsal fin membrane with scattered black bars, anal fin and lower lobe of caudal fin with white edge. Great Lakes, Arctic, Mississippi River basins from QC to AB, south to AL and LA. Introduced outside of native range. Occasional to common. Small to large rivers associated with sand and gravel runs. Whole body, protective resemblance carnivore. Non-guarding, open substrate lithopelagophil (A.1.2). Maximum size 460 mm TL.

199 WALLEYE—*Sander vitreus* (Mitchill). Elongate, deep bodied. Long, pointed snout, large mouth extending beyond middle of eye, large canine teeth, eye gray and opaque. Lateral line complete, lateral scales 77–104. Dorsal spines 19–22, dorsal rays 12–14, anal rays 12–14. Pyloric caeca 3, forked caudal fin. Brown to olive-yellow above, dark green wavy marks, 5–12 dusky saddles extend onto side as short indiscrete bars, side brassy to brown, white below. Large black spot on posterior edge of spinous dorsal fin, anal fin and lower lobe of caudal fin with white edge. Great Lakes, Arctic, Mississippi River basins from QC to NT, south to AR and AL. Introduced outside of native range. Occasional to common. Lakes and large, deep rivers associated with woody debris and submerged trees. Whole body, protective resemblance carnivore. Non-guarding, open substrate lithopelagophil (A.1.2). Maximum size 780 mm TL.

197 MANITOU DARTER—
Percina zebra

198 SAUGER—
Sander canadense

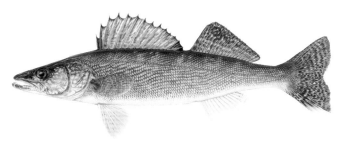

199 WALLEYE—
Sander vitreus

SAUGEYE—
Sander vitreus X *Sander canadense*

PYGMY SUNFISH FAMILY—ELASSOMATIDAE
(SPECIES PLATE 200)

The pygmy sunfish family was formerly included in the Centrarchidae, where it was considered a closely related family. The Elassomatidae is no longer considered neotonic Centrarchidae, rather the nearest common ancestors may be outside of the Percoidei (Johnson 1984). The family occurs in freshwater and consists of a single genus and 6 species (Nelson et al. 2004). Indiana possesses a single species.

The family is diagnosed by the absence of infraorbitals, basisphenoid, and endopterygoid; branchiostegal rays 5; gill membranes broadly united across isthmus; dentary and angular not penetrated by lateral line; no lateral line present on body; caudal fin rounded; cycloid scales; dorsal fin with 2–5 spines and 8–13 soft rays; and anal fin with 3 spines and 4–8 soft rays (Nelson 2006).

The species occurs in the former cypress swamps, marshes, and former wetlands of the Wabash River floodplain. The Banded pygmy sunfish is usually associated with submerged aquatic vegetation or overhanging terrestrial vegetation. Banded pygmy sunfish are water column, drift invertivores (Goldstein and Simon 1999). Spawning occurs as substrate-choosing phytophils (Simon 1999).

SUNFISH FAMILY—CENTRARCHIDAE
(SPECIES PLATES 201–217)

The Centrarchidae are a North American freshwater family that includes 8 genera and 31 species (Nelson et al. 2004). The family includes 6 genera and 17 species in Indiana.

The family is diagnosed by the presence of the suborbital and lachrymal bones; dentary and angular penetrated by lateral line; lateral line present on body, sometimes incomplete; anal fin spines usually 3 or fewer or 5 or more; dorsal fin usually with 13–15 spines; pseudobranch small and concealed; branchiostegal rays 6 or 7; gill membranes separate; and vertebrae 28–33 (Nelson 2006).

Most members of the family are nest-builders. They are important sport fish and have been widely introduced outside of native ranges. Courtship involves males constructing, cleaning, and defending nests from other males and predators. Males allow females to enter the nest and after spawning the male guards the eggs. After hatching, the male provides some protection. Most sunfish are water column, drift invertivores, while the black basses are whole body carnivores (Goldstein and Simon 1999).

KEY TO THE SUNFISHES AND PYGMY SUNFISH OF INDIANA

1 a) Caudal fin without a notch; spinous dorsal usually with 4 or 5 spines; anal fin usually with 5–6 soft rays; lateral line absent; size less than 50 mm .... **BANDED PYGMY SUNFISH**—*Elassoma zonatum*

   b) Caudal fin with a definite notch; spinous dorsal usually with 6 or more spines; anal fin usually with 8 or more soft rays; lateral line present; adults attain sizes greater than 50 mm 2

2 a) Anal fin spines usually 3, rarely 2 or 4....................................3

   b) Anal fin spines usually 5–8..15

3 a) Body more slender, its depth (A) going 3 times or more into SL (B) except in largest adults; mouth larger, upper jaw extending to or behind middle of eye; scales small, with 55 or more in lateral line........ **BLACK BASSES**—*Micropterus* (4)

b) Body deeper, its depth (A) going less than 3 times into SL (B); mouth smaller, upper jaw not extending behind middle of eye except in adults of a few species; scales larger, with fewer than 55 in lateral line..................**SUNFISHES**—*Lepomis* (6)

4 a) Mouth large, upper jaw extending far behind back of eye in fish more than 150 mm TL; spinous dorsal and soft dorsal nearly separate; margin of spinous dorsal strongly convex, the length of shortest spine near notch (A) less than half the length of longest spine (B); midside with a dark horizontal stripe; tail fin of young two-colored rather than three-colored, the rear part of the fin darker than the base..................
..................**LARGEMOUTH BASS**—*Micropterus salmoides*

b) Mouth smaller, upper jaw not extending much behind back of eye; spinous dorsal and soft dorsal well connected (if pull on spinous dorsal the soft dorsal fin is raised); margin of spinous dorsal gently rounded, the length of shortest spine near notch (A) more than half the length of the longest spine (B); midside with or without a dark horizontal stripe; tail fin of young distinctly three-colored with a prominent, dark vertical bar separating yellow or orange base from white fringe on rear margin of fin...5

5 a) Side with a dark horizontal stripe; lower side with a series of dark horizontal streaks in adults; juveniles with a prominent black spot at base of caudal fin; scales larger, usually 59–65 in lateral line and 23–26 around narrowest part of caudal peduncle; rays in soft dorsal usually 12–13................................
.... **SPOTTED BASS**—*Micropterus punctulatus*

b) Side plain or with a series of separate vertical bars; lower side without dark horizontal streaks; juveniles without a prominent black spot at base of caudal fin; scales smaller, usually 68–76 in lateral line and 29–31 around narrowest part of caudal peduncle; rays in soft dorsal usually 13–15.....
..................**SMALLMOUTH BASS**—*Micropterus dolomieu*

6 a) Tongue with a patch of teeth; mouth large, upper jaw extending to or behind middle of eye; several distinct dark lines radiating from eye............**WARMOUTH**—*Lepomis gulosus*

  b) Tongue without teeth; mouth smaller, upper jaw not extending behind middle of eye except in adult green sunfish; no distinct dark lines radiating back from eye 7

7 a) Pectoral fin shorter and tip rounded, usually not extending beyond front of eye when bent forward toward eye; mouth larger, upper jaw extending to beneath pupil of eye except in small young... 8

  b) Pectoral fin longer and tip pointed, usually extending far beyond front of eye when bent forward toward eye; mouth smaller, upper jaw not extending to beneath pupil of eye 13

8 a) Rear margin of gill cover (lying within base of but not including membranous opercular flap) stiff; membranous ear flap not greatly elongated 9

  b) Rear margin of gill cover thin and flexible; membranous ear flap elongated in adults, especially males............................. 11

9 a) Body slender, its depth (A) usually less than distance from tip of snout to front of dorsal fin (B); snout longer, its length (C) going less than 2 times into distance from back of eye to rear margin of ear flap (D); lateral line scales usually 41 or more..........................**GREEN SUNFISH**—*Lepomis cyanellus*

  b) Body deeper, its depth (A) greater than distance from tip of snout to front of dorsal fin (B); snout shorter, its length (C) going about 2 times into distance from back of eye to rear margin of ear flap (D); lateral line scales usually 40 or fewer 10

10 a) Soft dorsal with a prominent black spot near base of last few rays except in largest adults; lateral line usually incomplete; size small, length usually less than 65 mm .... **BANTAM SUNFISH**—*Lepomis symmetricus*

  b) Soft dorsal fin without a spot near base of last few rays; lateral line usually complete; size larger, length commonly more than 65 mm TL.........................**REDSPOTTED SUNFISH**— ....*Lepomis miniatus*

11 a) Gill rakers on first arch moderately long and thin, their length more than twice their width; 2 pit-like depressions in skull between eyes large, their width (A) about equal to distance between them (B) .... **ORANGESPOTTED SUNFISH**—*Lepomis humilis*

   b) Gill rakers on first arch short and thick, their length less than twice their width; 2 pit-like depressions in skull between eyes small, their width (A) much less than distance between them (B) 12

12 a) Ear flap without narrow white margin and red spot on an upwardly slanted ear flap; scales larger, lateral line scales 49 or fewer, opercle flexible posteriorly, with a narrow red membrane behind; gill rakers reduced to knobs.................... ... **NORTHERN LONGEAR SUNFISH**—*Lepomis peltastes*

   b) Ear flap black with narrow white margin; side of male with numerous scattered red and blue pigment flecks; gill rakers on first arch short, length about 2 times their width at base; pectoral rays usually 13–14... .... **LONGEAR SUNFISH**—*Lepomis megalotis*

13 a) Soft dorsal with a distinct black blotch near base of last few rays; gill rakers on first arch long and thin, their length more than twice their width; ear flap dark to its margin, without a light-colored border; ear flap without a red or orange spot ....**BLUEGILL**—*Lepomis macrochirus*

   b) Soft dorsal without a blotch near base of last few rays; gill rakers on first arch short and thick, their length less than twice their width; ear flap not dark to its margin, with a light-colored border; ear flap with a prominent red or orange spot in adults..14

14 a) Rear margin of gill cover (lying within base of but not including membranous ear flap) stiff; soft dorsal with distinct
spots; cheeks with wavy bluish lines...
....**PUMPKINSEED**—*Lepomis gibbosus*

   b) Rear margin of gill cover thin and flexible; soft dorsal
without distinct spots; cheeks without wavy bluish lines in
adults.............. **REDEAR SUNFISH**—*Lepomis microlophus*

15 a) Dorsal fin spines usually 11–13..16

   b) Dorsal fin spines usually 6–8...17

16 a) Anal fin much smaller than dorsal fin, with 6 spines and
10–11 rays; body depth (A) less than half the standard length
(B) .... **ROCK BASS**—*Ambloplites rupestris*

   b) Anal fin nearly as large as dorsal fin, with 7–8 spines and
13–15 rays; body depth (A) about half the standard length
(B) .... **FLIER**—*Centrarchus macropterus*

17 a) Dorsal fin spines usually 7–8; dark markings on sides consisting of irregularly arranged speckles and blotches............
........................**BLACK CRAPPIE**—*Pomoxis nigromaculatus*

   b) Dorsal fin spines usually 6; dark margin on sides consisting
of regularly arranged vertical bars...
.... **WHITE CRAPPIE**—*Pomoxis annularis*

200 BANDED PYGMY SUNFISH—*Elassoma zonatum* Jordan. Laterally compressed body. Upturned mouth with protruding lower jaw, large eye, head moderate. Cycloid scales on top of head. Lateral line scales 28–45. Dorsal fin 4–5 spines, dorsal rays 9–10; anal fin spines 3, anal fin rays 5–6. Caudal fin rounded. Black with greenish-gold flecks back, 1–2 large black spots on upper side below dorsal fin origin, 7–12 dark green to blue-black bars on side and below, fins black. Breeding male with greenish-gold flecks. Black fins, goldish-green bar beneath eye. Black bars on side. Black fins, goldish-green bar beneath eye. Atlantic and Gulf Coast north to southern IN in Mississippi River Embayment. Rare. Marshes and vegetated headwater streams over mud substrates. Drift, water column invertivore. Guarding, substrate-choosing phytophil (B.1.4). Maximum size 45 mm TL.

201 ROCK BASS—*Ambloplites rupestris* (Rafinesque). Deep, laterally compressed body. Snout pointed, large mouth, red eye, head moderate. Unscaled or partly scaled cheek. Lateral line scales 39–49, scale rows across breast (pectoral fin to pectoral fin) 21–25. Dorsal fin spines 11–13, anal fin rays 10–11. Light green above, brassy yellow flecks on side with 5 wide, dark saddles over back extending to midside, white to bronze breast and belly below. Black edges on dorsal, caudal, and anal fins. Great Lakes, Hudson Bay, and Mississippi River basins from Canada south to northern GA, west to MO. Common. Creeks to moderate-sized rivers and lakes associated with submerged vegetation, woody debris, and rocks. Invertivore/carnivore. Guarding, nest-spawning polyphil (B.2.2). Maximum size 265 mm TL.

202 FLIER—*Centrarchus macropterus* (Lacepede). Deep, laterally compressed body. Small mouth. Dorsal fin base about as long as anal fin base. Lateral line scales 36–44, dorsal spines 11–13, dorsal rays 13–15, anal spines 7–8, anal rays 13–17. Dusky gray back with 4 broad dark bars extending along side, large black teardrop beneath eye, silver side, many green and bronze flecks, interrupted rows of black along side, large red halo around large black spot on posterior dorsal fin, silver below. Brown-black spots usually with wavy lines on dorsal, caudal, and anal fins, black edge on front half of anal fin. Coastal Plain from Atlantic to Gulf Coast north into Mississippi Embayment in southeastern IN. Occasional. Marshes, lakes, and vegetated creeks, sloughs, and backwaters in pools over mud substrates. Drift, water column invertivore. Guarding, nest-spawning lithophil (B.2.3). Maximum size 190 mm TL.

200 BANDED PYGMY SUNFISH—
Elassoma zonatum

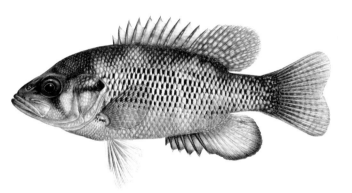

201 ROCK BASS—
Ambloplites rupestris

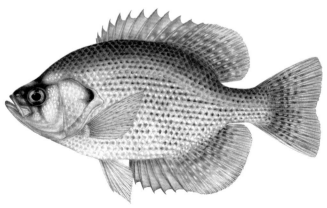

202 FLIER—
Centrarchus macropterus

203 GREEN SUNFISH—*Lepomis cyanellus* Rafinesque. Deep, more elongate, laterally compressed body. Long snout, large mouth with upper jaw extending beneath pupil. Short, round pectoral fins, usually not reaching past front of eye when bent forward. Short ear flap, stiff rear edge of gill cover (excluding ear flap). Complete lateral line, lateral line scales 41–53. Pectoral fin rays 13–14, anal fin rays 9. Long, slender rakers on first arch. Blue-green back and side, often yellow-metallic green flecks, sometimes dusky bars on side, blue wavy lines on cheek and opercle, yellow or orange edges on black ear flap, white below. Large black spot at rear of soft dorsal and anal fin bases. Great Lakes, Hudson Bay, and Mississippi River basins south to Gulf Slope. Abundant. Headwater streams to large rivers, ponds, and lakes in quiet pools, backwaters associated with rock rubble, vegetation, and muck substrates. Drift, water column invertivore. Guarding, nest-spawning polyphil (B.2.2). Maximum size 250 mm TL.

204 PUMPKINSEED—*Lepomis gibbosus* (Linnaeus). Deep, laterally compressed body. Small mouth, upper jaw not extending beneath eye, long pointed pectoral fin usually extends far past eye when bent forward. Short ear flap with stiff rear edge on gill cover (excluding ear flap). Complete lateral line, lateral line scales 35–47. Pectoral fin rays 12–13, anal fin rays 10. Short, thick rakers on first gill arch. Olive back and side, many gold and yellow flecks, wavy blue lines on cheek and opercle, bright red or orange spots on side, light-colored edge on black ear flap, dusky chain-like bars on side, white or red-orange below. Bold, dark brown wavy lines or orange spots on second dorsal, anal, and caudal fins. Atlantic Slope, Great Lakes, Hudson Bay, and upper Mississippi River basins. Common. Lakes, ponds, creeks to moderate-sized rivers associated with submerged aquatic plants. Drift, water column invertivore. Guarding, nest-spawning lithophil (B.2.2). Maximum size 400 mm TL.

205 WARMOUTH—*Lepomis gulosus* (Cuvier). Deep, slender, laterally compressed body. Pair of patch teeth on tongue. Large mouth with upper jaw extending beneath eye. Short ear flap with stiff rear edge on gill cover (excluding ear flap). Complete lateral line, lateral line scales 36–44. Pectoral fin rays 14, anal fin rays 9–10. Long thin rakers on first gill arch. Olive-brown above usually with purple sheen, dark brown mottling on back and upper side, often 6–11 hollow, dark brown bars on side, red spot on yellow edge of ear flap, cream to yellow below. Wavy bands on fins and pelvic fin black. Breeding male with bold patterns on body and fins, bright red-orange spot at base of second dorsal fin. Great Lakes and Mississippi River basins south to Gulf of Mexico along Atlantic Slope. Common. Lakes, ponds, marshes, and large rivers associated with submerged vegetation over mud substrates. Drift, water column invertivore/whole body, chasing carnivore. Guarding, nest-spawning polyphil (B.2.3). Maximum size 284 mm TL.

203 GREEN SUNFISH—
Lepomis cyanellus

204 PUMPKINSEED—
Lepomis gibbosus

205 WARMOUTH—
Lepomis gulosus

206 ORANGESPOTTED SUNFISH—*Lepomis humilis* (Girard). Deep, laterally compressed body. Fairly long snout, large mouth with upper jaw extending beneath eye. Thin, flexible rear edge on gill cover. Greatly elongate pores along preopercle edge, large sensory pits between eyes. Short, rounded pectoral fin usually not extending past eye when bent forward. Complete lateral line, lateral line scales 32–41. Pectoral fin rays 14, anal fin rays 9. Fairly long, thin rakers on first gill arch. Olive on back, silver-blue flecks on side, orange, red, or brown wavy lines on cheek and opercle, white to orange below. Fins unspotted. Breeding male with bright red-orange spots on side, red eye, belly, and edges on anal and dorsal fins, pelvic fins with black edge on white pelvic fins. Lower Great Lakes, Hudson Bay, and Mississippi River basins, south to Gulf Coast. Occasional. Creeks, small to large rivers, lakes, ponds, and marshes associated with submerged vegetation and woody debris in turbid waters. Drift, water column invertivore. Guarding, nest-spawning lithophil (B.2.3). Maximum size 100 mm TL.

207 BLUEGILL—*Lepomis macrochirus* Rafinesque. Deep, laterally compressed body. Small mouth with upper jaw not reaching to front of eye. Long, pointed pectoral fins usually reaching past eye when bent forward. Ear flap black to edge, thin, flexible rear edge on gill cover. Complete lateral line, lateral line scales 38–48. Pectoral fin rays 13, anal fin rays 11. Long, thin rakers on first gill arch. Olive back and side with yellow and green flecks, blue sheen over body, 2 blue streaks from chin to edge of gill cover, hollow bars extending to midside, large black spot on posterior margin at rear of dorsal fin and often with a dusky spot at rear of anal fin, white to yellow below. Clear to dusky fins with black pelvic fins. Great Lakes and Mississippi River basins south to Gulf and along Atlantic Slope. Abundant. Lakes, ponds, marshes and pools of creeks, and small to large rivers. Drift, water column insectivore. Guarding, nest-spawning lithophil (B.2.2). Maximum size 405 mm TL.

208 LONGEAR SUNFISH—*Lepomis megalotis* (Rafinesque). Deep, laterally compressed body. Large mouth with jaw not extending under eye. Ear flap thin and flexible. Short and rounded pectoral fin not reaching past eye when bent forward. Long ear flap that is horizontal and is usually bordered above and below by white edge. Scale rows on cheek 5–7, complete lateral line, lateral line scales 40–46. Pectoral fin rays 13–14, anal fin rays 9–10. Very short, thick rakers on first gill arch. Olive back and side, speckled with yellow flecks, wavy blue lines on cheek and opercle, dark red above, bright orange below, marbled and spotted with blue, white below. Fins without spots. Breeding male brilliant orange and blue, red eye, orange to red median fins, blue or black pelvic fins. Great Lakes, Hudson Bay, Mississippi River, and Gulf Slope from FL to TX. Abundant. Lakes, ponds, marshes and pools of creeks, and small to large rivers. Drift, water column insectivore. Guarding, nest-spawning lithophil (B.2.2). Maximum size 280 mm TL.

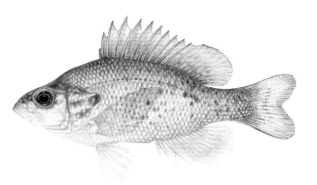

206 ORANGESPOTTED SUNFISH—
Lepomis humilis

207 BLUEGILL—
Lepomis macrochirus macrochirus

208 LONGEAR SUNFISH—
Lepomis megalotis

Family and Species Accounts of Indiana Fishes   293

209   REDEAR SUNFISH—*Lepomis microlophus* (Günther). Deep, laterally compressed body. Pointed snout, small mouth with upper jaw not extending under eye. Long, pointed pectoral fin usually extending past eye when bent forward. Short ear flap with thin flexible rear edge on gill cover. Complete lateral line, lateral line scales 34–47. Pectoral fin rays 13–14, anal rays 10. Light gold to green above, dusky gray spots or bars on silver side, white to yellow below. Fins mostly clear with dark mottling in soft dorsal fin. Breeding male brassy with dusky pelvic fins. Atlantic and Gulf Slope from SC to TX, north in Mississippi River basin to IN. Widely introduced. Common. Lakes, ponds, and marshes and small and moderate-sized rivers associated with aquatic vegetation and mud and sand substrates. Benthic and drift, crushing invertivore. Guarding, nest-spawning lithophil (B.2.2). Maximum size 250 mm TL.

210   REDSPOTTED SUNFISH—*Lepomis miniatus* (Jordan). Deep, laterally compressed body. Short snout, mouth large with upper jaw extending beneath eye. Short, rounded pectoral fin usually not reaching past eye when bent forward. Short ear flap with stiff rear main of gill cover. Complete lateral line, lateral line scales 35–41. Pectoral fins 13–14, anal fin rays 10. Moderately long, slender rakers on first gill arch. Dark olive above, white to yellow edge on black ear flap, red-orange patch on side just above ear flap, many black specks or rows or red-orange or yellow-brown spots on side, whitish-yellow or red-orange below. Clear to dusky fins. Breeding males darkly pigmented highlighting red-orange spots on side. Atlantic and Gulf Coastal Plain and Mississippi Embayment north to southern IN. Introduced into Tri-Lakes area of northern IN by stocking. Rare. Lakes, ponds, marshes, vegetated lowland creeks, streams, and small rivers over sand and mud substrates. Drift, water column invertivore. Guarding, nest-spawning lithophil (B.2.2). Maximum size 200 mm TL.

211   NORTHERN LONGEAR SUNFISH—*Lepomis peltastes* Cope. Deep, laterally compressed body. Large mouth with jaw extending under eye. Head convex. Ear flap thin and flexible. Short and rounded pectoral fin not reaching past eye when bent forward. Long ear flap that is slanted upward and is usually bordered above and below by white edge. Scale rows on cheek 5–7, complete lateral line, lateral line scales 33–40. Pectoral fin rays 13–14, anal fin rays 9–10. Very short, thick rakers on first gill arch. Olive back and side, speckled with yellow flecks, wavy blue lines on cheek and opercle, dark red above, bright orange below, marbled and spotted with blue, white below. Fins without spots. Breeding male brilliant orange and blue, red eye, orange to red median fins, black pelvic fins. Great Lakes from MI to northern OH, IN, west to IL. Common. Lakes, ponds, marshes and pools of creeks, and small to large rivers. Drift, water column insectivore. Guarding, nest-spawning lithophil (B.2.2). Maximum size 225 mm TL.

209 REDEAR SUNFISH—
Lepomis microlophus

210 REDSPOTTED SUNFISH—
Lepomis miniatus

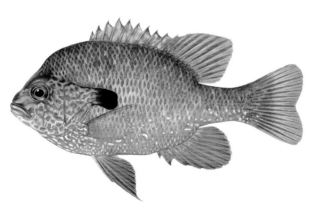

211 NORTHERN LONGEAR SUNFISH—
Lepomis peltastes

Family and Species Accounts of Indiana Fishes   295

212 BANTAM SUNFISH—*Lepomis symmetricus* Forbes. Deep, robust body little compressed laterally. Short snout, large mouth with upper jaw extending under eye. Short ear flap, stiff rear edge on gill cover. Short and rounded pectoral fin not reaching past eye when bent forward. Ear flap is black, usually bordered by white edge. Incomplete lateral line usually interrupted, lateral line scales 30–40. Pectoral fin rays 12–13, anal fin rays 10. Long, thin rakers on first gill arch. Dusky olive back and side, yellow flecks with dark brown spots on side, hollow bars on side of young, white edge on black ear flap, yellowish-brown below. Young with red dorsal and anal fins, adults with clear or dusky fins. Mississippi Embayment from southern IN to Gulf of Mexico, west from Coastal Plain to TX. Rare, possible imperiled species in IN. Marshes, ponds, sloughs, small creeks, and streams associated with submerged aquatic vegetation. Drift, water column insectivore. Guarding, nest-spawning lithophil (B.2.2). Maximum size 78 mm TL.

213 SMALLMOUTH BASS—*Micropterus dolomieu* Lacepede. Elongate, laterally compressed body. Large mouth with upper jaw reaching beneath eye, no tooth patch on tongue, opercle edge smooth. Anal fin base less than half dorsal fin base. Caudal fin shallowly forked. Lateral line scales 69–77, scales around caudal peduncle 29–32. Dorsal fin rays 13–14, anal fin spines 3, anal fin rays 11. Olive-brown above, dark mottling on back and side, red eye, side brown-black with black mottling and vertical elongate non-connected bars without a midlateral stripe on side, yellow-white below. Fins of young with tricolored caudal fin (yellow, black, and white edge). Great Lakes, Hudson Bay, and Mississippi River basins south to AL and OK. Widely introduced. Abundant. Small to large rivers in flowing pools and run habitats, clear, cool lake shallows over cobble and gravel substrates. Whole body carnivore. Guarding, nest-spawning lithophil (B.2.2). Maximum size 686 mm TL.

214 SPOTTED BASS—*Micropterus punctulatus* (Rafinesque). Elongate, laterally compressed body. Large mouth with upper jaw reaching past middle of eye, tooth patch present on tongue, opercle edge smooth. Anal fin base less than half dorsal fin base. First and second dorsal fin connected, caudal fin shallowly forked. Lateral line scales 60–68, scales around caudal peduncle 23–26. Dorsal fin rays 12, anal fin spines 3, anal fin rays 9–11. Yellow-brown above, dark olive mottling on back and side, red eye, side brown-black with black mottling and vertical wide, elongate non-connected bars on side connected with a midlateral black stripe. Lower quarter of body with rows of small black spots, yellow-white below. Fins of young with tricolored caudal fin (yellow, black, and white edge). Mississippi River basin south to Gulf of Mexico. Introduced elsewhere. Abundant. Creeks and small to large rivers in flowing pools and run habitats, occupies impoundment shallows over cobble and gravel substrates. Whole body carnivore. Guarding, nest-spawning lithophil (B.2.2). Maximum size 420 mm TL.

212 BANTAM SUNFISH—
Lepomis symmetricus

213 SMALLMOUTH BASS—
Micropterus dolomieu

214 SPOTTED BASS—
Micropterus punctulatus

215 LARGEMOUTH BASS—*Micropterus salmoides* (Lacepede). Elongate, laterally compressed body. Very large mouth with upper jaw reaching past eye, no tooth patch present on tongue, opercle edge smooth. Anal fin base less than half dorsal fin base. First dorsal fin highest at middle, low at posterior edge, dorsal fins nearly separate, caudal fin shallowly forked. Lateral line scales 60–72. Pectoral fin rays 14–15, dorsal fin spines 14–15, dorsal rays 13–14, anal fin spines 3, anal fin rays 11–12. Yellow-brown, green, or brassy above, dark olive mottling on back and side, eye brown, dark brown lines radiating from snout and back of eye to edge of gill cover, side brown-black with black mottling and vertical bars on side that are wider than tall connecting along midlateral black stripe, lower quarter of body with scattered black flecks, white below. Fins of young with bicolored caudal fin (yellow with black edge). Great Lakes, Hudson Bay, and Mississippi River basin south to Gulf, along Atlantic Slope from FL to Mexico. Introduced widely elsewhere. Abundant. Lakes, ponds, marshes, and backwaters associated with submerged vegetation, also found in pools of creeks and small to large rivers over sand and gravel substrates. Whole body carnivore. Guarding, nest-spawning lithophil (B.2.2). Maximum size 700 mm TL.

216 WHITE CRAPPIE—*Pomoxis annularis* Rafinesque. Deep, laterally compressed body. Mouth large with upper jaw reaching to beneath eye. Very long predorsal area with sharp head deflection over the eye. Dorsal fin base shorter than distance from eye to dorsal fin origin but about the same length as anal fin base. Dorsal spines 6, dorsal fin rays 14–15, anal spines 6, anal fin rays 17–19. Grayish-green above, silver side with 6–9 dusky, distinct hollow bars along side, bars are widest at top and are icicle-shaped, green flecks along side. Fins with spots on dorsal, caudal, and anal fins. Great Lakes, Hudson Bay, and Mississippi River basin south to Gulf Coast from AL to TX. Common. Pools of small creeks and backwaters of small to large rivers, lakes, and ponds. Invertivore/whole body carnivore. Guarding, nest-spawning phytophil (B.2.5). Maximum size 330 mm TL.

217 BLACK CRAPPIE—*Pomoxis nigromaculatus* (Lesueur). Deep, laterally compressed body. Mouth large with upper jaw reaching to beneath eye. Very long predorsal area with sharp head deflection over the eye. Dorsal fin base equal to anal fin base length. Dorsal spines 7–8, dorsal fin rays 15–16, anal spines 6, anal fin rays 17–19. Grayish-green above, wavy black lines, silver side with scattered green to black flecks along side, white below. Fins with spots on dorsal, caudal, and anal fins. Atlantic Slope, Great Lakes, Hudson Bay, and Mississippi River basin south to Gulf Coast. Common. Lakes, ponds, sloughs, and backwaters usually associated with submerged vegetation and woody debris over mud and sand substrates. Invertivore/whole body carnivore. Guarding, nest-spawning phytophil (B.2.5). Maximum size 420 mm TL.

215 LARGEMOUTH BASS—
Micropterus salmoides salmoides

216 WHITE CRAPPIE—
Pomoxis annularis

217 BLACK CRAPPIE—
Pomoxis nigromaculatus

SCULPIN FAMILY—COTTIDAE
(SPECIES PLATES 218–222)

The Cottidae (sculpins) is a large family of primarily marine fishes in the order Scorpaeniformes. About 70 genera and 300 species are distributed in marine and freshwater habitats around the world, primarily in the Northern Hemisphere (Nelson 2006).

Cottidae possess large heads and usually have spinous fins and spiny armature on the head and body (Nelson 2006). Along with large, flattened heads, sculpins have large mouths and large, dorsally placed eyes. The body tapers from the broad head to a relatively narrow caudal peduncle. Pectoral fins are large, spinous and soft dorsal fins are present, anal fin is spineless, pelvic fins bear a single spine and 2–5 soft rays. Most species are scaleless or nearly so, although the body can be covered with prickles, and their mucous covering results in a slippery texture. A lateral line is present but may be either complete or interrupted. Usually an air bladder is lacking or is rudimentary (Nelson 2006).

Sculpins are present throughout the freshwaters of North America; members of the genus *Myoxocephalus* are found in deep northern lakes and *Cottus,* the largest sculpin genus containing about 34 species worldwide, has 28 representatives in North America (Nelson 1994). They are usually bottom dwellers and are reported from a variety of habitats ranging from caves and spring runs to larger rivers and lakes (Smith 1979; Trautman 1981; Becker 1983; Burr and Warren 1986).

KEY TO THE SCULPINS OF INDIANA

1   a) Gill membranes meeting at acute angle, free from isthmus. Two to 4 conspicuous and partially naked preopercular spines on each side. Dorsal fins separated by space about equal to diameter of eye ....
........**DEEPWATER SCULPIN**—*Myoxocephalus thompsoni*

   b) Gill membranes broadly attached to isthmus. One conspicuous and partially naked preopercular spine on each side, other spines skin covered. Dorsal fins touching or narrowly joined...*Cottus* spp.

2 a) Lateral line complete 3

   b) Lateral line incomplete... 4

3 a) Lateral line complete. One midline chin pore. Preopercu-
      lar spine usually longer than 0.67 eye diameter and curved
      strongly inward. Upper head and body covered with prick-
      les, Pelvic fins with a single spine and 4 soft rays appearing
      as 4 units (spine and first ray encased in single fleshy mem-
      branes). Chin membranes with brain-like convolutions and
      folds (Not previously recorded from Indiana) ....
      .... **SPOONHEAD SCULPIN**—*Cottus ricei*

   b) Lateral line usually complete, ending near base of caudal fin.
      Dorsal fins usually not connected. Dark vertical bar crossing
      body at base of caudal fin broad and distinct (found in minor
      tributaries of the Ohio River drainage)....................................
      .... **BANDED SCULPIN**—*Cottus carolinae*

4 a) Pelvic rays 4, last ray a little shorter than the third. Caudal
      peduncle length less than postorbital distance. Last 2 rays of
      dorsal and anal fins arise from the same base. Palatine teeth
      usually present..5

   b) Pelvic rays usually 3, sometimes 4, last ray always much
      shorter than the third. Caudal peduncle length greater than
      postorbital distance. Last 2 rays of dorsal and anal fins sepa-
      rated, arising from separate bases. Palatine teeth usually
      absent ....**SLIMY SCULPIN**—*Cottus cognatus*

5 a) Large males with red margin to dorsal fin. Dorsal fin with
      distinct spots at anterior and posterior margins. First dorsal
      fin narrowly disconnected to base...
      ....**MOTTLED SCULPIN**—*Cottus bairdii*

   b) Dorsal fin with red margin and black stripe, no distinct spots
      at anterior and posterior margins of first dorsal fin. First
      dorsal fin slightly connected, bands beneath second dorsal
      fin distinct but faint anteriorly ....
      .... **BLUETHROAT SCULPIN**—*Cottus* cf. *bairdii* nov. sp.

218   MOTTLED SCULPIN—*Cottus bairdii* Girard. Robust body. Large head, palatine teeth present. Incomplete lateral line, usually 18–36 pores. Dorsal fins joined at base. Preopercular spines 3, pectoral fin rays 14–16, dorsal fin spines 6–9, dorsal rays 15–18, pelvic rays 4, anal fin rays 12–14. Brown above, dark brown to black mottling on back and side, uniformly speckled chin, 2–3 dark brown to black bars on body under second dorsal fin, light brown below. Large black spots at front, rear of first dorsal fin has black band, orange edge on first dorsal fin. Breeding male with black head and body. Atlantic, Arctic, and Mississippi River basins. Common. Headwater creeks, streams, small rivers, and springs associated with gravel and cobble substrates. Benthic, digging insectivore. Guarding, nest-spawning speleophil (B.2.7). Maximum size 150 mm TL.

219   BLUETHROAT SCULPIN—*Cottus* cf. *bairdii*. Robust body. Large head, palatine teeth present. Incomplete lateral line, usually 18–36 pores. Dorsal fins joined at base. Preopercular spines 3, pectoral fin rays 14, dorsal fin spines 6–7, dorsal rays 17–18, pelvic rays 4, anal fin rays 12. Brown above, dark brown to black mottling on back and side, chin without speckling, 2–3 dark brown to black bars on body under second dorsal fin, light brown below. No large black spots at front and rear of first dorsal fin, first dorsal fin with black band and orange edge. Breeding male with black head and body. Endemic to caves and karst regions in the Ohio River drainage in Indiana. Common. Headwater creeks, streams, small rivers, and springs associated with gravel and cobble substrates. Benthic, digging insectivore. Guarding, nest-spawning speleophil (B.2.7). Maximum size 189 mm TL.

220   BANDED SCULPIN—*Cottus carolinae* (Gill). Robust body. Large head, palatine teeth present. Complete lateral line, usually 28–34 pores. Dorsal fins separate to base. Preopercular spines 3, pectoral fin rays 16–17, dorsal fin spines 6–9, dorsal rays 15–18, pelvic rays 4, anal fin rays 11–14. Olive, tan, or reddish brown above, 4–5 brown to black saddles, last 3 extending onto side as sharply defined bars, mottled chin, light brown below. no large black spots at front and rear of first dorsal fin has black band, orange edge on first dorsal fin. Breeding male with black head and body. Mississippi River basin uplands. Common. Headwater creeks, streams, small rivers, and cave springs associated with gravel and cobble substrates. Benthic, digging insectivore. Guarding, nest-spawning speleophil (B.2.7). Maximum size 144 mm TL.

218 MOTTLED SCULPIN—
Cottus bairdii

219 BLUETHROAT SCULPIN—
Cottus cf. *bairdii*

220 BANDED SCULPIN—
Cottus carolinaev

221 SLIMY SCULPIN—*Cottus cognatus* Richardson. Elongate, robust body. Large head, no palatine teeth. Incomplete lateral line reaching to second dorsal fin, usually 12–26 pores. Dorsal fins separated to base. Preopercular spines 2–3, upper spine largest, pectoral fin rays 14–16, dorsal fin spines 7–9, dorsal rays 14–19, pelvic rays 3, anal fin rays 10–11, pores on chin 2. Dark brown or green above, dark gray mottling on back and side, usually 2 dark saddles under second dorsal fin, light brown below. Large black spots at front and rear of first dorsal fin often joined together, orange edge on first dorsal fin. Breeding male black or gray head and body, with orange band on dorsal fin. Great Lakes, Atlantic, Arctic, Mississippi River, and Pacific basins. Rare. Nearshore of Lake Michigan associated with littoral troughs usually over gravel and cobble substrates. Benthic, digging insectivore. Guarding, nest-spawning speleophil (B.2.7). Maximum size 80 mm TL.

222 DEEPWATER SCULPIN—*Myoxocephalus thompsoni* (Girard). Elongate body tapering to slender caudal peduncle. Wide, flat head, large mouth reaches beneath eye. Large disc-shaped scales on back and side above lateral line. Second dorsal fin taller than first dorsal fin, large pectoral fins. Complete lateral line. Preopercular spines 4, upper 2 spines directed obliquely upward appear as a single divided spine while lower 2 smaller and pointing downward. Dark brown to green mottling above, with 4–7 greenish saddles, on gray-brown back and side, white below. Fins with dark bars except on pelvics. Pelvic rays 3. Great Lakes and Arctic basins. Appears in IN nearshores in early spring after ice melt as juveniles. Rare. Lake Michigan depths to 366 m, but juveniles rise to surface to fill swim bladder and are often blown into shallow nearshore waters during spring. Benthic, digging insectivore. Guarding, nest-spawning speleophil (B.2.7). Maximum size 239 mm TL.

221   SLIMY SCULPIN—
      Cottus cognatus

222   DEEPWATER SCULPIN—
      Myoxocephalus thompsoni

GOBY FAMILY—GOBIIDAE
(SPECIES PLATE 223)

The family Gobiidae includes marine, estuarine, and some freshwater species. Nelson (2006) recognizes 210 genera and at least 195 species, including 5 subfamilies. The Gobiidae is the second-most species-rich family of vertebrates. The family has more marine species than any other fish family and also the most abundant freshwater fish on oceanic islands.

The Gobiidae can be diagnosed by possessing well-developed, united pelvic fins forming an adhesive or sucking disc; spinous dorsal, when present, separate from soft dorsal and with 2–8 flexible spines; scales cycloid or ctenoid (rarely absent); some species with prominent head barbels; and 5 branchiostegal rays (Nelson 2006).

The invasion of the Round goby (*Apollonia melanostomus*) and Tubenose goby (*Proterorhinus marmoratus*) into the Great Lakes resulted from ballast water discharge from ocean-going freighters. Populations were established in the Detroit River and Calumet Harbor (Jude et al. 1992). The Round goby is now found throughout the Great Lakes, including the St. Lawrence River.

STICKLEBACK FAMILY—GASTEROSTEIDAE
(SPECIES PLATES 224–226)

The sticklebacks are a group of small fishes that are related to the seahorses and pipefishes. The Gasterosteidae is a monophyletic family containing 5 genera that are distributed in the Northern Hemisphere (Nelson 2006). Members of the Gasterosteiformes have a small mouth at the end of a short or tubular snout and body armor of dermal plates. The pelvic girdle is not attached directly to the cleithra, and branchiostegal rays number between 1 and 5 (Nelson 2006). The combined Pegasiformes (sea moths), Syngnathiformes (pipefishes, seahorses, trumpet fish, and cornet fish), and Gasterosteiformes (sticklebacks) in this order are considered as a monophyletic group based on shared specialization in feeding apparatus.

The family Gasterosteidae is characterized by a slender maxillary that articulates anteriorally with the premaxilla; bran-

223   ROUND GOBY—*Apollonia melanostoma* (Pallas). Robust body with large, fused pelvic fins forming a single sucking disc ventrally. Blunt snout, wide, rounded head, large mouth reaching beneath eye, eye positioned high on head. Lateral line absent, no long, tubular anterior nostrils. Lateral scales 49–55. First gill arch with 12 rakers on anterior edge forming molariform pharyngeal teeth. Olive to slate gray above and on side, 5–6 dark brown to black saddles on back. Black, white, or red flecks in a checkerboard pattern on side, white below. Fins clear with exception of first dorsal fin, which has a large black spot on posterior 2 rays. Introduced. Exotic from the Black and Caspian seas. Introduced through ballast water into Calumet Harbor, IL, Lake Michigan, and has spread across the nearshore and direct tributaries. Abundant. Lake Michigan nearshore and moderate rivers and tributaries associated with a variety of substrates including artificial rock, gravel, mud, and cobble substrates. Benthic, digging insectivore. Guarding, nest-spawning speleophil (B.2.7). Maximum size 178 mm TL.

223   ROUND GOBY—
Apollonia melanostoma

chiostegal rays 3; well-developed dorsal and pelvic fin spines; soft dorsal fin preceded by 3–16 isolated well-developed spines, each with a triangular membrane, usually a short spine closely associated with a soft dorsal fin of 6–14 rays; pelvic fins thoracic in position, with a strong well-developed spine and 0–3 soft rays; and pelvic bones not attached to cleithra (Nelson 2006).

The Brook stickleback and Ninespine stickleback are native species in Indiana; however, the Brook stickleback has been widely introduced through bait bucket release. The Ninespine stickleback is Holarctic in distribution and occurs in Lake Michigan. The Threespine stickleback has invaded the Great Lakes and has been found throughout the Lake Michigan nearshore, usually associated with submerged aquatic vegetation in the various harbors and natural embayments.

KEY TO THE STICKLEBACKS OF INDIANA

1   a)   Sharp lateral keel present; dorsal spines 8–11. Caudal peduncle wider than deep. Caudal fin truncate to slightly notched .... **NINESPINE STICKLEBACK—** .... *Pungitius pungitius*

     b)   Sharp lateral keel absent; dorsal spines less than 6. Caudal peduncle deeper than wide. Caudal fin rounded 2

2   a)   Dorsal spines 4–6 .... **BROOK STICKLEBACK—** .... *Culaea inconstans*

     b)   Dorsal spines 3 .... **THREESPINE STICKLEBACK—** .... *Gasterosteus aculeatus*

225   THREESPINE STICKLEBACK—*Gasterosteus aculeatus* Linnaeus. Body elongate, laterally compressed with extremely narrow, long caudal peduncle. Bony keel along side of caudal peduncle, possessing 0–30 bony plates on side—fewer in freshwater populations. Gill membranes broadly joined across isthmus. Pelvic fin with a single spine (with cusp) and a single ray. Dorsal spines 3 (rarely 2–4). Silver-green to brown above, silver side, often with dark mottling, silver below. Clear fins. Breeding male with blue side, bright red belly, and red fins. Marine and freshwater. Arctic and Atlantic basins, western Hudson Bay, Pacific basin from AK to Baja California, Lake Ontario. Occasional. Lake Michigan nearshore associated with pelagic habitats or shallow vegetated areas over mud or sand substrates. Particulate-feeding invertivore. Guarding, nest-spawning ariadnophil (B.2.4). Maximum size 102 mm TL.

226   NINESPINE STICKLEBACK—*Pungitius pungitius* (Linnaeus). Body elongate, laterally compressed with extremely narrow, long caudal peduncle. Usually with a bony keel on caudal peduncle. No bony plates on side, small plates on lateral pores 0–8 on front half of body. Gill membranes joined to each other but not joined to isthmus. Pelvic fin with a single spine and a single ray. Short dorsal spines 9 (7–12) angled alternately to left to right. Gray to olive above, dark mottling on back and side, silver below. Breeding male with black belly and white pelvic fins. Marine and freshwater. Arctic, Atlantic, Pacific, and Great Lakes basins. Occasional. Lake Michigan nearshore associated with pelagic habitats or shallow vegetated areas over lakes, ponds, and pools of sluggish streams usually associated with sand substrates. Particulate-feeding invertivore. Guarding, nest-spawning ariadnophil (B.2.4). Maximum size 50 mm TL.

224   BROOK STICKLEBACK—*Culaea inconstans* Kirtland. Body deep, laterally compressed with extremely narrow, short caudal peduncle without a keel. Without large bony plates on side but possess small plates on lateral line pores. Gill membranes joined to each other but not connected to isthmus. Pelvic fin with single spine and single ray. Short dorsal spines 4–6. Olive above, green flecks with dark green mottling and a pale stripe along side, silver to white below. Breeding male is dark green to black. Atlantic, Arctic, Great Lakes, and Mississippi River south to OH and west to BC. Introduced widely through bait bucket release. Common. Lakes, ponds, marshes, headwater creeks, streams, and small rivers usually associated with submerged vegetation over mud or sand substrates. Particulate-feeding invertivore. Guarding, nest-spawning ariadnophil (B.2.4). Maximum size 87 mm TL.

224   BROOK STICKLEBACK—
Culaea inconstans

225   THREESPINE STICKLEBACK—
Gasterosteus aculeatus

226   NINESPINE STICKLEBACK—
Pungitius pungitius

FRESHWATER DRUM FAMILY—SCIAENIDAE
(*Species plate 227*)

The Sciaenidae (drums) is a large family of about 70 genera and 270 species, most found in marine and brackish waters of the Atlantic, Indian, and Pacific oceans. About 28 species are restricted to freshwaters of Atlantic drainages, most in South America. Freshwater drum, *Aplodinotus grunniens,* is the only species found in the freshwaters of the United States (Nelson 2006).

Diagnostic characteristic of the family Sciaenidae include a long dorsal fin with a deep notch separating 6–13 spines from a second portion that has a single spine and usually 25–35 soft rays; anal fin has 1–2 spines, both usually weak, but the second may be noticeably larger than the first (as in Freshwater drum), and 6–13 soft rays; lateral line scales extend to end of caudal fin; caudal fin slightly emarginate to rounded; head with large

227   FRESHWATER DRUM—*Aplodinotus grunniens* Rafinesque. Deep, slab-sided, and arched at dorsal fin origin, laterally compressed body. Small subterminal mouth, head with large cavernous canals and pores. Lateral line extends to end of caudal fin. First dorsal fin short possessing 10 spines, second dorsal long with 29–32 rays. Outer pelvic fin ray a long filament. Gray above, silver-gray sides, white below. Fins dusky gray. Arctic, Atlantic, Hudson Bay, Great Lakes basins south to Gulf of Mexico from GA to Mexico. Common. Large waterbodies including small to large rivers and Great Lakes over a variety of substrates. Invertivore/whole body carnivore. Non-guarding, open substrate pelagophil (A.1.1). Maximum size 890 mm TL.

cavernous canals (part of lateral line system); conspicuous pores on snout and lower jaw; preopercle is serrate or entire; chin barbels are present on some species; vomer and palatine without teeth; swim bladder usually with many branches; otoliths exceptionally large; and vertebrae 24–30 (Nelson 2006).

Freshwater drum, although wide ranging, is stable in its characters, exhibiting no geographic variation over much of its range (Smith 1979; Trautman 1981; Becker 1983). Scott and Crossman (1973) reported that, although meristic values appear stable, growth rates vary greatly throughout the range. No subspecies of freshwater drum have been proposed (Smith 1979), but a thorough systematic and taxonomic study has not been completed. Two combined characters distinguish Freshwater drum from other perciform fishes in the United States: includes only 1 or 2 anal fin spines, and a lateral line that extends to the end of the caudal fin.

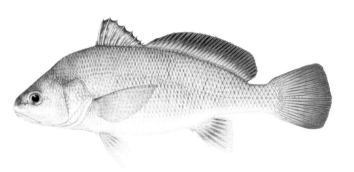

227   FRESHWATER DRUM—
Aplodinotus grunniens

Top 10 Fishing Spots in Indiana

LAKES AND RIVERS

Angling is among the most treasured pastimes in Indiana, with over 750,000 estimated people fishing the waters of the state each year. Based on my sampling experience at over 18,000 sites, I am often asked: Where are the best places to fish in Indiana? Although this depends on your objective, I present my top 10 fishing spots in Indiana, where I have caught some of the biggest fish in the state. Of course my methods are not hook-and-line, but the survey techniques used are a better estimate of population relative abundance. Table 5 presents the largest recorded individual fish species caught by hook-and-line in Indiana (Indiana DNR 2009) compared to global records of the largest individual ever recorded for each species.

My top fishing spot criteria is not only based on the maximum size of the target species but also takes into consideration the quality of the fishing experience, including the number of large individuals, number of individuals per distance, and site aesthetics. My top 10 list attempts to spread the experience equally across the northern, central, and southern sections of the state (Figure 19).

I hope that this list is visited by every Hoosier who reads this book. Please let me know if you enjoyed your experience!

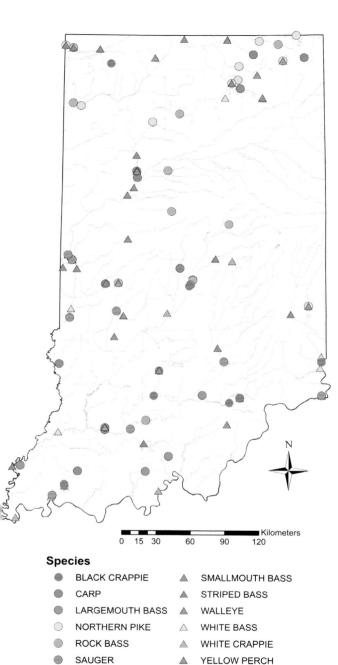

Species

● BLACK CRAPPIE	▲ SMALLMOUTH BASS
● CARP	▲ STRIPED BASS
● LARGEMOUTH BASS	▲ WALLEYE
● NORTHERN PIKE	△ WHITE BASS
● ROCK BASS	▲ WHITE CRAPPIE
● SAUGER	▲ YELLOW PERCH

Figure 19. Top fishing hot spots for ten fish game species in Indiana.

TABLE 5. GLOBAL AND STATE FISH RECORD WEIGHTS INCLUDING CATCH LOCATION

	Indiana			Global		
Species	Weight	Water Body	County	Record	Location	Date
Alligator gar				279 lbs	Rio Grande, TX	12/2/1951
Atlantic salmon	14 lbs 4 oz	Lake Michigan	Lake	79 lbs 2 oz	Tana River, Norway	4/11/1905
Black crappie	4 lbs 11 oz	Private lake	Jennings	4 lbs 8 oz	Kerr Lake, VA	3/1/1981
Blue catfish	104 lbs	Ohio River		111 lbs	Wheeler's Reservoir, TN	7/5/1996
Bluegill	3 lbs 4 oz	Pond	Greene	4 lbs 12 oz	Ketona Lake, AL	4/9/1950
Bowfin	16 lbs	Pine Lake	LaPorte	21 lbs 8 oz	Florence, SC	1/29/1980
Brook trout	3 lbs 15.5 oz	Lake Gage	Steuben	14 lbs 8 oz	Nipigon River, ON	7/1/1916
Brown bullhead				5 lbs 11 oz	Cedar Creek, FL	3/28/1995
Brown trout	29 lbs 0.48 oz	Lake Michigan	Lake	40 lbs 4 oz	Little Red River, AR	5/9/1992
Bigmouth buffalo	53 lbs 14.4 oz	Oak Hill Pond	Gibson	70 lbs 5 oz	Bussey Brake, LA	4/21/1980
Black buffalo				55 lbs 8 oz	Cherokee Lake, TN	5/3/1984
Black bullhead	4 lbs 14.4 oz	Potato Creek State Park	St. Joseph	8 lbs	Lake Waccabuc, NY	8/1/1951
Burbot	7 lbs 11 oz	Lake Michigan		18 lbs 11 oz	Angenmanelren, Sweden	10/22/1996
Channel catfish	37 lbs 8 oz	Lake	Vanderburgh	58 lbs	Santee-Cooper Reservoir, SC	7/7/1964
Chinook salmon	38 lbs	Trail Creek	LaPorte	97 lbs 4 oz	Kenai River, AK	5/17/1985
Cisco	3 lbs 12 oz	Big Cedar Lake	Whitley			

Coho salmon	20 lbs 12 oz	Lake Michigan	LaPorte	33 lbs 4 oz	Salmon River, Pulaski, NY	9/27/1989
Carp	43 lbs 4 oz	Pike Lake	Kosciusko	75 lbs 11 oz	Lac de St. Cassien, France	5/21/1987
Flathead catfish	79 lbs 8 oz	White River	Lawrence	91 lbs 4 oz	Lake Lewisville, TX	3/28/1982
Flier	3 lbs 0.8 oz	Stream	Jackson			
Freshwater drum	30 lbs	White River	Martin	54 lbs 8 oz	Nickajack Lake, TN	4/20/1972
Gizzard shad				4 lbs 6 oz	Lake Michigan, IN	3/2/1996
Goldeye	2 lbs 5 oz	Wabash River	Vermillion			
Goldfish				6 lbs 10 oz	Lake Hodges, CA	4/17/1996
Grass carp	65 lbs 3 oz	Private pond	Morgan			
Grass pickerel	1 lbs 10 oz	Pit	Fountain			
Green sunfish				1 lb	Dewart Lake, IN	6/9/1990
Greater redhorse				9 lbs 3 oz	Salmon River, NY	5/11/1985
Lake sturgeon				168 lbs	Georgian Bay, ON	5/29/1982
Lake trout	29 lbs 4 oz	Lake Michigan		72 lbs	Great Bear Lake, NT	8/19/1995
Lake whitefish				14 lbs 6 oz	Meaford, ON	5/21/1984
Largemouth bass	14 lbs 12 oz	Lake	Harrison	22 lbs 4 oz	Montgomery Lake, GA	6/2/1932
Longnose gar	22 lbs 5 oz	East Fork White River	Pike	50 lbs 5 oz	Trinity River, TX	7/30/1954
Muskellunge	42 lbs 8 oz	James Lake	Kosciusko	67 lbs 8 oz	Hayward, WI	7/24/1949
Northern pike	30 lbs 2 oz	Clear Lake	Steuben	55 lbs 1 oz	Lake of Grefeern, Germany	10/16/1986

continued

TABLE 5. *continued*

Species	Indiana			Global		
	Weight	Water Body	County	Record	Location	Date
Pink salmon	2 lbs 12.5 oz	Lake Michigan	Lake	13 lbs 1 oz	St. Mary's River, ON	9/23/1992
Rainbow trout	26 lbs 10 oz	Trail Creek	LaPorte	42 lbs 2 oz	Bell Island, AK	6/22/1970
Redear sunfish	3 lbs 10 oz	Lake	Brown			
Rock bass	3 lbs	Sugar Creek	Hancock	3 lbs	York River, ON	8/1/1974
Round whitefish				6 lbs	Putahow River, MB	6/14/1984
Sauger	6 lbs 1 oz	Tippecanoe River	Carroll	8 lbs 12 oz	Lake Sakakawea, ND	10/6/1971
Shortnose gar				5 lbs 12 oz	Rend Lake, IL	7/16/1995
Shovelnose sturgeon	14 lbs 8 oz	Wabash River	Fountain			
Silver carp	15 lbs 8 oz	West Fork White River	Greene			
Silver redhorse				11 lbs 7 oz	Plum Creek, WI	5/29/1985
Smallmouth bass	7 lbs 4 oz	Twin Lake	LaGrange	10 lbs 14 oz	Dale Hollow, TN	4/24/1969
Smallmouth buffalo				82 lbs 3 oz	Athens Lake, TX	6/6/1993
Spotted bass	5 lbs 5 oz		Vigo	9 lbs 9 oz	Pine Flat Lake, CA	10/12/1996
Spotted gar				9 lbs 12 oz	Lake Mevia, TX	4/7/1994
Striped bass	35 lbs 6 oz	Ohio River		67 lbs 8 oz	O'Neill Forebay, CA	5/7/1992

Species	Weight	Water	County	Weight	Location	Date
Walleye	14 lbs 4 oz	Kankakee River	Lake	25 lbs	Old Hickory Lake, TN	8/2/1960
	14 lbs 4 oz	Tippecanoe River	Pulaski			
Warmouth	1 lb 6 oz	North Dugger Pit	Sullivan	2 lbs 7 oz	Guess Lake, Holt, FL	10/19/1985
White bass	4 lbs 3 oz	Lake Freeman	Carroll	6 lbs 13 oz	Lake Orange, VA	7/31/1989
White catfish	9 lbs 12 oz	Pond	Wabash	18 lbs 14 oz	Inverness, FL	9/21/1991
White perch				4 lbs 12 oz	Messalonskee Lake, ME	6/4/1949
Yellow bass	2 lbs 15 oz	Morse Reservoir	Hamilton	2 lbs 4 oz	Lake Monroe, IN	3/27/1977
Yellow bullhead				4 lbs 4 oz	Mormon Lake, AZ	5/11/1984
Yellow perch	2 lbs 8 oz	Gravel pit	Vigo	4 lbs 3 oz	Bordentown, NJ	5/1/1865

Works Cited

Artyukhin, E. N. 2006. Morphological phylogeny of the order Acipenseriformes. *Journal of Applied Ichthyology* 22:66–69.

Bailey, R. M. 1980. Comments on the classification and nomenclature of lampreys—an alternative view. *Canadian Journal of Fisheries and Aquatic Sciences* 37:1217–1220.

Bailey, R. M., W. C. Latta, and G. R. Smith. 2004. An atlas of Michigan fishes with keys and illustrations for their identification. University of Michigan Museum of Zoology, Miscellaneous Publications 192.

Balon, E. K. 1975. Reproductive guilds of fishes: A proposal and definition. *Journal Fisheries Research Board of Canada* 32:821–864.

Bardack, D., and R. Zangerl. 1972. Lampreys in the fossil record. In M. W. Hardisty and I. C. Potter (eds.), *The Biology of Lampreys,* vol. 1, 67–84. New York: Academic Press.

Becker, G. C. 1983. *Fishes of Wisconsin.* Madison: University of Wisconsin Press,

Berra, T. M. 2001. *Freshwater Fish Distributions.* San Diego: Academic Press.

Blatchley, W. S. 1938. *The Fishes of Indiana.* Indianapolis: Nature Publication Company.

Boschung, H. T., Jr., and R. L. Mayden. 2004. *Fishes of Alabama.* Washington, D.C.: Smithsonian Books.

Braun, E. R. 1984. *A Fisheries Investigation of the Eel River.* Indianapolis: Indiana Department of Natural Resources, Division of Fish and Wildlife.

Burr, B. M., and R. L. Mayden. 1980. Dispersal of rainbow smelt, *Osmerus mordax* into the upper Mississippi River (Pisces: Osmeridae). *American Midland Naturalist* 104:198–201.

Burr, B. M., and M. L. Warren, Jr. 1986. *A Distributional Atlas of Kentucky Fishes.* Kentucky Nature Preserves Commission Scientific and Technical Series 4. Frankfort, Ky.

Carney, D. A., L. M. Page, and T. M. Keevin. 1993. Fishes of the Tippecanoe River, Indiana: An outstanding midwestern stream. *Proceedings of the Indiana Academy of Science* 101:201–209.

Castle, P. H. J. 1984. Notacanthiformes and Anguilliformes. In H. G. Moser and W J. Richard (eds.), *Ontogeny and Systematics of Fishes,* 62–93. Lawrence, Kans.: American Sociey of Ichthyologists and Herpetologists.

Cavender, T. M. 1986. Review of the fossil history of North American freshwater fishes. In C. H. Hocutt and E. O. Wiley (eds.), *The Zoogeography of North American Freshwater Fishes,* 699–724. New York: John Wiley and Sons.

Chenhan, L., and Z. Yongjun. 1988. Notes on the Chinese paddlefish, *Psephurus gladius* (Martens). *Copeia* 1988:482–484.

Coleman, A. P. 1922. Glacial and post-glacial lakes in Ontario. *University of Toronto Studies Biology, Publications Ontario Fisheries Research Laboratory* 21:5–76.

Cope, E. D. 1867. Synopsis of the Cyprinidae of Pennsylvania. *Transactions of the American Philosophical Society* 13(13):351–399.

———. 1868. On the distribution of fresh-water fishes in the Allegheny region of southwestern Virginia. *Journal of the Academy of Natural Sciences, Philadelphia* (Series 2) 6 (art. 5):207–247.

Crossman, E. J. 1978. Taxonomy and distribution of North American esocids. American Fisheries Society Special Publication 11, 13–26.

Emery, E. B., T. P. Simon, and R. Ovies. 1999. Influence of the Family Catostomidae on the metrics developed for a Great Rivers index of biotic integrity. In T. P. Simon (ed.), *Assessing the Sustainability and Biological Integrity of Water Resources Using Fish Communities,* 203–224. Boca Raton, Fla.: CRC Press.

Etnier, D. A., and W. C. Starnes. 1993. *The Fishes of Tennessee.* Knoxville: University of Tennessee Press.

Evenson, E. B., W. R. Farrand, D. F. Eschman, D. M. Mickelson, and L. J. Maher. 1976. Greatlakean substage: A replacement for Valderan substage in the Lake Michigan Basin. *Quarternary Research* 6:411–424.

Farrand, W. R., R. Zahner, and W. S. Benninghoff. 1969. Carry-Port Huron Interstade: Evidence from a buried bryophyte bed, Cheboygan County, Michigan. Geological Society of America Special Paper 123, 249–262.

Forbes, S. A., and R. E. Richardson. 1905. *The Fishes of Illinois.* Champaign: State of Illinois Natural History Laboratory.

———. 1920. *The Fishes of Illinois.* Champaign: State of Illinois Natural History Laboratory.

Foster, N. R. 1967. Comparative studies on the biology of killifishes (Pisces: Cyprinodontidae). Ph.D. diss., Cornell University, Ithaca, N.Y.

Gardiner, B. G. 1984. Sturgeons as living fossils. In N. Eldridge and S. Stanley (eds.). *Living Fossils.* 148–152. New York: Springer-Verlag.

Gerking, S. D. 1945. Distribution of Indiana fishes. *Investigations of Indiana Lakes and Streams* 3:1–137.

Goldstein, R. M., and T. P. Simon. 1999. Toward a united definition of guild structure for feeding ecology of North American freshwater fishes. In T. P. Simon (ed.), *Assessing the Sustainability and Biological Integrity of Water Resources Using Fish Communities,* 123–202. Boca Raton, Fla.: CRC Press.

Gosline, W. A. 1948. Some possible uses of x-ray in ichthyology and fisheries research. *Copeia* 1948:58–61.

Grande, L. 1980. *Paleontology of the Green River Formation, with a Review of the Fish Fauna.* Laramie: Geological Survey of Wyoming.

———. 1985. Recent and fossil clupeomorph fishes with materials for revision of the subgroups of clupeoids. *Bulletin American Museum of Natural History* 181:231–372.

Grande, L., and W. E. Bemis. 1991. Osteology and phylogenetic relationships of fossil and recent Paddlefishes (Polyodontidae) with contributions on the interrelationships of Acipenseriformes. Society of Vertebrate Paleontology Memoirs 1, *Journal of Vertebrate Paleontology* 11 Supp.

———. 1998. A comprehensive phylogenetic study of amiid fishes (Amiidae) based on comparative skeletal anatomy. An empirical search for interconnected patterns of natural history. Society of Vertebrate Paleontology Memoirs 4, *Journal of Vertebrate Paleontology* 18 Supp.

Greenwood, P. H. 1973. Interrelationships of osteoglossomorphs, In P. H. Greenwood, et al. (eds.), *Interrelationships of Fishes*. 307–332. London: Academic Press.

Hardisty, M. W., and I. C. Potter. 1971a. The behavior, ecology, and growth of larval lamprey. In M. W. Hardisty and I. C. Potter (eds.), *The Biology of Lampreys,* vol. 1, 85–125. New York: Academic Press.

———. 1971b. Paired species. In M. W. Hardisty and I. C. Potter (eds.), *The Biology of Lampreys,* vol. 1, 249–277. New York: Academic Press.

———. 1982. *The Biology of Lampreys.* vols. 1–4b. New York: Academic Press.

Hubbs, C. L., and M. D. Cannon. 1935. The darters of the genera Hololepis and Villora. University of Michigan Museum of Zoology, Miscellaneous Publications 30.

Hubbs, C. L., and K. F. Lagler. 1964. *Fishes of the Great Lakes Region.* Ann Arbor: University of Michigan Press.

Hubbs, C. L., and I. C. Potter. 1971. Distribution, phylogeny, and taxonomy. In M. W. Hardisty and I. C. Potter (eds.), *The Biology of Lampreys,* vol. 1, 1–65. New York: Academic Press.

Hubbs, C. L., and L. P. Schultz. 1941. Contributions to the ichthyology of Alaska, with descriptions of two new fishes. University of Michigan, Museum of Zoology, Occasional Paper Number 431.

Indiana Department of Natural Resources (IDNR). 2009. *Fishing Guide.* Indianapolis: Indiana Department of Natural Resources, Division of Fish and Wildlife.

Johnson, G. D. 1984. Percodei: Development and relationships. In H. G. Moser and W. J. Richards (eds.), *Ontogeny and Systematics of Fishes.* 464–498. Lawrence, Kans.: American Society of Ichthyologists and Herpetologists.

Jordan, D. S. 1877. On the fishes of northern Indiana. *Proceedings Academy of Natural Sciences, Philadelphia* 29:42–104.

Jordan, D. S., and B. W. Evermann. 1890. Description of a new species of fish from Tippecanoe River, Indiana. *Proceedings of the United States National Museum* 1890:3–4.

Jude, D. J., R. H. Reider, and G. R. Smith. 1992. Establishment of Gobiidae in the Great Lakes basin. *Canadian Journal of Fisheries and Aquatic Sciences* 49:416–421.

Kay, L. K., R. Wallus, and B. L. Yeager. 1994. *Reproductive Biology and Early Life History of Fishes in the Ohio River Drainage,* vol. 2, *Catostomidae.* Chattanooga: Tennessee Valley Authority.

Khirdir, K. T., and C. B. Renaud. 2003. Oral fimbriae and papillae in parasitic lampreys (Petromyzontiformes). *Environmental Biology of Fishes* 66:271–278.

Kingsley, J. S. 1899. *Textbook of Vertebrate Zoology.* New York: Henry Holt and Company.

Koelz, W. 1929. Coregonid fishes of the Great Lake. *Bulletin United States Bureau Fisheries* 43:297–643.

Kuehne, R. A., and R. W. Barbour. 1983. *The American Darters.* Lexington: University of Kentucky Press.

Laird, C. A., and L. M. Page. 1996. Nonnative fishes inhabiting the streams and lakes of Illinois. *Illinois Natural History Survey Bulletin* 35:1–51.

Lauder, G. V., and K. F. Liem. 1983. The evolution and interrelationships of the actinopterygian fishes. *Bulletin of the Museum of Comparative Zoology* 150:95–197.

Lee, D. S., C. R. Gilbert, C. H. Hocutt, R. E. Jenkins, D. E. McAllister, and J. R. Stauffer, Jr. 1980. *Atlas of North American Freshwater Fishes.* Raleigh: North Carolina State Museum of Natural History.

Leverrett, F., and F. B. Taylor. 1915. *The Pleistocene of Indiana and Michigan and the History of the Great Lakes.* Monograph U.S. Geological Survey 53, 1–529.

Lindsey, C. C., and C. S. Woods. 1970. *Biology of Coregonid Fishes.* Winnepeg: University of Manitoba Press.

Lundberg, J. G. 1982. The comparative anatomy of the toothless blindcat, Trogloglanis pattersoni Eigenmann, with a phylogenetic analysis of ictalurid catfishes. University of Michigan Museum of Zoology, Miscellaneous Publications 163.

Margulies, D., O. S. Burch, and B. F. Clark. 1980. Rediscovery of the gilt darter (*Percina evides*) in the White River, Indiana. *American Midland Naturalist* 104:207–208.

Mayden, R. L., B. M. Burr, L. M. Page, and R. R. Miller. 1992. The native freshwater fishes of North America. In R. L. Mayden (ed.), *Systematics, Historical Ecology, and North American Freshwater Fishes,* 827–863. Palo Alto, Calif.: Stanford University Press.

Mayden, R. L., F. B. Cross, and O. T. Gorman. 1987. Distributional history of the rainbow smelt, *Osmerus mordax* (Salmoniformes: Osmeridae), in the Mississippi River basin. *Copeia* 1987:1051–1054.

McGowan, M. F., and F. H. Berry. 1984. Clupeiformes: Development and relationships. In H. G. Moser and W. J. Richards (eds.), *Ontogeny and Systematics of Fishes,* 108–126. Lawrence, Kans.: American Society of Ichthyologists and Herpetologists.

Nelson, G. J. 1969. Gill arches and the phylogeny of fishes, with notes on the classification of vertebrates. *Bulletin American Museum of Natural History* 141:475–552.

Nelson, J. S. 1984. *Fishes of the World,* 2nd ed. New York: John Wiley and Sons.

———. 1994. *Fishes of the World,* 3rd ed. New York: John Wiley and Sons.

———. 2006. *Fishes of the World,* 4th ed. New York: John Wiley and Sons.

Nelson, J. S., E. J. Crossman, et al. 1994. *Common and Scientific Names of Fishes from the United States and Canada,* 5th ed. Bethesda, Md.: American Fisheries Society.

Nelson, J. S., E. J. Crossman, H. Espinoza-Perez, L. T. Findley, C. R. Gilbert, R. N. Lea, and J. D. Williams. 2004. *Common and Scientific Names of Fishes from the United States and Canada,* 6th ed. Bethesda, Md.: American Fisheries Society.

Page, L. M. 1983. *Handbook of Darters.* Neptune, N.J.: T.F.H. Publications.

Page, L. M., and B. M. Burr. 1986. Zoogeography of fishes in the lower Ohio—upper Mississippi basin. In C. H. Hocutt and E. O. Wiley (eds.), *The Zoogeography of North American Freshwater Fishes,* 287–324. New York: John Wiley and Sons.

———. 1991. *A Field Guide to Freshwater Fishes: North America North of Mexico.* Boston: Houghton-Mifflin.

Page, L. M., P. A. Ceas, D. L. Swofford, and D. G. Buth. 1992. Evolutionary relationships within the Etheostoma squamiceps complex (Percidae, subgenus Catonotus) with descriptions of five new species. *Copeia* 1992:615–646.

Patterson, C. 1982. Morphology and interrelationships of primitive actinopterygian fishes. *American Zoologist* 22:214–259.

Pearson, J. 2001. Cisco population status and management in Indiana. Indianapolis: Indiana Department of Natural Resources, Division of Fish & Wildlife.

Potter, I. C. 1980. The Petromyzontiformes with particular reference to paired species. *Canadian Journal of Fisheries and Aquatic Sciences* 37:1595–1615.

Renfro, J. L., and L. G. Hill. 1970. Factors influencing aerial breathing and metabolism of gars (*Lepisosteus*). *Southwest Naturalist* 15:45–54.

Ross, S. T. 2001. *The Inland Fishes of Mississippi.* Jackson: University of Mississippi Press.

Scharpf, C. 2009. Checklist of freshwater fishes of North America, including subspecies and undescribed forms. American Currents.

Schofield, P. J., J. D. Williams, L. G. Nico, P. Fuller, and M. R. Thomas. 2005. Foreign Nonindigenous Carps and Minnows (Cyprinidae) in the United States: A Guide to Their Identification, Distribution, and Biology. U.S. Geological Survey Scientific Investigations Report 2005-5041.

Scott, W. B., and E. J. Crossman. 1973. Freshwater fishes of Canada. *Fisheries Research Board of Canada Bulletin* 184.

Simon, T. P. 1990. Bowfin, *Amia calva* Linnaeus. In. R. Wallus, T. P. Simon, and B. L. Yeager (eds.). *Reproductive Biology and Early Life History of Fishes in the Ohio River Drainage,* vol. 1, *Acipenseridae through Esocidae.* 90–97. Chattanooga: Tennessee Valley Authority.

———. 1999. Assessment of Balon's reproductive guilds with application to midwestern North American freshwater fishes. In T. P. Simon (ed.), *Assessing the Sustainability and Biological Integrity of Water Resources Using Fish Communities,* 97–122. Boca Raton, Fla.: CRC Press.

———. 2005. Life history of the Tippecanoe darter, Etheostoma tippecanoe Jordan and Evermann, in the Tippecanoe River, Carroll County, Indiana. Miscellaneous Papers of the Indiana Biological Survey Aquatic Research Center 5, 1–16.

———. 2007. Biodiversity of fishes in the Wabash River: Status, indicators, and threats. *Proceedings of the Indiana Academy of Science* 115:136–148.

Simon, T. P., G. Bright, F. Veraldi, J. R. Smith, and J. R. Stahl. 2006. New records of the Oriental weatherfish, Misgurnus anquillicauda-

tus, in the Lake Michigan basin, Indiana (Cypriniformes: Cobitidae). *Proceedings of the Indiana Academy of Science* 115:32–36.

Simon, T. P., and A. L. Kiley. 1993. Rediscovery of the harlequin darter,
Etheostoma histrio Jordan and Gilbert, in the White River drainage,
Indiana. *Proceedings of the Indiana Academy of Science* 102:279–281.

Simon, T. P., and R. Wallus. 2004. *Reproductive Biology and Early Life
History of Fishes in the Ohio River Drainage,* vol. 3, *Ictaluridae—
Catfish and Madtoms.* Boca Raton, Fla.: CRC Press.

———. 2006. *Reproductive Biology and Early Life History of Fishes in
the Ohio River Drainage,* vol. 4, *Percidae—Perch, Pikeperch, and
Darters.* Boca Raton, Fla.: CRC Press.

Simon, T. P., J. O. Whitaker, Jr., J. S. Castrale, and S. A. Minton. 2002.
Revised checklist of the vertebrates of Indiana. *Proceedings of the
Indiana Academy of Science* 111:182–214.

Smith, P. W. 1979. *The Fishes of Illinois.* Champaign: Illinois University
Press.

Todd, T. N. 1981. Allelic variability in species and stocks of Lake
Superior ciscoes (Coregoninae). *Canadian Journal of Fisheries and
Aquatic Sciences* 38:1808–1813.

Todd, T. N., and G. R. Smith. 1980. Differentiation in Coregonus
zenithicus in Lake Superior. *Canadian Journal of Fisheries and
Aquatic Sciences* 37:2228–2235.

Todd, T. N., G. R. Smith, and L. E. Cable. 1981. Environmental and
genetic contributions to morphological differentiation in ciscoes
(Coregoninae) of the Great Lakes. *Canadian Journal of Fisheries and
Aquatic Sciences* 38:59–67.

Trautman, M. B. 1981. *Fishes of Ohio.* Columbus: Ohio State University
Press.

Underhill, J. C. 1986. The fish fauna of the Laurentian Great Lakes,
the St. Lawrence Lowlands, Newfoundland and Labrador. In C. H.
Hocutt and E. O. Wiley (eds.), *The Zoogeography of North American
Freshwater Fishes,* 105–136. New York: John Wiley and Sons.

Vasetskiy, S. G. 1971. Fishes of the family Polyodontidae. *Journal of
Ichthyology (USSR)* 11:18–31. [English translation.]

Vladykov, V. D. 1951. Fecundity of Quebec lamprey. *Canadian Fish
Culturist* 10:1–14.

Vladykov, V. D., and E. Kott. 1979. Satellite species among the Holarctic
lampreys. *Canadian Journal of Zoology* 57:860–867.

Whitaker, J. O., Jr., and J. R. Gammon. 1988. *Endangered and Threatened Vertebrate Animals of Indiana, Their Distribution and Abundance.* Indianapolis: Indiana Academy of Science Monograph 5.

Whitaker, J. O., Jr., and D. C. Wallace. 1973. Fishes of Vigo County,
Indiana. *Proceedings of the Indiana Academy of Science* 82:448–464.

White, M. M. 2000. Genetic variation in white bass. *Transactions of the
American Fisheries Society* 129:879–885.

Wiley, E. O. 1976. The phylogeny and biogeography of fossil and recent
gars (Actinpterygii: Lepisosteidae). University of Kansas Museum of
Natural History Miscellaneous Publication 64.

———. 1986. A study of the evolutionary relationships of Fundulus
topminnows (Teleostei: Fundulidae). *American Zoologist* 26:121–130.

Woods, A. J., J. M. Omernik, C. S. Brockman, T. D. Gerber, W. D. Hosteter, and S. H. Azevedo. 1998. Ecoregions of Indiana and Ohio (two-sided color poster with map, descriptive text, summary tables, and photographs). U.S. Geological Survey, Reston, Va. Scale 1:500,000.

Glossary

abbreviate heterocercal Tail in which the vertebral axis is prominently flexed upward, only partly invading upper lobe of caudal fin; fin fairly symmetrical externally.

actinotrichia Fin supports that are precursors of fin rays or spines; also called lepidotrichia.

adherent Attached or joined together, at least at one point.

adhesive egg An egg that adheres on contact to substrate material or other eggs; adhesiveness of entire egg capsule may or may not persist after attachment.

adipose fin A fleshy, rayless median dorsal structure, located posterior to the true dorsal fin.

adnate Congenitally united; conjoined; keel-like.

adnexed Flag-like.

adult Sexually mature as indicated by production of gametes.

alevin A term applied to juvenile catfish, trout, and salmon after yolk absorption; exhibiting no post-yolk-sac larval phase.

allopatric Having separate and mutually exclusive areas of geographical distribution.

anadromous Fishes that ascend rivers from the sea to spawn.

anal Pertaining to the anus or vent.

anal fin Unpaired median fin immediately behind anus or vent.

anlage Rudimentary form of an anatomical structure; primordium; incipient.

antero-hyal Anterior bone to which branchiostegal rays attach; formerly ceratohyal.

anus External orifice of the intestine; vent.

auditory vesicle Sensory anlage from which the ear develops; clearly visible during early development.

axillary process Enlarged accessory scale attached to the upper or anterior base of pectoral or pelvic fins.

barbel Tactile process arising from the head of various fishes.

basibranchials Three median bones on the floor of the gill chamber, joined to the ventral ends of the 5 gill arches.

body depth at anus Vertical depth of body at anus, not including finfolds.

branched ray Soft fin ray with 2 or more branches distally.

branchial arches Bony or cartilaginous structures supporting the gills, filaments, and rakers; gill arches.

branchial region The pharyngeal region where branchial arches and gills develop.

branchiostegals Struts of bone inserting on the hyoid arch and supporting, in a fanwise fashion, the branchiostegal membrane; branchiostegal rays.

buoyant egg An egg that floats free within the water column; pelagic.

caeca Finger-like outpouchings at boundary of stomach and intestine.

catadromous Fishes that go to sea from rivers to spawn.

caudal fin Tail fin.

caudal peduncle Area lying between posterior end of anal fin base and base of caudal fin.

cement glands Discrete or diffuse structures that permit a larva to adhere to a substrate.

cephalic Pertaining to the head.

cerotohyal See antero-hyal.

cheek Lateral surface of head between eye and opercle, usually excluding preopercle.

chorion Outer covering of egg; egg capsule.

choroid fissure Line of juncture of invaginating borders of optic cup; apparent in young fish as a trough-like area below lens.

chromatophores Pigment-bearing cells; frequently capable of expansions and contractions that change their size, shape, and color.

cleavage stages Initial stages in embryonic development where divisions of blastomeres are clearly marked; usually include first through sixth cleavages (2–64 cells).

cleithrum Prominent bone of pectoral girdle, clearly visible in many fish larvae.

coelomic Pertaining to the body cavity.

confluent Coming together to form one.

ctenoid scale Scale with comb-like margin; bearing cteni or needle-like projections.

cycloid scale Scale with evenly curved, free border, without cteni.

demersal egg An egg that remains on the bottom, either free or attached to substrate.

dentary Major bony element of the lower jaw, usually bearing teeth.

dorsal fins Median, longitudinal, vertical fins located on the back.

early embryo Stage in embryonic development characterized by formation of embryonic axis.

egg capsule Outermost, encapsulating structure of the egg, consisting of one or more membranes; the protective shell.

egg diameter In nearly spherical eggs, greatest diameter; in elliptical eggs given as two measurements, the greatest diameter or major axis and the least diameter or minor axis.

egg pit The pit or pocket in a redd (nest) into which a trout female deposits one batch of eggs.

emarginate Notched but not definitely forked, as in the shallowly notched caudal fin of some fishes.

emergence The act of leaving the substrate and beginning to swim; swim-up.

epaxial Portion of the body dorsal to the horizontal or median myoseptum.

epurals Modified vertebrae elements that lie above the vertebrae and support part of the caudal fin.

erythrophores Red or orange chromatophores.

esophagus Alimentary tract between pharynx and stomach.

eye diameter Horizontal measurement of the iris of the eye.

falcate Deeply concave, as a fin with middle rays much shorter than anterior and posterior rays.

finfold Median fold of integument that extends along body of developing fishes and from which median fins arise.

fin insertion Posteriormost point at which the fin attaches to the body.

fin origin Anteriormost point at which the fin attaches to the body.

focal point Location of a fish maintaining a stationary position on or off the substrate for at least a 10-second period.

fork length Distance measured from the anteriormost point of the head to the end of the central caudal rays.

frenum A fold of skin that limits movement of the upper jaw.

ganoid scales Diamond- or rhombic-shaped scales consisting of bone covered with enamel.

gas bladder Membranous, gas-filled organ located between the kidneys and alimentary canal in teleosts; air bladder or swim bladder.

gastrula Stage in embryonic development between blastula and embryonic axis.

gill arches See branchial arches.

gill rakers Variously shaped bony projections on anterior edge of the gill arches.

granular yolk Yolk consisting of discrete units of finely to coarsely granular material.

greatest body depth Greatest vertical depth of the body excluding fins and finfolds.

guanophores White chromatophores; characterized by presence of iridescent crystals of guanine.

gular fold Transverse membrane across throat.

gular plate Ventral bony plate on throat, as in *Amia calva*.

gular region Throat.

head length Distance from anteriormost tip of head to posteriormost part of opercular membrane, excluding spine; prior to development of operculum, measured to posterior end of auditory vesicle.

head width Greatest dimension between opercles.

heterocercal Tail in which the vertebral axis is flexed upward and extends nearly to the tip of the upper lobe of the caudal fin; fin typically asymmetrical externally, upper lobe much longer than lower.

homocercal Tail in which the vertebral axis terminates in a penultimate vertebra followed by a urostyle (the fusion product of several vertebral elements); fin perfectly symmetrical externally.

horizontal myoseptum Connective tissue dividing epaxial and hypaxial regions of the body; median myoseptum.

hypaxial That portion of the body ventral to the horizontal myoseptum.

hypochord A transitional rod of cells that develops under the notochord in the trunk region of some embryos.

hypochordal Below the notochord; referring to the lower lobe of the caudal fin.

hypurals Expanded, fused, hemal spines of last few vertebrae that support the caudal fin.

incipient Becoming apparent.

incubation period Time from fertilization of egg to hatching.

inferior mouth Snout projecting beyond the lower jaw.

interorbital Space between eyes over top of head.

interradial Area between the fin rays.

interspaces Spaces between parr marks of salmonids.

iridocytes Crystals of guanine having reflective and iridescent qualities.

isocercal Tail in which vertebral axis terminates in median line of fin, as in Gadiformes.

isthmus The narrow area of flesh in the jugular region between gill openings.

jugular Pertaining to the throat; gular.

juvenile Young fish after attainment of minimum adult fin-ray counts and complete absorption of the median finfold and before sexual maturation.

keeled With a ridge or ridges.

larva Young fish between time of hatching and attainment of juvenile characteristics.

late embryo Stage prior to hatching in which the embryo has developed external characteristics of its hatching stage.

lateral line Series of sensory pores and/or tubes extending backward from head along sides.

lateral line scales Pored or notched scales associated with the lateral line.

lepidotrichia See actinotrichia.

mandible Lower jaw, comprised of 3 bones: dentary, angular, and articular.

maxillary The dorsalmost of the 2 bones in the upper jaw.

Meckel's cartilage Embryonic cartilaginous axis of the lower jaw in bony fishes; forms the area of jaw articulation in adults.

melanophores Black chromatophores.

mental Pertaining to the chin.

myomeres Serial muscle bundles of the body.

myosepta Connective tissue partitions separating myomeres.

nares Nostrils, openings leading to the olfactory organs.

narial Pertaining to the nares.

nasal Pertaining to region of the nostrils, or to the specific bone in that region.

notochord Longitudinal supporting axis of body that is eventually replaced by the vertebral column in teleostean fishes.

notochord length Straight-line distance from anteriormost part of head to posterior tip of notochord; used prior to and during noto-chord flexion.

obtuse With a blunt or rounded end; an angle greater than 90 degrees.

occipital region Area on dorsal surface of head, beginning above or immediately behind eyes and extending backward to end of head; occiput.

oil globule(s) Discrete sphere(s) of fatty material within the yolk.

olfactory buds Incipient olfactory organs.

ontogenetic Related to biological development.

operculum Gill cover.

optic vesicles Embryonic vesicular structures that give rise to the eyes.

otoliths Small, calcareous, secreted bodies within the inner ear.

over yearling Fish having spent at least one winter in a stream; applies to trout and salmon.

palatine teeth Teeth on the paired palatine bones in the roof of the mouth of some fishes.

parapatric Distribution of species or other taxa that meet in a very narrow zone of overlap.

pectoral fins Paired fins behind head, articulating with pectoral girdle.

peduncle Portion of body between anal and caudal fins.

pelagic Floating free in the water column; not necessarily near the surface.

pelvic bud Swelling at site of future pelvic fin; anlage of pelvic fin.

pelvic fins Paired fins articulating with pelvic girdle; ventral fins.

pericardium Cavity in which the heart lies.

peritoneum Membranous lining of abdominal cavity.

perivitelline space Fluid-filled space between egg proper and egg capsule.

pharyngeal teeth Teeth on the pharyngeal bones of the branchial skeleton.

physoclistic Having no connection between the esophagus and the pneumatic duct; typical of perciform fishes.

physostomus Having the swim bladder connected to the esophagus by the pneumatic duct; typical of cypriniform fishes.

plicae Wrinkle-like folds found on the lips of some catostomids.

postanal length Distance from posterior margin of anus to the tip of the caudal fin.

postanal myomeres Myomeres posterior to an imaginary vertical line through the body at the posterior margin of the anus; the first postanal myomere is the first myomere behind and not touched by the imaginary line.

postero-hyal Posterior bone to which branchiostegal rays attach, formerly epihyal.

postorbital length Distance from posterior margin of eye to posterior edge of opercular membrane.

preanal length Distance from anteriormost part of head to posterior margin of anus.

preanal myomeres The number of myomeres between the anteriormost myoseptum and an imaginary vertical line drawn at the posterior margin of anus, including any bisected by the line.

predorsal scales Scales along dorsal ridge from occiput to origin of dorsal fin.

prejuvenile Developmental stage immediately following acquisition of minimum fin ray complement of adult and before assumption of adult-like body form; used only where strikingly different from juvenile.

premaxillary The ventralmost of the 2 bones included in upper jaw.

primordium Rudimentary form of an anatomical structure; anlage.

principal caudal rays Caudal rays inserting on hypural elements; the number of principal rays is generally defined as the number of branched rays plus 2.

procurrent caudal rays A series of much shorter rays anterior to the principal caudal rays, dorsally and ventrally, not typically included in the margin of the caudal fin.

pronephic ducts Ducts of pronephic kidney of early development stages.

pterygiophore Bones of the internal skeleton supporting the dorsal and anal fins.

redd An excavated area or nest into which trout spawn.

retrorse Pointing backward.

rostrum Snout.

scute A modified, thickened scale, often spiny or keeled.

semibuoyant Referring to eggs that neither float nor sink but remain suspended in the water column.

sigmoid heart The S-shaped heart that develops from the primitive heart tube.

soft rays Bilaterally paired, usually segmented, fin supports.

spines Unpaired, unsegmented, unbranched fin supports, usually (but not always) stiff and pungent.

spiracle Opening behind the eye of a separate duct or can that leads to the gill chamber in sharks, rays, and primitive bony fishes This is not the gill opening.

squamation Covering of scales.

standard length In larvae, straight-line distance from anteriormost part of head to the most posterior point of the notochord or hypural complex.

stellate Referring to a melanophore that is expanded into a star-like shape.

stomodeum Primitive invagination of the ectoderm that eventually gives rise to the mouth.

superior mouth Condition when the lower jaw extends upward and the mouth opens dorsally.

sympatric Species inhabiting the same or overlapping geographic areas.

terminal mouth Condition when lower and upper jaws are equal in length and the mouth opens terminally.

total length Straight-line distance from anteriormost part of head to tip of tail; all older literature references not stated differently are assumed to be total length.

urostyle Terminal vertebral element in higher teleosts, derived from the fusion and loss of several of the most posterior centra of the more primitive forms; usually modified for caudal fin support.

vent Anus.

vermiculate Having worm-like markings.

vitelline vessels Arteries and veins of yolk region.

water-hardening Expansion and toughening of egg capsule due to absorption of water into the perivitelline space.

Weberian apparatus First 4 vertebrae of cypriniform fishes modified for sound amplification.

width of perivitelline space Distance between yolk and outer margin of egg capsule.

xanthophores Yellow chromatophores.

yearling A fish in its second year.

yolk Food reserve of embryonic and early larval stages, usually seen as a yellowish sphere diminishing in size as development proceeds.

yolk diameter Greatest diameter of yolk; more accurately measurable prior to embryo formation.

yolk sac A bag-like ventral extension of the primitive gut containing the yolk.

yolk-sac depth Greatest vertical depth of yolk sac.

yolk-sac larva A larval fish characterized by the presence of a yolk sac.

yolk-sac length Horizontal distance from most anterior to most posterior margin of yolk sac.

Index

Books in the Indiana Natural Science Series

THOMAS P. SIMON, Ph.D., has published more than 150 scientific papers and 10 books on the natural history and ecology of North American freshwater fishes. He is a Fellow of the Indiana Academy of Science and former Director of the Indiana Biological Survey.

JOSEPH R. TOMELLERI holds an M.S. in biology and has worked full-time as a scientific illustrator since 1985. He has illustrated more than 950 fishes, which have appeared in more than 1,000 publications.

APR 2 4 2012